STUDY GUIDE FOR ORNSTEIN
PSYCHOLOGY
THE STUDY OF HUMAN EXPERIENCE ⊙ THIRD EDITION

SHELLEY PATNOE
SAN JOSE STATE UNIVERSITY

HARCOURT BRACE JOVANOVICH, PUBLISHERS
SAN DIEGO NEW YORK CHICAGO AUSTIN WASHINGTON, D.C.
LONDON SYDNEY TOKYO TORONTO

Copyright © 1991, 1988, 1985 by Harcourt Brace Jovanovich, Inc.

All rights reserved. No part of this publication may be reproduced or transmitted
in any form or by any means, electronic or mechanical, including photocopy, recording,
or any information storage and retrieval system, without permission in writing from the
publisher.

Requests for permission to make copies of any part of the work should be mailed to:
Permissions Department, Harcourt Brace Jovanovich, Inc., 8th Floor, Orlando, Florida 32887.

ISBN: 0-15-572688-9

Library of Congress Catalog Card Number: 90-82911

Printed in the United States of America

STUDY GUIDE FOR ORNSTEIN AND CARSTENSEN'S
PSYCHOLOGY
THE STUDY OF HUMAN EXPERIENCE ⊙ THIRD EDITION

TO THE STUDENT

HOW TO USE THIS STUDY GUIDE

GENERAL STUDY QUESTIONS

The first section in each chapter of the Study Guide is made up of questions designed to help you focus on the main ideas in the corresponding chapter. You might want to glance over them before you read the chapter. After reading the chapter, answer each of the questions using just three or four sentences. This will give you a good understanding of the major points in the chapter so the details of the material will be easier to learn.

OUTLINE OF KEY TERMS AND CONCEPTS

The purpose of this section is to summarize the main terms and concepts covered in each chapter. These terms and concepts are listed in outline form that parallels the organization of the material in the text.

One way to use this section is to write out a brief definition or description that explains or describes each entry in more detail. If you put each term on a small card with the definition on the back, you can test yourself and discard those items you have mastered.

This outline section can also be useful as a quick review of the entire chapter, especially when preparing for exams. After careful study, individual entries should trigger meaningful associations that bring to mind larger chunks of information.

COMPLETION ITEMS

This section contains a series of sentences in which you are to fill in the missing words. Each item consists of one or several sentences in which blanks have been left for you to insert key words. In each case, the missing information is printed in the margin directly across from the blank. If you cover up the answers in the margin, you can test your knowledge of details in the chapter. This will give you an idea of which material in the chapter you need to study further.

Rather than just reading items, be sure to actually fill them in. Correct answers are reinforced, or rewarded, by the knowledge that you have responded correctly; incorrect answers are immediately corrected when you look at the answer in the margin. Remember, you will gain the most from this section if you (1) avoid looking at the answers until you have responded and (2) actually write in your responses rather than just thinking them.

SELF-QUIZ

This section is made up of a series of multiple-choice and true-false items that, in addition to the Completion Items, are representative of the questions you are likely to see on your exams. First read the item carefully, then circle the the answer you think is correct. Check your answers against the Answer Key at the end of the Self-Quiz section.

THINKING ABOUT THE PSYCHOLOGY OF YOUR OWN EXPERIENCE

The purpose of this section is twofold. First, it should prompt you to consider how the ideas in the corresponding chapter relate to your own life and it should help stimulate some new and productive insights into your own personality and life experience. Second, the personal nature of this thinking exercise is based on the premise that we tend to remember better, and assimilate more completely, knowledge that we can apply to ourselves in some way.

SUGGESTED STUDY PROGRAM

Step 1 Read over the General Study Questions.
Step 2 Read the Outline of Key Terms and Concepts in the Study Guide.
Step 3 Read and study actively the corresponding chapter in the text.
Step 4 Answer the General Study Questions.
Step 5 Repeat step 2 and add your own notations to the entries.
Step 6 Work on the Completion Items section in the Study Guide.
Step 7 Go back to the text to study the content in more depth, concentrating on those areas requiring further study as revealed in your results from the previous step.
Step 8 Take the Self-Quiz in the Study Guide.
Step 9 Repeat step 6.
Step 10 Work on the exercises in Thinking about the Psychology of Your Own Experience in the Study Guide to help assimilate the content to your personal frame of reference.
Step 11 Go over the general study questions once more to see how thoroughly you understand them. Review for your exam as much as you feel is necessary using the Outline of Key Terms and Concepts and Completion Items sections for the purpose of quick review.

The closer you follow this recommended study strategy, the more you will learn.

CONTENTS

To the Student   v
    Chapter 1   The Study of Human Experience   1

PART I   The World of the Developing Person   11
    Chapter 2   Human Development: Birth to Adulthood   13

PART II   The Biological World   27
    Chapter 3   The Brain and the Nervous System   29
    Chapter 4   Genetics and Evolution   39
    Chapter 5   Sensory Experience   50

PART III   The Mental World   61
    Chapter 6   Perceiving the World   63
    Chapter 7   Consciousness and the Nature of the Mind   74
    Chapter 8   The Basics of Learning   85
    Chapter 9   Remembering and Forgetting   96
    Chapter 10   Thinking and Language   107
    Chapter 11   The Measurement of Intelligence   119

PART IV   The World of the Self   129
    Chapter 12   Emotions and Happiness   131
    Chapter 13   Needs and Goals   142
    Chapter 14   Personality   154
    Chapter 15   Psychological Disorders   166
    Chapter 16   Psychotherapies   179

PART V   The Social World of the Adult   193
    Chapter 17   Social Psychology   195
    Chapter 18   Human Intimacy   208
    Chapter 19   Health Psychology   216
    Chapter 20   Adapting to the Modern World   228
    Chapter 21   Old Age   234

1
THE STUDY OF HUMAN EXPERIENCE

GENERAL STUDY QUESTIONS

After reading Chapter 1, you should be able to answer the following questions:

1. How does scientific psychology differ from everyday psychology?

2. What is replication and why is it important?

3. In what three ways do psychologists define and test ideas?

4. What are the three ways in which observations are made? Describe each briefly.

5. What are the elements of the experimental method?

6. In an experiment, what is the difference between the experimental group(s) and the control group?

7. An experimental psychologist has an interesting idea about interpersonal attraction. What is the first step taken in designing an experiment to test it?

8. What are the two methods used to minimize experimenter bias?

9. Why do psychologists use statistics?

10. What are the two forms of statistical "average" used by psychologists? How are they different from one another?

11. What is a correlation? When are correlations used by psychologists? What is the difference between a negative correlation and no correlation?

12. What is a "natural experiment?"

13. What seventeenth century thinker set in motion the modern study of mind-brain relationships? What did he believe was the source of human knowledge?

14. The British empiricists believed that knowledge was gained through association. The association of what?

15. Why did John B. Watson propose that psychologists study behavior rather than the mind?

16. What justification is there for studying animals when psychologists are really interested in human beings?

17. What is the fundamental assumption underlying modern behaviorism?

18. What is the difference between the biological approach and the cognitive approach? What is a question that would be asked by someone using the biological approach? What is a question that would be asked by someone using the cognitive approach?

19. What aspect of human cognition makes terrorism very effective?

20. What is the focus of the social environment perspective?

21. The clinical approach offers what kind of information?

22. The field of health psychology offers new understanding of what relationships?

23. How does the humanistic approach differ from the clinical approach?

24. What three general perspectives are used to organize the presentation of how men and women differ?

25. The material in the textbook is organized into four concentric circles with biology being the innermost circle. What are the other three circles?

OUTLINE OF KEY TERMS AND CONCEPTS

Scientific psychology versus everyday psychology
    Aims and virtues of science
        Systematic and formal
        Specific rules
Order, unity, and simplicity
Repeatability
Scientific ideas and tests
    Observation
        Case Histories
        Measurements
            Qualitative measurement
            Quantitative measurement
        Tests
        Questionnaires
        Demonstrations
        Experiments
            Hypotheses
            Independent variable
            Dependent variable
        Sample
            Subjects
            Experimental group

    Control group
Thinking like a psychologist
    The Dutton and Aron experiment
    Experimenter bias
    Replication
    Double-blind procedure
Statistics
    Significant difference
    Mean
    Median
    Correlation
        Negative
        Positive
    Natural experiment
Moments from the history of psychology
    René Descartes
        Innate knowledge
        Pineal
    British empiricists
        John Locke
        David Hume
        John Stuart Mill
        Association of ideas
    John Watson
        Behaviorism
    Copernicus
    Charles Darwin
        Natural selection
        Theory of evolution
        Comparative psychology
        Ethology
    William James
        Principles of Psychology

    Wilhelm Wundt
Perspectives on human experience
    Behaviorism
        John Watson
        B. F. Skinner
    Biological approach
        Wilder Penfield
    Cognitive approach
        Mental errors
        New and surprising events
    Social environment approach
    Clinical approach
        Biological malfunction
            Aphasia
        Psychoanalysis
        Multiple personalities
    Health, mind and the brain
        Health psychology
        Psychoimmunology
    Humanistic approach
        Abraham Maslow
        Self-actualization
    Perspectives
        Biological
        Clinical-psychodynamic
        Social-cognitive
    Being female, being male
        Sex
        Gender
        Gender identity
            Biological theories
            Social learning and cognitive theories
            Clinical-psychodynamic theories

COMPLETION ITEMS

experience
behavior

1. Psychology is a science of human _____ and _____.

systematic, formal

2. Science differs from ordinary inquiry in that it is a _____ and _____ process of gathering information.

order

3. One of the most fundamental assumptions of science is that there is _____ and unity in the world. One of the ways in which scientific knowledge is refined and checked is through attempts to establish the reliability of findings by repeating or _____ them.

replicating

4. Ordinary guesses are vague, and we do not have all the information, so confirmation is haphazard. Scientific psychology is more specific: ideas

observation
demonstration, experiment
case histories, measurements and tests, questionnaires

experimental

independent

double-blind

Statistical
mean
median
Correlation

positive

1.0

0

group

innate

pineal

association

introspection

observable

behavioristic

environmental

selection

laboratory

electrical

are defined and tested by _____,
_____, and _____.

5. Formal observations are made in three ways: _____, _____, and _____.

6. In the _____ method, the researcher intervenes, arranges a situation, controls all the parts of an experience, and records the results.

7. The control group is similar to the experimental group in every respect except for the _____ variable.

8. In order to prevent the experimenter from biasing the results of the study, the _____ procedure keeps the experimenter in the dark about which is the experimental group and which is the control group.

9. _____ procedures are used to evaluate research data. The _____ is the arithmetic average of a set of scores, and the _____ is the middle score in a distribution. _____ is a statistical procedure designed to evaluate the strength and direction of the relationship between two variables.

10. When high scores on X are associated with high scores on Y, a _____ correlation is said to exist between those variables. When a perfect relationship exists between two variables, this would be expressed quantitatively as a correlation of _____. If there were exactly no relationship between the variables measures, the correlation coefficient would be _____.

11. Most scientific conclusions are not about individual differences but about _____ differences.

12. René Descartes believed that much human knowledge was _____. He proposed that abilities of the "mind" direct the body through an interactive process that occurs in the _____ organ of the brain.

13. The British empiricists believed that all knowledge comes from experience through an _____ of ideas.

14. In the late nineteenth century, researchers used the technique of _____ to study the workings of their own minds and to analyze the contents of their experience. In view of the disagreement that often resulted from application of the latter approach, John Watson argued that _____ behavior provided a more appropriate object of study for the development of psychology as a science. An important assumption of the _____ approach, which followed from Watson's proposal, is that behavior changes insofar as there are changes in _____ conditions.

15. British naturalist Charles Darwin proposed that human beings, along with all other life on earth, have evolved from a common ancestor through a process which he called natural _____.

16. Wilhelm Wundt played an important role in the development of psychology as a science by establishing the first _____ of psychology.

17. Neurosurgeon Wilder Penfield found that _____ stimulation of particular areas of the brain resulted in a subject reporting specific experiences from his or her past.

cognitive
attention

writing

capture

sudden
gradual

social

hurry

clinical

multiple

immune

psychoimmunology
humanistic

growth

actualized

gender
Gender identity

genes
women

males
social learning

identify

Freud

personality

18. The word "_____" comes from the Latin verb which means "to know." Studies of divided _____ by Ulric Neisser and his colleagues indicate that people can learn to do two complex activities simultaneously, such as reading on one subject while _____ on another.

19. After your second midterm of the day you find yourself trying to unlock the door of the room you lived in last semester, instead of your new room in the quiet end of the dorm. This is an example of a _____ error.

20. The disproportionate influence of terrorism on international social behavior reflects the fact that _____ threats register intensely in our awareness, whereas _____ changes go largely unnoticed.

21. The study of how other people and our environment affect us is referred to as the _____ environmental perspective. The results of the study in which divinity students were used as subjects suggested that when people are in a _____ they are unlikely to stop and help someone in need.

22. The _____ approach is based on the idea that studying a person who is unable to perform a function can help us to understand how that function usually operates.

23. The case study of Billy Milligan illustrates the clinical condition known as _____ personality.

24. The results of a study by Barthrop and colleagues, indicated substantial weakening of the _____ system in people grieving over their spouses who had been killed in a train wreck. This study exemplifies the kind of work being done in the field of _____.

25. The _____ approach emphasizes the positive aspects of human experience. Abraham Maslow, the founder of this point of view, believed that a person's natural inclination is toward _____ and development. He referred to those people whose inner potentials are most fully developed as self-_____ individuals.

26. Sex is a biological fact but _____ is a cultural construction. _____ refers to our sense of self as a male or a female.

27. One biological theory of gender differences emphasizes that these differences emerged because of different strategies used by males and females to insure that their _____ are passed along. This theory was supported by a cross-cultural study showing that _____ prefer mates who are powerful and wealthy, whereas _____ value youth and attractiveness in their partners.

28. The _____ theorists conceptualize gender as a product of social experience. Girls and boys learn to act like girls and boys by imitating role models. According to cognitive theorists, the first step in acquiring gender identity is for a child to _____ his or her own sex.

29. In contrast to the cognitive theorists, _____ believed that the process of moving through a fixed series of stages from birth to about age 6 results in the formation of _____ and the acquisition of gender.

CHAPTER 1 / THE STUDY OF HUMAN EXPERIENCE

SELF-QUIZ
MULTIPLE-CHOICE ITEMS

1. Which of the following *is not* among the ways in which knowledge developed from scientific psychology tends to differ from that derived from personal experience in everyday life?
   a. It is more conservative.
   b. It is more directly oriented to the individual.
   c. It is more objective.
   d. It is more generally applicable and reliable.

2. The goal of science is to find
   a. order in things that appear disordered.
   b. unity in apparent diversity.
   c. both a and b.
   d. none of the above.

3. Which of the following is *not* among the advantages of experiments over other methods of scientific inquiry?
   a. Experiments are the most repeatable.
   b. Experiments are the most controllable.
   c. Experiments are the most precise.
   d. Experiments are the most representative of everyday life.

4. According to the text, the first step in an experiment is to
   a. identify the independent variable.
   b. measure the dependent variable.
   c. control the dependent measures as completely as possible.
   d. develop a hypothesis.

5. Results of the Dutton and Aron experiment about interpersonal attraction tend to support the hypothesis that exposure to _____ increases a man's feelings of attraction to a woman in whose presence such exposure occurs.
   a. danger
   b. the outdoors environment
   c. success-inducing experiences
   d. failure-inducing experiences

6. Statistical tests are used to evaluate the
   a. control group's effects on the independent variable.
   b. control group's effects on the dependent variable.
   c. significance of the experimental outcome.
   d. importance of the experiment.

7. A correlation of 1.0 between two variables means that
   a. there is essentially no relationship between them.
   b. there is a perfect correlation between them.
   c. high scores on one variable are associated with low scores on the other.
   d. an important scientific discovery has been made.

8. A *negative correlation* is indicated when the relationship between the variables measured is as follows:
   a. the more X happens, the less Y happens
   b. the less X happens, the less Y happens
   c. the less X happens, the less Y happens
   d. there is essentially no relationship between X and Y

9. According to seventeenth-century philosopher René Descartes, the _____ is the organ in the brain where the mind and body interact.
   a. hypothalamus
   b. pituitary
   c. pineal
   d. occipital lobe

10. In the early nineteenth century, _____ was the primary method used by psychological researchers.
    a. the opinion survey
    b. controlled experimentation
    c. introspection
    d. psychoanalytic hypnotic age regression

11. The fundamental assumptions of which of the following approaches in contemporary psychology coincide most closely with the philosophical tradition of British empiricism?
    a. psychoanalysis
    b. humanism
    c. behaviorism
    d. cognitive theory

12. Which of the following areas of psychology was *not* influenced by Darwin's theory of natural selection?
    a. psychoanalysis
    b. Piaget's work on child development
    c. the study of emotions
    d. all of the above were influenced by Darwin's theory.

13. Wilhelm Wundt is credited with having established the first
    a. laboratory of psychology.
    b. psychological clinic.
    c. licensing and certification standards for professional psychologists.
    d. eloquent synthesis of psychology.

14. A biologically oriented psychologist studies
    a. the mind.
    b. thoughts.
    c. the brain.
    d. consciousness.

15. The social environmental perspective focuses on the ways in which _____ and our environments affect us.
    a. our inner potentials
    b. unconscious motives
    c. sublimated needs and drives
    d. other people

16. The research by Bathrop and colleagues with people whose spouses had been killed in a train wreck, indicated that the stress of grief may seriously affect
    a. people's attitudes toward medical intervention.
    b. communication patterns between surviving members of the victim's family.
    c. the immune system.
    d. the surviving spouse's self concept.
17. Which of the following approaches is best known for basing its understanding of human personality on studies of people who are scientific geniuses and world leaders?
    a. behaviorism
    b. cognitive theory
    c. humanism
    d. psychoanalytic theory
18. Which of the following refers to our sense of self as either male or female?
    a. sex
    b. gender
    c. sex role
    d. gender identity
19. Social learning theorists conceptualize gender as the product of
    a. hormones.
    b. parental pressure.
    c. social experience.
    d. schools.
20. According to the text, psychology is the science of
    a. the brain
    b. the mind
    c. human nature and thought
    d. human experience and behavior

TRUE-FALSE ITEMS

1. T F The first assumption of science is that the world of natural events and processes is essentially ordered.
2. T F The dependent variable is the one that is manipulated or changed in an experiment so that its effects on other variables can be assessed.
3. T F The results of the Dutton and Aron experiment shows that male subjects who met a woman on a wobbly bridge wrote stories with far less sexual imagery than did those subjects who met her on a secure bridge.
4. T F The independent variable in Dutton and Aron's experiment was the kind of bridge upon such the subjects stood.
5. T F Statistical procedures are used to evaluate research evidence.
6. T F Most scientific conclusions are based on average group differences.
7. T F The correlation between a man's height and the length of his trousers is likely to be negative.
8. T F The British empiricists believed that much human knowledge is innate.

9. T F Introspection is the method whereby the contents of one's own experience are examined.
10. T F Neurosurgeon Wilder Penfield made his startling discoveries about the effects of electrical stimulation of the brain while performing a preoperative test on a human brain tumor patient.
11. T F More people are murdered every two hours in the United States than were killed by terrorists in the entire summer of 1986.
12. T F When others are around, we are more likely to help someone in distress.
13. T F One characteristic of the humanistic approach as advocated by Abraham Maslow, is the belief that the highest possibilities of human nature have been underrated.
14. T F Gender is a construction that is the same from culture to culture.
15. T F Evolutionary theories of gender differences suggest that it is in the male's interest to impregnate as many females as possible in order to assure survival of his genes.

ANSWER KEY TO SELF-QUIZ

MULTIPLE-CHOICE ITEMS

1. b 2. c 3. d 4. d 5. a 6. c 7. b 8. a 9. c 10. c 11. c 12. d 13. a 14. c 15. a 16. c 17. c 18. d 19. c 20. d

TRUE-FALSE ITEMS

1. T 2. F 3. F 4. T 5. T 6. T 7. F 8. F 9. T 10. T 11. T 12. F 13. T 14. F 15. T

THINKING ABOUT THE PSYCHOLOGY OF YOUR OWN EXPERIENCE

1. You are the star of your own life. You see things from one single perspective: one person, born of two parents in one time and place. You may be unaware of the assumptions you have about yourself and about human experience. One way to find out where your knowledge is limited, is to read textbooks such as this one.

Another way is to select several fellow students who have different backgrounds from yours and discuss some important questions with them: Are the sexes different? Are people "programmed" to behave in specific ways? Are there significant differences between the races? Are some people more intelligent than others, and if so, how did they get that way? Add your own questions.

At the end of the course, try this again and see how different your answers are then.

2. In Chapter 1, experimental evidence is reviewed that indicates that how attracted you are to someone of the opposite sex may depend on the emotion-arousing aspects of the environmental circumstances at the time. Can you think of an event in your own life that fits this hypothesis? What about the time you went to the Boardwalk on a first date, or to that scary slasher movie? Was the relationship between you and the other person affected in any way? If so, did the effects endure? Could such knowledge provide a mechanism through which one person could manipulate another?

PART I

THE WORLD OF THE DEVELOPING PERSON

2
HUMAN DEVELOPMENT: BIRTH TO ADULTHOOD

GENERAL STUDY QUESTIONS

After reading Chapter 2, you should be able to answer the following questions:

1. What is the difference between physical maturation and psychological maturation? What is adaptation?

2. How do developmental psychologists use the term "egocentrism"?

3. What are "critical periods"? Why are they important?

4. What effect does the ability to move around have on an infant's cognitive development?

5. Piaget's theory rests on three assumptions. What are they?

6. What are schemata? How do they change and grow? What are operations?

7. What is social referencing?

8. According to Piaget, there are four stages of cognitive development. What are they and when do they occur?

9. Egocentrism and decentration are important indicators of what? Why?

10. What are the three major criticisms of Piaget's theory?

11. According to Kohlberg's theory, what are the three levels of moral development? An individual's level of moral development is indicated by what?

12. What are the major criticisms of Kohlbergs theory?

13. What are the five different perspectives of mother-infant attachment presented in the chapter?

14. What is the classic test of the nature of mother-child attachment? What are the three basic patterns of attachment that have been observed?

15. Erikson divides psychosocial development into how many stages? Each stage is associated with a crisis, what are they?

16. In what ways is gender identity shaped by social factors?

17. Where does the word "puberty" come from? What are some of the other physical changes associated with adolescence?

18. What effect does adolescent egocentrism have on psychosocial development?

19. How has the expression of adolescent sexuality changed over the last forty years? What are some of the differences between young men and women in their sexual attitudes?

20. In what two ways does life-span psychology differ from child developmental psychology?

21. What important similarity is there in Jung and Bühler's thinking about adult development?

22. Describe instrumental and companionship-based marriages. Are males or females happier within marriage? For whom is it most beneficial?

23. Is it a good idea to have a baby in order to improve a bad marriage? Why or why not?

24. What is the most stressful period of the divorce process? How long after a divorce does it take for adults to regain their sense of equilibrium?

25. What is a midlife crisis? What personality types are prone to depression in midlife?

OUTLINE OF KEY TERMS AND CONCEPTS

Reflexes
Maturation
    Physical maturation
    Psychological maturation
Adaptation
Egocentrism
Critical periods
Life before birth
    In utero
    Germinal period
    Embryonic period
    Fetal period

The newborn: The first two weeks
    Reflexes
    Cognition
    Preferences in perception
Physical growth in the early years
    Sequence of motor development
    Milestones in language development
Cognitive development
    Piaget's theory
        Assumptions
            Knowledge guides action
            Knowledge through experience and actions

                Complexity of mental structures and
                    biological age
                Schema
                Assimilation
                Accommodation
                Operations
        Social referencing
            Stages of cognitive development
                Sensorimotor stage (0–2 years)
                    Representational or symbolic thought
                    Object permanence
                Preoperational stage (2–7 Years)
                    Conservation
                Concrete operations (7–12 years)
                Formal operations (12 years to adult)
            Egocentrism
            Decentration
        Criticisms of Piaget's theory
    Moral Development
        Kohlberg's theory
            Levels of moral reasoning
                Premoral
                Conventional morality
                Postconventional morality
                Sociomoral perspective
        Criticisms of Kohlberg's theory
    Psychosocial development
        Attachment
            Separation anxiety
            Stranger anxiety
            Psychologist's views and studies
                Bowlby and Ainsworth
                Harlow and Harlow
                Sigmund Freud
                Jean Piaget
                Schaffer and Emerson
            The strange situation
                Patterns of attachment
                    Unattached
                    Securely attached
                    Insecurely attached
            Play
        Erikson's theory
            The eight ages of man
                Basic trust versus mistrust
                Autonomy versus shame and doubt
                Initiative versus guilt
                Industry versus inferiority
                    Identity versus role confusion
                Intimacy versus isolation
                Generativity versus self-absorption
                Integrity versus despair
        Development of gender roles
        Adolescence
            Physical development
                Puberty
            Cognitive development
                Questioning and idealism
            Psychosocial development
                Egocentrism
                Identity and turbulence
                Sexuality
        Adulthood
            Jung's theory
            Bühler's theory
            Erikson's theory
            Early adulthood
                Occupational choice
                Role model
                Mentor
            Marriage
                Instrumental marriage
                Companionship-based marriage
            Becoming a parent
            Divorce
        Middle age
            Midlife crisis
            Menopause
            Empty nest period

COMPLETION ITEMS

human development 1. Life-span psychologists argue that _____ is a life-long process that continues until death.

Reflexes 2. _____ are unlearned responses to environmental stimulation and are present at birth.

Physical

Psychological

3. _____ maturation is controlled by information contained in the genes and is assumed to be relatively unaffected by experience. _____ maturation is the development of mental abilities that result from the normal growth of the brain and nervous system.

adaptation

4. The changes an individual makes to adjust to environmental conditions are referred to as _____.

Critical periods

5. _____ are times in life when specific environmental or biological events *must* occur or development will fail to proceed normally.

ovum

embryo

fetal

6. The *in utero* period of the _____ begins at the moment of fertilization and ends about two weeks later when the fertilized egg is implanted in the uterus. Once attached to the uterine wall, the ovum becomes an _____. The embryonic period lasts until about the ninth week of pregnancy at which time the _____ period begins with the baby's first independent reaction to the world.

simpler

7. The text suggests that the world of the infant may not be so much confused as it is _____ and more selective than the adult world.

faces

new

8. In a study by psychologist Robert Fantz, newborn babies looked longer at patterned discs than at single-colored ones, and the longest at pictures of _____. Research evidence suggests that the infant comes into the world with a predisposition to search out _____ features of the environment.

sensory

distance

perceptual

9. Physical growth during infancy affects all of the child's _____ systems. As the head grows, the eyes become farther apart, making it difficult to judge accurately the _____ between an object and oneself. These constant changes contribute to the instability of the infant's _____ and mental worlds.

initiate, terminate

Cognitive

10. Somewhere between 6 and 8 months the child begins to locomote and a whole new world opens up. For the first time, infants can _____ and _____ social situations. _____ development soars once locomotion begins.

exciting

distracted

11. Children who are 3 years of age and younger, tend to focus on the next _____ event in their environment. By 6 years of age, the child's attention is more under control, and he or she is less easily _____ by irrelevant stimuli.

cognitive

evolutionary
adaptive

action

12. The most influential theory of _____ development was proposed by psychologist Jean Piaget, whose theory is rooted in _____ theory. He believed that our mental abilities develop because they have _____ value. A fundamental assumption of Piaget's theory of cognitive development is that knowledge develops through experience and _____.

schemata

accommodation

13. According to Piaget's theory, the _____ are our knowledge of how things are organized and related to each other. They are assumed to change by the processes of assimilation and _____.

17

COMPLETION ITEMS

knowledge

accommodate

Operations

concepts

permanence

conservation

egocentric

reasoning

continuous

descriptions

cognitive
reasons

individual

experience

masculine

attachment

14. Assimilation presumably occurs when children encounter a new event and try to assimilate it into their existing _____ structures or schema. When young children cannot assimilate new events into existing schemata, they must change their thinking to _____ the new information.

15. _____ are rules for transforming and manipulating information. They are reversible. For example, if you have four of anything and take two away, you will have two. The reverse is if you have two of anything and add two, you will have four. This operation reflects a basic fact about the physical world. Piaget proposed that children gain _____ by performing operations on things.

16. One of the most important accomplishments of the early phase of the sensorimotor stage is object _____: babies learn that something continues to exist even when they cannot see it.

17. Piaget believed that before the age of six or seven, children have not yet formed the _____ rule, which permits them to understand that the amount of an object may remain the same even though its outward appearance changes.

18. From the standpoint of Piaget's theory, infants are totally _____, in the sense that they know no differences between themselves and other people or objects in the world.

19. One criticism of Piaget's theory is that he seems to underestimate the _____ abilities of children and to overestimate their verbal abilities. Another criticism follows from research evidence indicating that development is more _____ and diverse than Piaget allows. Many critics feel that the "stages" of development postulated by Piaget are useful as generalized _____ of the thought of an "ideal" child at different points of development, but they are probably not adequate explanations of the course of intellectual growth.

20. Kohlberg's theory of moral reasoning, like Piaget's, is based on the _____ abilities of the child. Kohlberg's theory focuses on people's _____ for doing what they think is right and how moral reasoning and behavior change as schemata become more complex.

21. One criticism of Kohlberg's theory of moral reasoning is that its "stages" might not hold true in a culture in which there is less emphasis on _____ rights. Other critics argue that the stages of moral development are not fixed and can be greatly modified by _____. Carol Gilligan has pointed out a sex bias in Kohlberg's theory, whereby reasoning, which is seen as characteristic of the highest stages, tends to reflect traditionally _____ values.

22. Due to human beings' long period of immaturity, the relationships formed in the first few years have a special quality. That special quality is the _____ between the infant and the mother or primary caregiver.

object

separation anxiety
stranger anxiety

survival
food

needs
object permanence

communication

ages

mistrust

autonomy

guilt

inferiority
role

relationships

generativity

gender

social
gender roles

think
behavior

puberty

imagine

egocentric
self

23. After the age of about 8 months, because they have learned the concept of _____ permanence, infants often show extreme distress when the mother leaves. This distress is known as _____. They also become afraid of strangers, a fear called _____.

24. Bowlby and Ainsworth believe that attachment is innate and that strong attachments have a _____ function. Harlow and Harlow found that _____ is not the primary basis for attachment. Freud, on the other hand, believed that the basis for attachment lies in the fact that the mother gratifies the baby's _____, especially for food. Piaget believed that attachment is a function of the concept of _____ while other theorists believe that social interaction and _____ serve as the basis for the development of attachment.

25. Erik Erikson divides psychosocial development into eight stages that he calls the "eight _____ of man." According to his theory, the first year of life is characterized by the crisis of basic trust versus _____. During the second year of life, if their parents will allow them to work through difficult problems on their own, children will develop a sense of self or _____.

26. During the third to fifth years of life, if children's initiative or innovation is condemned by the family, they will suffer _____. From age 6 to puberty, the principal life crisis is one that Erikson describes as that of industry versus _____. During adolescence, the focal life crisis is that of identity versus _____ confusion.

27. During the period known as "early adulthood," Erikson considers the major crisis to be one that centers around the development of lasting, intimate _____. In middle adulthood, the choice is between concern for others or a preoccupation with oneself, a crisis of _____ versus self-absorption.

28. One of the central tasks of childhood is the acquisition of _____. At the point that children identify their own sex they begin selectively to adopt behaviors that are consistent with the _____ definitions of male or female. These social roles are termed _____.

29. In the gender literature the largest differences are found in the way we _____ about gender and the smallest in actual _____.

30. In early adolescence, "pudginess" is a sign that the changes of _____ are fast approaching. Many adolescents become idealistic for the first time because now they can _____ an ideal world and what an ideal society might be like.

31. Although adolescents tend to be intellectually idealistic, at the same time they remain emotionally _____. This characteristic is manifested in their extreme _____-consciousness.

COMPLETION ITEMS

sexually

virginity

passage

Emotional

enduring

biologically

experience

diverse

differentiation

instrumental

gender

husbands
wives

good friends

women's
men's

declines
improves

One-half
18 months

midlife crisis

empty nest

fewer
better

32. In the last few decades, attitudes toward sex have changed, and adolescents, girls in particular, have become more active _____ than ever before. Even with the liberalizing of attitudes in our society, losing _____ seems to be a different experience for boys and girls. For boys, it is almost a rite of _____ into manhood.

33. _____ involvement with the partner is often more important for young women than it is for young men. Young men typically have more sexual partners than do young women, while young women generally have more _____ relationships.

34. Life-span development differs from child developmental psychology in two important ways. First, child development is more _____ based while adult development is a function of _____ independent of maturation. Second, in contrast to child development, adult development is highly _____. It is commonly referred to as the process of _____.

35. Some researchers class marriages into two subtypes: _____ and companionship-based. Instrumental marriages are traditional marriages, based on clear role distinctions influenced heavily by _____ roles. In companionship-based marriages, roles tend to be shared.

36. Throughout marriage _____ are more satisfied with their relationships than are their _____. According to Levenson and Gottman, couples that stay together are, first and foremost, _____.

37. The transition to parenthood changes _____ lives more than _____ in both positive and negative ways. We know that marital satisfaction for both men and women _____ after the birth of a child and _____ after the children leave home.

38. _____ of new marriages end in divorce. Fifteen percent will occur within _____ of the birth of the first child.

39. A _____ occurs when a person discovers that he or she is not happy with life, and that goals either have not been attained or do not bring expected satisfactions.

40. The _____ period, when children leave home and become independent, is often thought to be a time of crisis for the family. Researchers have found that the best predictor of adjustment during menopause is the number of children in the home. The _____ the children, the _____ the woman adjusts.

SELF-QUIZ

MULTIPLE-CHOICE ITEMS

1. _____ is the development of mental abilities that result from the normal growth of the brain and nervous system.
   a. Physical maturation
   b. Psychological maturation

CHAPTER 2 / HUMAN DEVELOPMENT: BIRTH TO ADULTHOOD

c. Adaptation
d. Egocentrism

2. Trevarthen's research has indicated that the spontaneous lip movements of newborns are
   a. more frequent in girls than in boys.
   b. negatively correlated with the incidence of retardation.
   c. the same as required for adult speech.
   d. different in different cultures.

3. The authors of the text characterize the world of the newborn as
   a. a blooming, buzzing confusion.
   b. simpler and more selected than the adult world.
   c. a transitory one where there are no permanent objects.
   d. fearsome and frightening.

4. By about the age of 5 years, the human brain has generally attained _____ of its adult size.
   a. 25 percent
   b. 50 percent
   c. 75 percent
   d. 95 percent

5. Piaget assumed that
   a. knowledge guides action.
   b. knowledge develops through experience and action.
   c. the growth of capacity, or mental structures, is cognitive development.
   d. all of the above.

6. According to Piaget's theory, _____ are the knowledge of how things are organized and relate to each other.
   a. accomodations
   b. assimilations
   c. schemata
   d. abstract symbols

7. According to Piaget's theory, _____ are the rules for transforming and manipulating information.
   a. operations
   b. accomodations
   c. assimilations
   d. decentrations

8. According to Piaget's theory, a 4-year-old child would be expected to be in the _____ stage of development.
   a. formal operational
   b. concrete operational
   c. preoperational
   d. sensorimotor

9. In Piaget's terms, a child who shows that he or she understands that a given quantity of water remains the same although it is poured into a different-shaped container, is demonstrating attainment of
   a. assimilation.
   b. accomodation.
   c. the stage of formal operations.
   d. conservation.

10. According to Piaget's theory, the _____ phase of life is totally egocentric.
    a. sensorimotor
    b. preoperational
    c. concrete operations
    d. formal operations

11. Which of the following levels of Kohlberg's theory of moral development is characterized by conformity as means of avoiding disapproval and dislike by others?
    a. premoral
    b. preconventional morality
    c. conventional morality
    d. postconventional morality

12. Which of the following would be most likely to be evaluated by Kohlberg's method as having attained the highest levels of moral reasoning?
    a. a political conservative
    b. a political liberal
    c. a woman
    d. a man with traditional feminine values

13. According to Carol Gilligan's analysis, which of the following values would be likely to be viewed as reflective of the lowest level of moral reasoning using Kohlberg's method?
    a. individuality
    b. rationality
    c. caring
    d. detachment

13. The attachment of an infant to its mother is an important event in development. A securely attached child
    a. has difficulty becoming independent later in childhood.
    b. interacts less with other children.
    c. is more advanced in cognitive and social skills.
    d. is more advanced in cognitive skills but not social skills.

14. According to Erikson's theory, _____ is the central crisis of the adolescent years.
    a. autonomy versus shame and doubt
    b. initiative versus guilt
    c. industry versus inferiority
    d. identity versus role confusion

15. According to Erikson's theory, the crisis of the aging years is that of integrity versus
    a. inferiority.
    b. despair.
    c. self-absorption.
    d. ego-diffusion.
16. Common to all theories of gender development is a consensus
    a. that mothers are responsible for the acquisition of gender identity.
    b. about the power of gender in the lives of young children.
    c. that if left alone, children show no clear preference for sex-typed toys.
    d. the largest difference between girls and boys is in their behavior.
17. According to the text, the emergence of formal operations and the capacity for abstract thought during adolescence results in
    a. an intense period of questioning and idealism.
    b. a lessening in egocentrism and an increase in empathy.
    c. a disruption in the relationship with parents.
    d. the ability to learn algebra, finally.
18. In a 1978 survey, _____ of the girls questioned said they would like to first have sexual intercourse "on a first or second date."
    a. less than 1 percent
    b. about 5 percent
    c. almost a third
    d. over half
19. Which of the following is *not* one of the hallmarks of the beginning of adulthood:
    a. growing to your full stature
    b. beginning a career
    c. getting married
    d. beginning a family
20. The people most satisfied with marriage are
    a. wives.
    b. husbands.
    c. wives with children.
    d. husbands with children.
21. According to the text, which of the following couples are *least* likely to divorce?
    a. a couple married when they were teenagers
    b. a couple who were high school dropouts
    c. a yuppie couple who never see each other
    d. a couple in a traditional marriage with an unemployed husband
22. Which of the following women is *least* likely to suffer depression during the "empty-nest" period?
    a. a Black woman with one child
    b. a Jewish woman with three children
    c. a Protestant woman with four children
    d. all of these women would become depressed during this period.

TRUE-FALSE ITEMS

1. T F The reason developmental psychologists now study adult development is because they agree that children are simply small adults.
2. T F Physical maturation is profoundly affected by experience.
3. T F The embryonic period of *in utero* development begins at the moment of fertilization.
4. T F Newborns have been found to look longer at pictures of human faces than at single-color discs.
5. T F The order in which motor skills develop is the same for all children.
6. T F The human brain attains 95 percent of its adult size within the first two years.
7. T F In Piaget's view, the complexity of mental structures is determined largely by biological age.
8. T F According to Piaget, knowledge is acquired through physical manipulation of the environment.
9. T F According to Piaget's theory, higher order thinking begins in the formal operational stage.
10. T F One criticism of Piaget's theory is that it seems to overestimate the reasoning abilities of children and underestimate their verbal abilities.
11. T F In Kohlberg's theory, the highest level of moral reasoning is reflected by conformity to obtain rewards.
12. T F Youths in Turkey were found to display the same sequence of moral development as do children in the West.
13. T F The bulk of research evidence shows that people who score at the higher levels of Kohlberg's measure of moral reasoning, tend to *behave* more "morally" than do individuals who score at the lower levels.
14. T F Generally, human infants do not become attached to the people with whom they interact unless those people provide caregiving functions to the child.
15. T F Erikson's theory conceptualizes human development as a process which continues throughout the lifespan.
16. T F Gender identity refers to society's expectations of how a male or female should behave.
17. T F Girl babies have been found to react more to the human voice than do boy babies.
18. T F Puberty officially begins for boys when they have their first sexual experience.
19. T F To raise a well-adjusted child it is important that parents maintain a laissez-faire attitude.
20. T F Psychological factors are the most important influence in occupational choice.
21. T F According to the text a bad marriage is better than no relationship at all.
22. T F Mothers who work outside of the home report that their lives are no more stressful than the lives of unemployed women.
23. T F People of all classes consider their 20s to be the prime of life.
24. T F Menopause is characterized by hot flashes, irritability, drying spells, and depression in most women between the ages of 48 and 51.

ANSWER KEY TO SELF-QUIZ

MULTIPLE-CHOICE ITEMS

1. b 2. c 3. b 4. d 5. d 6. c 7. a 8. c 9. d 10. a 11. c 12. b 13. c 14. d 15. b 16. b 17. a 18. a 19. a 20. b 21. c 22. a

TRUE-FALSE ITEMS

1. F 2. F 3. F 4. T 5. T 6. F 7. T 8. T 9. T 10. F 11. F 12. T 13. T 14. F 15. T 16. F 17. T 18. F 19. F 20. F 21. T 22. T 23. F 24. F

THINKING ABOUT THE PSYCHOLOGY OF YOUR OWN EXPERIENCE

1. You read in Chapter 2 that adolescence "is often an intense period of questioning, searching, and rebellion." In this regard, consider the following: (1) How "intense" or "turbulent" was this period for you? (2) What were the principal issues or problems on which your own "questioning, searching, and rebellion" focused? (3) How completely do you feel you have resolved any of the issues or problems that were the object of that questioning, searching, and/or rebellion? (4) How has any of this, do you think, affected the way you see yourself and your relationships with other people?

Next, find someone over the age of 50 who you feel you can talk to. It might be someone you are related to or someone you have met through work or school. Ask this person to tell you about what it was like when he or she was an adolescent. If you feel it is appropriate, ask this person the four questions you answered above. You may be surprised at the similarity of his or her experience to your own. Perhaps this person can comment on the importance of the issues of adolescence from the vantage point of middle age (which some theorists consider to be a second adolescence because of all the changes that occur.)

2. It was also noted in Chapter 2 that "adolescence and young adulthood are often marked by a search for one's own identity." In some sense this may be a search that goes on more or less intensely throughout life. To be sure, there are no "age limits" on the search for identity, and adults in contemporary society apparently feel freer than ever before to acknowledge openly that they are 50 or 60 years old and still do not know "what they want to be when then grow up." At the heart of the search for identity or "self," is the definition of one's own values—the question of just what it is that is more important to us in life and the priorities we assign to those things. Regrettably, although we learn many things over the course of our formal education, values clarification is not often among them. Here is an exercise you might want to try in one of your quiet moments, to give you a feel for how values clarification ties in with self-definition or identity. Write out (not just *think* out) an answer to the question "Who am I?" As you write, just describe yourself as you are. When you finish, write out an answer to the following question: "How and what do I *want* to be?"

In the process of writing and comparing your answers to these two questions, especially if you do the same exercise every few months or so, you may find that you have gained some interesting insights. Periodic self-appraisal of this sort can also be helpful in defining realistic goals and in evaluating your own progress toward developing and carrying through a fulfilling life plan.

PART II

THE BIOLOGICAL WORLD

3
THE BRAIN AND THE NERVOUS SYSTEM

GENERAL STUDY QUESTIONS

After reading Chapter 3, you should be able to answer the following questions.

1. According to the text, in what structure does experience reside?

2. Which part of the brain was the last to evolve? What human activities is it responsible for?

3. Which part of the brain is the "oldest"? What functions does it govern?

4. If you were asleep and someone stimulated your RAS, what would you do?

5. What is stored in the cerebellum? What was the cerebellum's original function?

6. The four f's of survival: feeding, fighting, fleeing, and "sexual activity" are governed by what part of the brain?

7. What is the "master gland of the brain"? How does it regulate the body? What part of the brain tells it what to do?

8. Surgery on what part of the brain results in emotional deficiencies in humans?

9. The cortex performs what three functions?

10. What would you be unable to do if your frontal lobes were destroyed or removed?

11. What part of the brain analyzes sensory input?

12. Stimulating the temporal lobe will result in what kind of feeling?

13. The two hemispheres of the brain specialize in different functions. What functions does each control? Is it possible to function normally with only one hemisphere?

14. What has happened to someone who has been commisurotomized? What can be learned from such a person?

15. Besides thinking, what does the brain do for us?

16. What is the "language of the brain"?

17. Draw a neuron and label its parts.

18. What are neurotransmitters? What do they determine?

19. What is the myelin sheath and what does it do?

20. There are three nervous systems. What are they and what do they do?

21. Besides the nervous systems, what way does the brain have of controlling the body?

22. What is a hormone and what does it do? How is it regulated?

23. In what way is the brain modifiable?

24. What are the three types of hemispheric organization in left-handers? Which is the most common?

OUTLINE OF KEY TERMS AND CONCEPTS

Architecture of the brain
    Cortex
Archeology of the brain
    Levels of functions
    Archaic nature of the nervous system
Keeping alive
    Brain stem
    Reticular activating system (RAS)
    Thalamus
    Cerebellum
    Limbic system
    Homeostasis
    Four F's of survival
    Hypothalamus
    Pituitary
    Hormones
    Hippocampus
    Amygdala
Creating anew
    Convoluted

Data processing center
Talents
Executive branch
Frontal lobes
    Loss of self
Sensory and motor areas
    Homunculus
Parietal lobes
    Agnosia
    Amorphosynthesis
Temporal lobes
    Aphasia
Occipital lobes
    Visual cortex
Two hemispheres
    Corpus callosum
    Lateral specialization
    Planum temporale
    The "split brain"
    Workings of the normal brain

Brain "minds" the body
  Running the body
  Organ of adaptation
Language of the brain
  Neurons
    Cell body
    Axon
    Dendrite
  Neural impulse: Action potential
  Neuron and neurotransmission
    Neurohormones
    Neurotransmitters
    Resting potential
    Action potential
    Absolute refractory period
    Myelin sheath
      Insulation
      Acceleration of transmission
      Isolation
    Neurotransmission
      Electrical
      Chemical
      Synapse
      Presynaptic neuron
      Postsynaptic neuron
      Synaptic vesicles
      Synaptic cleft
      Neurotransmitters
        Acetylcholine (ACh)
          Curare
        Chemical pathways
        Norepinephrine
        Dopamine
          Parkinson's disease
          L-Dopa
        Serotonin
          LSD
          Mood
        Body humors
          Bile
          Phlegm
The nervous system
  Central nervous system
    Reflexes
    Afferent neurons
    Efferent neurons
    Interneurons
  Peripheral nervous system
    Somatic nervous system
    Autonomic nervous system
      Sympathetic nervous system
      Parasympathetic nervous system
The brain's chemical system
  Neuroendocrine system
    Lock and key principle
    Hormones and the pituitary
      Neurosecretory cells
      Thyroid releasing hormone
    Adrenal glands
      Adrenal cortex
      Adrenal medulla
The individual brain
  Brain growth and experience
    Language in the first month of life
    Right- and left-handedness
      Mixed dominance
    Sex differences in the brain
  The changing brain
    Short-term changes
      Eggs and ACh
      Carbohydrates and serotonin
    Long-term alterations

COMPLETION ITEMS

atoms

pharmacy

cortex

1. In a single human brain, the number of potential interconnections between cells is greater than the number of _____ in the known universe. The brain is a _____; it produces more chemical substances than any other organ of the body.

2. The _____ was the last part of the brain to evolve and produces the most distinctive human activities such as language and art.

archeology
four

stem
thalamus

limbic

hypothalamus

hippocampus

data
executive

frontal

planning

complex

parietal
agnosia

aphasia

visual

callosum

language

draw

alpha

problem

thinking

body

neuron

dendrite

3. In addition to an architecture, the brain has what we could call an _____. Like an archeological dig; there are layers to the brain—_____ different levels of functions that developed as the brain evolved.

4. Most sensory information from the outside world enters the lower brain _____. Information is then relayed to appropriate parts of the cortex by the _____.

5. The _____ system is the area of the brain that regulates vital body processes. Functions such as eating, drinking, and body temperature are regulated by the _____. The structure in the brain that determines whether incoming information matches stored information is known as the _____.

6. The cortex is comprised of specialized cells arranged in columns, which act as _____ processing centers. The cortex serves as the _____ branch of the brain, responsible for decision-making and judgments.

7. The _____ lobes lie at the intersection of the neural pathways that convey information from the parietal areas of the brain about people and events. If they are destroyed or removed, the individual becomes incapable of _____, carrying out, or understanding a complex action or idea.

8. The more _____ the function, the more space devoted to it in the brain.

9. Sensory input is analyzed by the _____ lobes. Damage to these areas can result in a form of _____, which means "not knowing."

10. Severe damage to certain areas of the left temporal lobe may result in a language impairment known as _____.

11. The occipital lobes of the brain are sometimes known as the _____ cortex.

12. The cerebral cortex is divided into two hemispheres connected by a large structure called the corpus _____. The left hemisphere controls the right side of the body, as well as logical activities and _____.

13. Dr. Bogen found that split-brain patients could still write with their right hand, but could not _____ very well.

14. In EEG recordings, _____ wave activity indicates an awake brain on "idle," and beta waves indicate an awake brain actively processing information. Recent research has indicated that people can apparently use their left and right hemispheres at will when engaged in _____ solving.

15. The brain as a whole is not primarily designed for _____ and rational activity. Its main job is to regulate or "mind" the _____.

16. The major constituent of the brain is the nerve cell or _____. The "transmitter" end of this cell is called the axon, and the "receiving" end is known as the _____.

33

COMPLETION ITEMS

action

refractory

myelin

chemical

conservation

acetylcholine

dopamine

humors

barrier

central

afferent

efferent

voluntary

emergency

shape

hormone

emergency
medulla

cardiovascular

more

pruning

right

left

serotinin
cortex

17. Communication between neurons occurs by the process of neurotransmission. The neural impulse of a firing neuron is the _____ potential. After it fires, the neuron is temporarily depleted of energy and does not fire again while it is in what is called the _____ period.

18. The fatty substance coating some neurons is called the _____ sheath.

19. The action potential inside a neuron is electrical, but the transmission of the neural impulse from one neuron to the next is _____. The space between the axon of one neuron and the dendrite of the next is called the _____.

20. The drug curare is fatal because it causes paralysis by interfering with the neurotransmitter known as _____. Parkinson's disease is caused by a lack of the neurotransmitter _____.

21. The ancient Greeks mistakenly believed that mood states are determined by specific body _____ such as bile and phlegm.

22. A special network of cells called the "blood-brain _____" keeps toxins in the blood from reaching the brain.

23. The brain and spinal cord together make up the _____ nervous system. Information is brought into the brain from the sensory system by way of the _____ neurons. Messages from the brain to muscles and glands are carried by the _____ neurons.

24. The somatic nervous system controls the _____ movements of the body. The parasympathetic system acts like a brake on the sympathetic system and returns the body to normal after some sort of _____ reaction.

25. It is the _____ of the drug or neurotransmitter molecule that is the "key" to activating a particular receptor cell in the brain.

26. The pituitary is the control gland of the endocrine system. When the thyroid gland receives TRH, it produces its own _____ known as thyroxin.

27. The adrenal glands start up in _____ situations. When activated by the ANS, the adrenal _____ secretes epinephrine and norepinephrine. Both of these hormones stimulate the _____ system.

28. There are many _____ connections in the brain of an infant than in an elderly adult. Development seems to be a matter of _____ original connections rather than making new ones.

29. In most right-handed people, language and other sequential abilities are present in the _____ hemisphere.

30. The representation of analytic and sequential thinking is more clearly present in the _____ hemisphere of males than in females.

31. A meal rich in carbohydrates increases the brain's supply of _____. Rats raised in a negatively ionized atmosphere have a _____ 9 percent larger than those raised in and atmosphere which is nonionized.

CHAPTER 3 / THE BRAIN AND THE NERVOUS SYSTEM

SELF-QUIZ
MULTIPLE-CHOICE ITEMS

1. In the text, the brain is compared to a
   a. ramshackle house.
   b. Rolls Royce engine.
   c. bowl of noodle soup.
   d. radio transmitter.

2. The _____ was the last part of the brain to evolve.
   a. brain stem
   b. limbic system
   c. cortex
   d. thalamus

3. The brain stem structure which controls level of arousal is called the
   a. LAR.
   b. RAS.
   c. EPT.
   d. MOA.

4. The limbic system includes
   a. the hypothalamus.
   b. the pituitary.
   c. the hippocampus.
   d. all of the above.

5. The _____ lobes are classified by many psychobiologists as part of the limbic system.
   a. occipital
   b. parietal
   c. frontal
   d. temporal

6. The sensory and motor areas are at the juncture of the _____ lobes in the brain.
   a. frontal and occipital
   b. frontal and parietal
   c. parietal and occipital
   d. occipital and temporal

7. Aphasia is most likely to result from severe damage to the left _____ lobe.
   a. frontal
   b. parietal
   c. occipital
   d. temporal

8. After temporal lobe stimulation, some people report feeling
   a. lost.
   b. sleepy.
   c. in two places at once.
   d. afraid.

9. Which of the following *is not* among those functions predominantly controlled by the right brain hemisphere?
    a. language
    b. the left side of the body
    c. spatial judgments
    d. artistic activities
10. Communication between the two brain hemispheres takes place through the
    a. hypothalamus.
    b. temporal lobe.
    c. corpus callosum.
    d. planum temporale.
11. Research by Galin and Ornstein indicated that there is more alpha wave activity in the right than in the left hemisphere when a person is
    a. arranging blocks.
    b. writing a letter.
    c. putting together a jigsaw puzzle.
    d. doing any of the above.
12. The _____ is the transmitter end of the neuron.
    a. cell body
    b. axon
    c. dendrite
    d. synapse
13. The neural impulse of a firing neuron is the
    a. neurotransmission
    b. action potential
    c. absolute refractory period
    d. synaptic action
14. Which of the following *is not* among the main functions of the myelin sheath?
    a. insulation
    b. acceleration of neural transmission
    c. isolation of the neuron
    d. secretion of neurotransmitters
15. The drug curare causes death by interfering with which of the following neurotransmitters?
    a. acetylcholine
    b. norepinephrine
    c. dopamine
    d. serotonin
16. Loss of which of the following is most likely to cause insomnia?
    a. acetylcholine
    b. norpinephrine
    c. dopamine
    d. serotonin
17. Which of the following *is not* one of the types of neurons found in the spinal cord?
    a. afferant neurons

b. efferent neurons
c. interneurons
d. all of the above are found in the spinal cord

18. You wake up from a nap and find your room on fire. Which system will be immediately activated?
    a. autonomic system
    b. sympathetic system
    c. parasympathetic system
    d. all three

19. In what way does the brain grow in response to certain experiences?
    a. the existing neurons fire more often
    b. more neurons are formed
    c. the existing neurons become larger
    d. the existing neurons fire more easily

20. A rich meal of which of the following is most likely to increase the available levels of ACh in the brain?
    a. sugars
    b. starches
    c. eggs
    d. tryptophan

TRUE-FALSE ITEMS

1. T F The memory for certain types of simple learned responses is stored in the cerebellum.
2. T F The limbic system is involved in the maintenance if homeostasis.
3. T F Eating, drinking, sleeping, waking, body temperature, heart rate, sex, and emotions are all regulated by the hypothalamus.
4. T F Of all animals, human beings have the most enfolded cortex.
5. T F The case of Phineas Gage illustrates the important role of the temporal lobes in planning and comprehending complex actions, as well as in presentation of the "self".
6. T F More brain area is devoted to the back than to the tongue.
7. T F Wernicke's aphasia is most likely to result from damage to the left parietal lobe.
8. T F Only in human beings do the brain hemispheres specialize for different functions.
9. T F In 95 percent of fetuses, the left hemisphere is larger than the right.
10. T F The two hemispheres are essentially two separate systems, and thus, two separate brains.
11. T F The primary component of hemispheric specialization is the type of information processes and not how the brain processes that information.
12. T F The brain as a whole *is not* primarily designed for thinking.
13. T F Once a neuron fires, it immediately fires again.
14. T F The neural impulse from one neuron to the next is electrical.
15. T F "Re-uptake" refers to the process by which a neurotransmitter returns to the axon of the presynaptic neuron.
16. T F The drug LSD seems to block the firing of ACh neurons.

17. T F Information is brought into the brain through the efferent neurons.
18. T F It is norepinephrine that carries the message of the sympathetic division of the ANS.
19. T F In the "lock-and-key" principle described in the text, it is the *size* of the neurotransmitter or drug molecule which is the "key."
20. T F Most left-handers have brains in which language is controlled by the right hemisphere.
21. T F Air full of negatively charged ions will have a negative effect on your mood. (F)

ANSWER KEY TO SELF-QUIZ

MULTIPLE-CHOICE ITEMS

1. a 2. c 3. b 4. d 5. c 6. b 7. d 8. c 9. a 10. c 11. b 12. b 13. b 14. d 15. a 16. d 17. d 18. b 19. c 20. c

TRUE-FALSE ITEMS

1. T 2. T 3. T 4. T 5. F 6. F 7. F 8. T 9. T 10. F 11. F 12. T 13. F 14. F 15. T 16. F 17. F 18. T 19. F 20. F 21. F

THINKING ABOUT THE PSYCHOLOGY OF YOUR OWN EXPERIENCE

1. Do you jog, work out with weights, or engage regularly in any other kind of vigorous, physically demanding, maybe even exhausting kind of training? If not, do you know someone who does? Many people who "get into" this kind of thing report that they do so regularly because they enjoy it and "feel better" when they do. Interestingly, however, these same people also often say that if they should *have to* miss a few days of their training regimen, for business or other reasons, they begin to "feel awful," physically, emotionally, and intellectually, and that the only thing that seems to bring them out of this bad feeling state is a renewal of their exercise program. Indeed, it is almost as if the person *needs* his or her "exercise fix"!

Which of the facts of brain chemistry covered in Chapter 3 is most relevant to these observations? Might these facts help to explain the apparent "addiction" to physical training that develops in some people? What, if anything, might this same mechanism have to do with development of the "stress-addicted" or "high-drive" personality? How might the same mechanism also be involved in the development of "self-abusive" behaviors, such as head banging and tongue biting in emotionally disturbed children.

2. There are many people who seem to have very different ways of viewing the world. One important difference between people may be in the way they use their hemispheres.

Do you know some people who seem organized around the special abilities of the right hemisphere—painting, drawing, dance, music—but seem less proficient in language skills? Similarly, do you notice the same for the left hemisphere?

What other divisions in the brain seem to suggest to you possible differences in personality?

4
GENETICS AND EVOLUTION

GENERAL STUDY QUESTIONS

After reading Chapter 4, you should be able to answer the following questions.

1. What is the double helix? What are the four chemical bases it is made up of? Why is it important to us?

2. What is a codon? According to the text, what is the fundamental difference between humans and turtles, at the molecular level?

3. How do organisms grow? After the DNA spirals split in half, what happens?

4. What carries an individual's genetic program? How many chromosomes do each of us have and where do they come from?

5. Where did you get your eye color? What color eyes do you suppose your first child will have? What does it depend on?

6. Who determines the sex of the child, the mother or the father? Which sex is more fragile?

7. In what two ways can generations differ in characteristics? Under what conditions does a mutation have an effect on the evolution of the species?

8. Why do scientists prize identical twins?

9. What is the "range of reaction"?

10. Do you believe that humans are determined by nature or by nurture? What difference does it make?

11. Why is the principle of adaptation important?

12. What are the four important hominid characteristics that marked the change from prehuman to human beings?

13. What is the most sophisticated tool human beings have?

14. What is the crucial factor in evolution? What determines which offspring survives? Which traits get passed on?

15. The term "fitness" refers to what?

16. Who or what is "the blind watchmaker"?

17. Why does the environment play a much greater role in the development of the human brain than that of any other animal?

18. What does an ethologist study? What is a stable strategy and why is it important?

19. What purpose does the neotenic face serve?

20. What are fixed-action patterns?

21. Sociobiology attempts to account for what? What is the difference between inclusive fitness and reproductive fitness?

22. What is parental investment? How does this help explain some parent-child conflicts?

23. What is the difference between the phylogenetic and the selectionist viewpoints?

24. What is the sociobiological explanation for the differences in male and female sexual behavior? What are some of the problems with this explanation?

25. According to the text, what is our most important characteristic?

OUTLINE OF KEY TERMS AND CONCEPTS

Genetic code
  DNA
  Four chemical "building blocks"
    Adenine
    Thymine
    Guanine
    Cytosine
  Codon
  Double helix
    Mitosis

Watson's and Crick's discovery
Chromosomes
  Dominant and recessive genes
    Genotype
    Phenotype
  Sex
    Chromosome pair 23
    X and Y
    Ratios for human species
  Birth Defects

    Trisome in pair 21
        Downs syndrome
    Trisome in pair 23
        Feminine characteristics in male
  Mutations
  Twins
    Identical (Monozygotic)
    Fraternal
Genetics, behavior and experience
  Inherited traits
    Eye color
    Family characteristics
  Range of reaction
    Schizophrenia
      Family histories
      Genetic similarity and concordance
The beginnings: Our heritage
  Nature-nurture issue
    Nature
      Innate characteristics
    Nurture
      Environment
  Principle of adaptation
    Adaptive value
Origins and development of human beings
  Evolutionary time
  Prehumans
    Hominids
      Ramapithecus
      Australopithecus
      Homo Habilis
    Modern humans
      Homo erectus
        Upright man
        Terra Amata
      Neanderthal
      Homo sapiens
        Cro-Magnon
Hunting, gathering, and agricultural revolution
  Hunter-gatherers
  Agricultural revolution
    Civilizations
Process of adaptation and evolution
  Charles Darwin
    On the Origin of Species

    Natural selection
      Population
        Artificial selection
    Adaptive value and fitness
      Survival of the fittest
      Vitamin D synthesis
        Skin color
  Impact of Darwin's theory
    Our view of ourselves
    Copernicus's discovery
    "Monkey trial"
    The Blind Watchmaker
  Human adaptation
    Bipedalism
    Immaturity at birth
      The brain
      Mother-father-infant relationship
  Dexterity and tool use
    Specialized tools
    Homo erectus
    Cro-Magnon
  Ethology and biological fixed action patterns
    Imprinting
    Prepared reaction
    Stable strategy
    Cuteness and attraction
    Fixed-action patterns
  Sociobiology
    Evolution and genetics
      Individual
      Group
      Population
      The gene
    Inclusive fitness
      Altruism
      Schizophrenia
    Parental investment
      Reproductive fitness
      Parent-child conflicts
    Effects of one gene on behavior
      Phylogenetic viewpoint
        Specialized computational programs
      Selectionism viewpoint
        Judgment and choice

COMPLETION ITEMS

gene

DNA

double helix

bases
blueprint

codons

structural, functional

mitosis

chromosome

46
genotype

phenotype
dominant
recessive

sex

father's

mutation

replication
molecules

range of reaction

experience

1. The _____ is the basic unit of biological heredity in all living things. Genes are made of a substance called _____, which is an acronym for deoxyribonucleic acid. The DNA molecule consists of two chains twisted into a _____.

2. The rungs of the ladder contain the genetic information consisting of four chemical substances or _____. Virtually every living thing gets its _____ for growth and development from these bases.

3. Groups of three bases are called _____. The order in which the bases appear along the double helix spells out exactly what _____ and _____ proteins to make, when to make them and where to put them.

4. Organisms grow by a process of cell divisions called _____, during which the DNA spirals separate, yet each new cell has exactly the same genetic code as the original cell.

5. Genes are arranged, like beads on a string, on a _____, which carries an individual's entire genetic program.

6. Humans have a total of _____ chromosomes. All the genes a person carries are called his or her _____. The portion of all of one's genes that is expressed is called the _____.

7. When a _____ gene is present, the trait it represents will be expressed. A _____ gene will normally be expressed only if it is contributed to the offspring's genetic program by *both* parents.

8. Chromosome pair 23 determines an individual's _____. Females have two X chromosomes in pair 23, and males have one X and one Y chromosome in that pair. A child's sex is thus determined at conception by the _____ contribution to his or her genetic makeup.

9. A _____ is a spontaneous change in the structure of one or more genes. This can happen in a variety of ways: a mistake when the chromosomes are combined at conception; mistakes in DNA _____; or physical damage to DNA _____, which can be caused by environmental events such as radiation.

10. Most complex human abilities are determined by an interplay between inheritance and environment; these are the kinds of abilities governed by what is called the _____. The specific genetic endowment may predispose an individual to an ability or trait but whether the predisposition develops into a reality depends largely on _____.

nature
nurture

adapted
environment

hominids

Ramapithecus

Australopithecus

tools

cooperative

erectus

complexity

fire

Neanderthals

intelligent

symbolism

hunting
agriculture

civilization

On the Origin of Species
genetics

fittest
succeeding

11. The _____ view holds that we are governed by our innate characteristics. In contrast, the _____ view asserts that people are the result of their environment and that it is life circumstances that makes a person into what he or she becomes.

12. When an organism changes to fit better into its environment it has _____. Any trait has adaptive value if it helps an organism to function better in its _____.

13. Our prehuman ancestors, who were _____, were descended from tree-dwelling animals.

14. Our first human like ancestor was _____, who first appeared sometime between 9 and 13 million years ago.

15. The first hominid we could call our *direct* ancestor was _____, who was followed by *Homo habilis*. *Homo habilis*, it is believed, survived primarily because of the ability to use _____ and to hunt effectively in groups.

16. The change from prehuman to human involved the development of four important characteristics: increasingly upright stance, increased use of tools, increased size of the brain, and emergence of a _____ society.

17. About one and a half million years have passed since the emergence of one of the first modern humans, *Homo* _____, in which time the brain has doubled in size. What most distinguished this species from its predecessors was a large brain and the _____ of behavior that it made possible. We know from the archaeological find at Terra Amata that this species had a culture that was very advanced, with elaborate shelters, clothing, and apparently the controlled use of _____.

18. In the culture of _____, the cave men of popular folklore, there was division of labor, increased inventiveness, organized conflict, and apparently even spiritual worship.

19. In the remains of Cro-Magnon we have found the earliest predecessors of our own species. *Homo sapiens*, which means "_____ man."

20. A major innovation of Cro-Magnon is art, which along with language, is a significant milestone in human evolution because it signifies a mind capable of abstraction, _____, and invention.

21. For most of history, human beings have lived in _____ and gathering societies. The invention of _____ liberated humans from the uncertainties of the nomadic life as hunter-gatherers, promoted the development of more stable societies, and is thus seen as marking the beginning of _____ as we know it.

22. English naturalist Charles Darwin proposed his theory of how adaptation occurs in his book, _____. Darwin's theory, combined with modern _____, is the basis of the modern theory of evolution.

23. Darwin's theory came to be identified with the idea of "survival of the _____." The advantage of a new trait is not seen in the individual who inherits it but in _____ generations.

Natural

evolution

animal

human nature

feedback

bipedal
visual

tool

immaturity

womb

language

Ethology

imprinting
Fixed

neotenic

survival
inclusive

investment

phylogenetic
selectionist

24. _____ selection is the process by which the environment selects the individuals best adapted to it. The resulting change in the population is _____.

25. Darwin's theory placed human beings as members of the _____ kingdom, subject to the same forces that act on all animals, and it launched the scientific inquiry of _____.

26. The evolutionary process of human adaptation is most appropriately viewed as a positive _____ loop.

27. Humans are _____, which means that we walk on two feet instead of on all four. A more sophisticated _____ system developed along with upright posture. Hands were freed from weight-bearing responsibilities, making _____ use possible.

28. Developmental _____ at birth was the evolutionary "solution" to the problem created by the thicker pelvis and larger brain and head of the human infant. The major portion of the brain's development occurs outside of the _____.

29. Those areas of the brain that control fine motor movements and that become further developed in toolmaking are the same ones involved in _____.

30. _____ is the professional study of behavior under natural conditions. The tendency for a newly hatched duckling to follow around a moving object is called _____. _____ action patterns are unlearned behaviors, generic to a species, which appear or are released in the presence of certain sign stimuli.

31. A baby's cute _____ face is characterized by a proportionally larger forehead, eyes, and cheeks than are characteristic of adults.

32. Sociobiology emphasizes the importance of individual genes as determinants of behavior. According to this view, much of our social behavior can be seen as the outcome of our genes "trying" to ensure their own _____ through *us* as their temporary hosts. The concept of _____ fitness associated with this view, accounts for a number of human behaviors that make no sense from the standpoint of Darwin's "survival of the fittest" idea.

33. Parental _____ refers to any behaviors that enhance the survival potential of an offspring.

34. The _____ view assumes that organisms evolved to suite their environment. The _____ viewpoint assumes that specific selection mechanisms operate in human judgment and choice.

COMPLETION ITEMS

SELF-QUIZ

MULTIPLE-CHOICE ITEMS

1. Which of the following is *not* one of the four chemical "building blocks" of DNA?
   a. adenine
   b. thymine
   c. guanine
   d. rybonine

2. The order in which the four chemical building blocks of DNA appear along the double helix is called the
   a. nucleosphere.
   b. genetic code.
   c. nucleosine program.
   d. trisome 23.

3. A person who has two X chromosomes in pair 23 is most likely to
   a. have blue eyes.
   b. be afflicted with Downs syndrome.
   c. be a female.
   d. be a male.

4. Most complex human abilities are determined by an interplay between inheritance and the environment. These kinds of abilities are governed by
   a. a gene.
   b. the range of reaction.
   c. the range of convenience.
   d. the environment.

5. The "nature" view emphasizes the importance of _____ in the determination of behavior.
   a. early experience
   b. learning
   c. the environment
   d. instincts

6. If someone were to chart the entire history of the earth on a single year's calendar, making midnight on December 31 represent today, everything that has happened in recorded history would occur in the _____ of the year.
   a. final minute
   b. final day
   c. final week
   d. last two months

7. Archeological evidence from a cave in Iraq indicates that _____ had organized funeral ceremonies.
   a. *Homo habilis*
   b. *Homo erectus*
   c. *Australopithecus*
   d. Neanderthals

8. According to the text, _____ made possible the beginning of civilization as we know it.
    a. tool use
    b. agriculture
    c. the development of art
    d. the development of spiritual worship
9. Charles Darwin's theory was oriented primarily to describing the mechanism by which organisms
    a. reproduce.
    b. adapt to their environment.
    c. grow in intelligence.
    d. survive mutations.
10. The match between the traits of a population and its environment is called
    a. adaptation.
    b. natural selection.
    c. fitness.
    d. evolution.
11. According to the text, an increasingly sophisticated _____ developed along with bipedalism.
    a. visual system
    b. sense of smell
    c. ability to remain calm and relaxed when confronted with sudden changes in the environment.
    d. all of the above
12. At birth a human baby's brain is _____ percent of its adult weight.
    a. 25%
    b. 40%
    c. 50%
    d. 75%
13. The _____ evolved faster than any other human organ(s).
    a. brain
    b. sex organs
    c. hand
    d. skin
14. Tinburgen found that _____ serves as the critical sign that releases attack behavior in the stickleback fish.
    a. rapid movement
    b. changes in speed of movement
    c. a red underbelly
    d. a high-frequency humming sound
15. The sociobiological approach emphasizes the gene as the determinant of
    a. physical traits such as eye and hair color
    b. racial and ethnic characteristics
    c. behavior
    d. schizophrenia

16. Consistent with the concept of inclusive fitness, the probability of _____ has been shown to increase with increases in the number of genes in common.
    a. Down's syndrome
    b. self-awareness
    c. aggressive attack
    d. altruism
17. It seems that natural selection in human beings works mainly
    a. on the individual.
    b. on the gene.
    c. by the process referred to by Darwin as "speciology".
    d. through chromosome pair 21.
18. According to the text, our most important characteristic is
    a. the ability to mate at any time.
    b. the ability to go beyond our inheritance.
    c. the ability to think.
    d. the ability to use tools.

TRUE-FALSE ITEMS

1. T F The chromosome is the basic component of heredity in all living things.
2. T F Each fragment on a DNA strand contains all the information to conceive a new double helix.
3. T F All of an individual's genes are present in the nucleus of every cell of the body.
4. T F There are 105 females born for every male.
5. T F More males than females die at almost every age level.
6. T F The position taken in your text is that most complex human activities are determined by genetic inheritance rather than environment.
7. T F The identical twin of a schizophrenic is no more likely to suffer from the disorder than is a fraternal twin.
8. T F Adaptation is the natural fit of the organism to the environment.
9. T F The preponderance of available archaeological evidence indicates that Neanderthals most probably *were* just the kind of brutish, dim-witted creatures they are depicted to be in popular folklore.
10. T F Agriculture made possible the origin of civilization as we know it.
11. T F Many anthropologists use the fact that production of vitamin D within the body is stimulated by exposure to sunlight to explain skin color differences between different human populations.
12. T F The major portion of the brain's development occurs inside the womb.
13. T F Those areas of the brain that control fine motor movements are also involved in language.
14. T F Ethologist Konrad Lorenz demonstrated that baby goslings can be imprinted to a human.
15. T F Ethologists have shown that fixed action patterns are actually overlearned habit patterns.

16. T F Altruistic behavior is more adequately accounted for by Darwin's "survival of the fittest" idea than it is by the concept of inclusive fitness.
17. T F The selectionist viewpoint assumes that organisms evolved to suit their environment.
18. T F Variability is the key to evolutionary fitness.

ANSWER KEY TO SELF-QUIZ

MULTIPLE-CHOICE ITEMS

1. d 2. b 3. c 4. b 5. d 6. a 7. b 8. b 9. b 10. c 11. a 12. a 13. a 14. c 15. c 16. d 17. a 18. b

TRUE-FALSE ITEMS

1. F 2. T 3. T 4. F 5. T 6. F 7. F 8. F 9. F 10. T 11. T 12. F 13. T 14. T 15. F 16. F 17. F 18. T

THINKING ABOUT THE PSYCHOLOGY OF YOUR OWN EXPERIENCE

1. Do you think that knowledge derived from recent advances in modern cellular biology and genetics will have an impact on the future course of human evolution? If so, why? If not, why not? What are some reasons why the findings and applied implications of such research might evoke vigorously critical reactions based on theological considerations? How might such research in cellular biology have an important political as well as medical and psychological impact on life in our society. Do you think there should be some kind of governmental restriction on this research? If so, how might this kind of monitoring be managed? What are the dangers inherent in such research? What are the benefits that might be realized from it. How do you think you would feel about these issues if you were soon to be a parent?

2. If you were suddenly transported back a hundred and fifty years in time but remained in the same place, could you survive? What things would you need to know and how would you learn them? What are some of the skills and abilities you have developed that you wouldn't need (eg. driving fast, watching three television shows at once). If you were designing the human species, what would you change to allow us to adapt to the twenty-first century?

5
SENSORY EXPERIENCE

GENERAL STUDY QUESTIONS

After reading Chapter 5, you should be able to answer the following questions.

1. What does "deconstruction" mean and what does it have to do with sensation?

2. In what way are our senses censors?

3. Give an example of sensory adaptation, change, and comparison.

4. Psychophysics is the study of what?

5. What is the difference between absolute threshold and difference threshold?

6. List the four major related principles of psychophysics.

7. What is transduction and why is it important?

8. What two "miracles" do the senses perform? Which one of these miracles still mystifies scientists?

9. Which sense is responsible for the control of almost all the basic actions necessary for living in the human world? What are its basic functions?

10. Which part of the eye begins its development as part of the brain? What are its three main layers of nerve cells?

11. Why is the "blind spot" blind?

12. What is the major difference between rods and cones? What are the three different kinds of cones?

13. Where is the greatest concentration of cones?

14. How do our eyes adapt to seeing in the dark? Where is color? How do we see it?

15. What is the most common form of color blindness? Why is there no such thing as red-blue color blindness?

16. What three pathways merge to produce a unified perception of an object?

17. What is lateral inhibition? How does it work? What does it help us see?

18. Cells in the visual cortex respond best to what?

19. In what way is sensory experience determined by movement?

20. How does the ear work? How can sound be painful?

21. In what ways are the visual system and the auditory system alike?

22. Which sense is the "most direct"? In what way?

23. What are the four basic elements of taste?

24. Which parts of the body are most sensitive to touch? The different nerve endings in the skin send their information to the brain by way of what two systems?

25. What three factors determine adaptation level? What is the anchoring effect?

OUTLINE OF KEY TERMS AND CONCEPTS

Reflecting and selecting the world
   Deconstruction
   Selectivity
      Inclusion/exclusion
How the senses simplify and organize the world
   Sensory adaptation
      Adaptation
      Comparison
How physical and psychological worlds are related
   Psychophysics
      Thresholds
         Absolute threshold
         Just noticeable difference (j.n.d.)
      General principles of sensation
         Weber's law
            Proportional relationship
         Fechner's law
            Relative intensity
         Power law
How physical energy is changed into experience
   Transduction
Vision
   Detecting
      Layout of surroundings
      Change or sequence
      Controlling movement
   Cornea
   Pupil
   Iris
      Circular muscles
      Radial muscles
   Lens

- Retina
  - Intermediate layer
    - Bipolar cells
    - Ganglia
    - Horizontal cells
    - Amacrine cells
  - Ganglion cells
- Blind spot
- Photoreceptors
  - Rods
  - Cones
  - Fovea
  - Dark Adaptation
- Color vision
  - Psychological primaries
  - Opponent process
    - After images
  - Color blindness
- What the eye tells the brain
  - Optic chiasma
  - Lateral geniculate nucleus (LGN)
  - Visual cortex
  - Tectum
  - Secondary visual cortex
    - Tectopulvinar system
    - Geniculostriate system
    - Magnocellular division
    - Parvocellular division
  - Lateral inhibition
  - Receptive fields in retina and visual cortex
    - Receptive field
    - Feature analyzers
    - Simple cells
    - Complex cells
    - Hypercomplex cells
    - Modules of sensory analysis
  - What the brain tells the eye
    - Movement-produced stimulation
    - Saccades
- Hearing
  - Sound waves
    - Amplitude
    - Frequency
  - Structure of the ear
    - Auditory canal
    - Ear drum
    - Middle ear
      - Hammer
      - Anvil
      - Stirrup
    - Cochlea
      - Basilar membrane
      - Oval window
      - Organ of corti
      - Round window
  - What the ear tells the brain
    - Tuning curve
    - Auditory cortex
      - Cochlear nucleus
      - Superior olive
      - Medial geniculate
      - On/off/on-off cells
      - Frequency sweep detectors
- Chemical senses
  - Smell
    - Olfactory cilia
    - Olfactory epithelium
  - Taste
    - Papillae
    - Taste buds
- Skin senses
  - Touching and feeling
    - Pacinian corpuscle
    - Lemniscal system
    - Spinothalamic system
- Internal senses
  - Somesthetic system
  - Proprioception
  - Kinesthesis
    - Joint position receptors
  - Vestibular senses
    - Otolith organs
      - Semicircular canals
    - Ampulla
- Relativity of sensory experience
  - Adaptation level
    - Focal stimuli
    - Background stimuli
    - Residual stimuli
    - Anchoring effect

COMPLETION ITEMS

outposts

biological

exclusion

constant
adaptation

comparison
change

physics

threshold

just noticeable difference

experience

intensity

Power

neural firing

touch
electrical
transduction

Vision

camera
images
cornea

pupil

focus

retina
brain

1. The senses are the _____ of the brain and connect the physical and psychological worlds.

2. The first major basis of selection is the _____ nature of the senses themselves. Sensory selectivity involves both inclusion and _____.

3. The senses respond most vigorously to beginnings and endings of events and respond less to _____ stimulation. This decline in response is called sensory _____.

4. Sensory systems operate primarily by _____. A sensory _____ is a difference in a stimulus from one moment to the next.

5. Using the methodology and techniques of _____ as their model the first psychologists tried to determine how changes in the outside world affected the internal world of human experience.

6. The absolute _____ is the minimum strength for a stimulus to be noticed by an observer 50 percent of the time. The minimum increase in a physical stimulus necessary for a person to notice a difference in the stimulus is called the _____ (j.n.d.).

7. Ernst Weber noted that equal changes in physical intensity do not produce equal changes in _____. Gustav Fechner found that it is not the absolute differences between stimuli but the relative _____ differences that our senses are designed to notice.

8. The so-called _____ law states that within each sensory system equal ratios of stimulus intensity produce equal ratios of change in experience.

9. Although each sense responds to a different form of physical energy, the brain has only one way of receiving and responding to information: _____.

10. Physical energy, such as waves in the air and mechanical pressure _____, are transformed into _____ or chemical action. This process is called _____.

11. _____ is the dominant sense of human beings, responsible for almost all the basic actions necessary for living in the human world.

12. The eye does not work like a _____. It is neural impulses and not _____ that are received by the brain. Light first enters the eye through the _____, a transparent membrane that covers the front of the eye.

13. Like the aperture of the camera, the size of the opening of the _____ of the eye determines how much light is let in. The interocular muscles pull the lens and change its shape so as to _____ on objects at different distance.

14. The _____ is the key structure of vision. It begins its development as part of the _____ but becomes part of the eye in the embryonic stage.

CHAPTER 5 / SENSORY EXPERIENCE

nerve	15. All the axons from the eye's ganglion cells leave the eye at the same point, where they are bundled together to form the optic _____.
photoreceptor	Since there are no _____ cells at the point where these cells come together to form this structure, this part of the eye cannot respond to light and is thus commonly referred to as
blind	the _____ spot.
rods	16. The photoreceptor cells known as the _____ respond best to wavelengths of 480 nm, which we experience as the blue-green end
cones	of the color spectrum. The _____ are those retinal cells responsible for color vision.
fovea	17. More brain cells receive input from the area in the center of the retina, known as the _____, than from any other part of the eye.
primary	18. The cones operate like a color television camera, with three color sensors; red-yellow, green, and blue, the three _____ colors of
cones	light from which all others can be made. The _____ are those photoreceptor cells that quickly adapt to the dark.
psychological primaries	19. Four colors, called _____, are seen as pure. There are red, green, blue, and yellow. Like all other colors, the primaries are associ-
wavelengths	ated with specific _____ of light.
opponent	20. The brain's method for color coding is called an _____ process. If you stare at a red square against a white background for a minute and then look only at the white background, you will see an after-
opponent	image of its _____ color, green.
genetic	21. Color blindness is a _____ defect in one of the three color systems and occurs primarily in men. The most common form is
red-green	_____ color blindness.
geniculate	22. The lateral _____ nucleus (LGN) is a kind of switching station in the thalamus that alerts the visual cortex to visual input.
	23. The two types of cell divisions within the LGN, the magnocellular and
parvocellular	_____, project to different parts of the
primarily visual cortex	_____ in a way that results in three complementary visual pathways. In the visual cortex, the information from the two areas is
shading	combined to produce the perception of color and _____.
	24. The physiological mechanism that underlies visual experience, through which the brightness of one object is compared to surrounding brightness,
lateral	is called _____ inhibition. Whenever a cell fires, it
inhibits	_____ the cells next to it from firing.
	25. The area of stimulation that a cell responds to is called the
receptive	_____ field. The function of the cells in the visual cortex is different from that of cells in the optic tract: the cortical cells respond best to specific features in the environment and are called
feature analyzers	_____.
Amplitude	26. _____ refers to the height of a sound wave; frequency refers to the number of cycles the wave makes each second. The loudness of a sound is determined by its amplitude, and the frequency of
pitch	the wave determines its _____.

membrane

Corti

context
pitch

on-off

olfactory

smell

papillae
skin
pacinian

lemniscal

spinothalamic

Proprioception

kinesthesis
vestibular

otolith
adapt

adaptation level
anchoring

27. When the stirrup beats on the cochlea at the oval window, a structure called the basilar _____ begins to move, thus creating a "traveling wave." Once the membrane's movements bend the outer hair cells of the organ of _____, pressure waves are transduced into neural firing.

28. Hearing, like vision, is affected by _____. The judgments of the loudness of a tone is influenced by its _____.

29. There are three different types of cells in the auditory cortex; "on cells" respond when a tone starts; "off cells" respond when the tone stops; and "_____ cells" respond when there is any change in the stimulus.

30. The receptors for smell are the _____ cilia, located at the end of the nasal cavity.

31. The neural information about _____ is sent to the brain without any intermediate nerves.

32. The surface of the tongue is covered with small bumps called _____, each of which has 200 taste buds around it.

33. The _____ is the largest sense organ of the body.

34. The _____ corpuscles in the skin respond to mechanical pressure.

35. The _____ system is comprised of large nerve fibers that conduct information directly from the skin to the cortex.

36. Internal pains, such as those resulting from surgery or a toothache, are conveyed to the brain by the slow nerve fibers of the _____ system.

37. _____ is the sense by which we know where each part of the body is in relationship to other parts.

38. The sense of movement is called _____. The sense of balance is one of the so-called _____ senses.

39. In human beings, the organs of balance are in the inner ear next to the cochlea and are called the _____ organs. These organs are unique among the senses in that they do not _____ to continuous change.

40. The _____ approach allows us to quantify comparative sensory experience. One important finding is the _____ effect, which is the effect of the preceding stimuli on the judgment of subsequent stimuli.

SELF-QUIZ

MULTIPLE-CHOICE ITEMS

1. Our sensory systems are designed to notice
   a. food.
   b. danger.
   c. change.
   d. the outside world.

2. Electromagnetic energy is sensed as
   a. odor or aroma.
   b. sound.
   c. movement.
   d. light.
3. The sensory systems operate primarily by
   a. deconstruction.
   b. adaptation.
   c. comparison.
   d. chance.
4. The absolute threshold is the minimum strength for a stimulus to be noticed by an observer _____ percent of the time.
   a. 25
   b. 50
   c. 75
   d. 100
5. Transduction refers to the process by which each sensory organ transforms physical energy into
   a. j.n.d.'s.
   b. absolute thresholds.
   c. neural firing.
   d. images.
6. Which of the following is *not* among the basic functions of vision as described by Gibson?
   a. detecting the layout of surroundings
   b. detecting change or sequence
   c. detecting and controlling movement
   d. focusing and directing attention
7. Which of the following is not among the types of cells found in the intermediate layer of the retina?
   a. bipolar
   b. ganglion
   c. horizontal
   d. amacrine
8. _____ are the photoreceptors for color vision.
   a. Rods
   b. Cones
   c. Ganglia
   d. Amacrine cells
9. Which of the following is *not* one of the three systems of color information sent from the eye to the brain?
   a. red-yellow component
   b. red-green component
   c. blue-yellow component
   d. dark-light component

10. Staring at a _____ square against a white background evokes a green after-image when that square is taken away.
    a. blue
    b. red
    c. yellow
    d. black
11. Our perception of color is
    a. much more precise than our ability to see movement.
    b. much less precise than out ability to see movement.
    c. affects our ability to see movement.
    d. no different than our perception of movement.
12. In the visual cortex of the cat, it is the _____ cells that are the orientation detectors.
    a. amacrine
    b. hypercomplex
    c. complex
    d. simple
13. Which of the following is not one of the three bones of the middle ear?
    a. hammer
    b. anvil
    c. cochlea
    d. stirrup
14. The frequency of a sound wave governs the _____ .
    a. medium through which the wave travels
    b. pitch
    c. loudness
    d. direction
15. Which of the following is not among the types of cells in the auditory cortex?
    a. on-on
    b. off
    c. on
    d. on-off
16. Selection and analysis of sound signals takes place in the
    a. cochlea.
    b. basilar membrane.
    c. round window.
    d. auditory cortex.
17. Which sense organ has the most direct line to the brain?
    a. vision
    b. hearing
    c. smell
    d. taste

18. Which system conveys to the brain information concerning sensations in the internal environment, such as deep pain or nausea?
    a. vestibular system
    b. kinesthetic system
    c. proprioception system
    d. somesthetic system
19. Which of the following is not among the three factors determining adaptation level, according to Helson's theory?
    a. focal stimuli
    b. subliminal stimuli
    c. background stimuli
    d. residual stimuli

TRUE-FALSE ITEMS

1. T F The "rodent eliminator" described at the beginning of the chapter, works by emitting fumes that are toxic only to rats and mice.
2. T F Our sensory systems are designed to respond to constant stimulation.
3. T F Perception seems to be mostly a matter of comparing absolute differences between stimuli.
4. T F Our sensory systems operate primarily by comparison.
5. T F The absolute threshold is the minimum intensity required for a stimulus to be noticed by an observer every time it is presented.
6. T F The absolute threshold is the amount of energy required to activate the sensory system but not for us to experience the stimulus.
7. T F The minimum increase in a physical stimulus necessary for us to notice a difference is called the difference threshold, or the just noticeable difference (j.n.d.).
8. T F Weber's law is based on the observation that equal changes in the physical intensity of a stimulus do not produce equal changes in experience.
9. T F Light is focused on the retina by changes in the shape of the pupil and iris.
10. T F There are more rods than cones in the eye.
11. T F More brain cells receive input from the fovea than from any other part of the eye.
12. T F Color blindness is a genetic defect.
13. T F There are two visual pathways in the optic tract that serve specialized functions.
14. T F The hypercomplex cells in the visual cortex are the orientation detectors.
15. T F The pitch of a sound is determined by its frequency.
16. T F The first stop after a signal has left the ear on its way to the brain is the cochlear nucleus.
17. T F The taste buds respond to sour, bitter, sweet, salty, and temperature.
18. T F The immediate pain from a sudden, sharp blow to the knee would most like be sent quickly to the brain by the spinothalamic system.
19. T F We receive kinesthetic feedback only when we are moving.
20. T F The anchoring-effect is the effect of the preceding stimuli on the judgment of subsequent stimuli.

ANSWER KEY TO SELF-QUIZ

MULTIPLE-CHOICE ITEMS

1. c 2. d 3. c 4. b 5. c 6. d 7. b 8. b 9. a 10. b 11. b 12. d
13. b 14. b 15. a 16. d 17. c 18. d 19. b

TRUE-FALSE ITEMS

1. F 2. F 3. F 4. T 5. F 6. F 7. T 8. T 9. F 10. T 11. T 12. T
13. T 14. F 15. T 16. T 17. T 18. F 19. F 20. T

THINKING ABOUT THE PSYCHOLOGY OF YOUR OWN EXPERIENCE

1. The evolution of many of our senses produced an adaptive advantage. One of the most striking of these is color vision. There is no color in nature, but the different wavelengths of light are perceived more precisely in the human visual system than in most other animals. Originally, this aided our ancestors in many ways, for example in determining whether a piece of fruit was ripe or not.

Demonstrate this for yourself by using a color television set to follow the action of a ball game (tennis, football, or basketball). Watch first in black and white and then in color. You will immediately see how color makes the complex action easier to follow.

2. Sensory judgments are not the only judgments that are made within the context of adaptation level. For example, how did you react to your grade on the last midterm you took. Suppose you earned an 82% on the exam. Were you pleased? How do you decide whether your are pleased or not? It depends doesn't it? It depends on how hard you worked, how well prepared you were for the exam, and the exam situation itself. It also depends on what you expected based on how you have done in the past. An 82% in psychology might cause you to be disappointed but an 82% in calculus might be the occasion for a party. Or, an 82% on any exam taken in a too-hot room might be cause for joy. It depends. Think of the important areas of your life such as school, relationships, work, or health, and consider how your feeling are influenced by the comparisons you make.

PART III

THE MENTAL WORLD

6
PERCEIVING THE WORLD

GENERAL STUDY QUESTIONS

After reading Chapter 6, you should be able to answer the following questions.

1. What is perception? What does it depend on?

2. What two characteristics of the environment have been studied by ecological psychologists?

3. How does the mental system go about interpreting meaning from raw sensory information?

4. What are the two components of perceptual analysis? What is a percept?

5. What is a gestalt? Describe the four rules that govern the organizing principles of perception.

6. What does it mean to "go beyond the information given"? How do assumptions affect our perceptions?

7. List some of the different kinds of constancy we experience? Why are they important to us?

8. Why are psychologists interested in illusions? What are some of the illusions described in the text?

9. What is a "critical period"?

10. What is the difference between sensation and perception?

11. Can blind people draw? Which sense is closest to vision in its ability to convey information?

12. How do ocular accommodation, binocular disparity and binaural disparity help us perceive distance?

13. What five cues from the environment help us perceive distance?

14. What two movement cues give us information about distance?

15. In what way is perception an act of creation? Which theory of perception emphasizes this approach?

16. What is the difference between the ecological and constructivist approach to perception?

17. What is the computational approach to visual perception? According to this view, what is the mind's first operation?

18. What is the progression of internal analysis proposed by Marr's computational approach?

19. What should scientists find in the brain if Marr's theory is correct?

20. Triesman proposes two stages in object perception. What are they?

OUTLINE OF KEY TERMS AND CONCEPTS

Perception
   Organization
   Active process
      Reception
      Selection
      Computation
      Creation
Process of perception
   Affordance
   Invariance
Rules of organization
   Perceptual organization
   Interpretation
   Simplicity
Gestalt: Principles of organization
   Figure-ground
   Proximity
   Similarity
   Good continuation
Interpretation
   Going beyond information given
   Unconscious inferences
   Assumptive world
   Needs and values
How perceptual experience changes
   Assimilation
   Accommodation
Constancy
   Shape constancy
   Size constancy
   Brightness and color constancy
   Illusions
      Comparative size
      Ponzo illusion
      Müller-Lyer illusion
   Adapting to the environment
   Adapting to distortion
Perception: Innate or learned
   Development of perception
   Recovery from blindness
Cultural effects on perception
Perception of space
   Internal cues to distance
      Ocular accommodation
      Binocular disparity
      Binaural disparity
   External stationary cues to distance
      Interposition
      Perspective
      Size
      Brightness
      Texture gradient
   External movement cues to distance
      Motion parallax
      Optical expansion
Theories of perception
   Ecological approach
   Constructivist approach
   Criticism of these approaches
   Deconstruction, computation, and reconstruction
      Marr's theory
         Computational approach
         Zero-crossings
            Raw primal sketch
            Two-dimensional sketch
            Three-dimensional representation
      Neural spatial frequency channels
      Triesman's two-stage theory

COMPLETION ITEMS

Perception
1. _____ is the organization of sensory information into simple, meaningful patterns.

2. Our perceptions begin with the information our senses receive, and the processes involve not only reception and selection but also acts of
computation, creation _____ and _____.

affords
3. What an organism perceives depends on what elements exist in the environment—what the environment _____.

invariant
4. Each object in the external environment offers to the perceiver certain _____ features, which are constant patterns of stimulation.

5. The perceptual system is so specialized for organizing sensory information that it attempts to organize disconnected things into a
pattern _____ even when there is none.

6. Two important components of perceptual analysis are organization and
interpretation _____. The minds fusion and coordination of separate
perceptual organization stimuli into something meaningful is _____.

simplified
7. When something is organized, it is _____. Because of the vast amount of information in the world, it is important that we
simplify _____ it so we can act quickly.

organization
8. The rules of perceptual _____ are the basis of the Gestalt approach to psychology.

9. In line with the assumption of the Gestalt approach, an object or figure tends
whole to be perceived as _____, and not as the sum of its parts.

Ambiguous
10. "_____ figures" are those in which figure-ground articulation is unclear.

proximity
11. The Gestalt principle of _____ refers to the fact that when elements are close together they tend to be perceived as a unit.

Like
12. _____ elements tend to be grouped together.

13. One of the most noticeable perceptual operations is one that "cleans up"
straightens information and "_____ it out".

14. We are usually unaware of the act of perception, and we make uncon-
inferences scious _____—that is, we draw conclusions about reality on the basis of suggestions and cues brought in by the senses.

15. The research by psychologists Adelbert Ames and his colleagues followed
assumptions from the hypothesis that if our _____ or inferences about a stimulus change, so will our perceptions of it.

16. Bruner and Goodman found that children from poor families experienced
larger coins as _____ than did children from wealthy families.

17. Perceptual experience changes in the same ways that children's schemata
assimilation change as they get older: by _____ and accommodation. We constantly update schemata as our search of the external environ-
interpretation ment relays information that requires new _____.

Accommodation
18. _____ is the process by which schemata change to fit new information, if the discrepancy between the outside world and schemata is great enough.

CHAPTER 6 / PERCEIVING THE WORLD

constancy	19. The main purpose of the reception, organization, and interpretation by the perceptual processes is to achieve _____, the perception of a stable, constant world.
Shape	20. _____ constancy refers to the fact that the same object is experienced as the same, regardless of the angle from which it is seen.
increase	21. As someone walks toward you from the horizon, that person's image on your retina can _____ by more than 100 times.
the same relative	22. Although the brightness and color of an object vary in different illuminations, we perceive them to be _____. We experience color as we do brightness because we see it _____ to the surrounding environment.
larger farther away	23. When the moon is near the horizon, it appears much _____ than when it is overhead because when it is at the horizon we see it across many cues to depth and distance—the ground, sea, mountains, and so on. The moon seems _____ when we look up at it with no cues to distance.
illusion	24. The Müller-Lyer _____ is one in which two lines of equal length are made to appear unequal by having the arrows at the ends of each line point in different directions.
retina	25. The optical image that is cast on our _____ is upside-down from what we actually "see".
consistent	26. Nineteenth century psychologist, George Stratton, reasoned that if perception is a process of adaptation to the environment, then it ought to be possible to learn to adapt to an entirely different arrangement of visual information, as long as it is _____.
adapted	27. Ivo Kohler discovered that subjects who wore various kinds of distorting lenses _____ to the new optical arrangement within a few weeks.
corneal hands	28. The man who was blind from birth and who was given sight by means of a successful _____ transplant had no idea what a lathe was, even though he was experienced in its use, until he closed his eyes and examined it thoroughly with his _____.
size	29. Pygmies of the Congo, who dwell mostly in dense forest and thus rarely see across large distances, do not seem to develop as strong a concept of _____ constancy as we do.
schemata	30. People from different cultures may not be "fooled" by the same optical tricks as we are because they do not share the same _____.
right Zulus	31. Illusions such as the Müller-Lyer and Ponzo depend to a certain extent on living in a world in which _____ angles and straight lines predominate. Some African tribes such as the _____, who live in round huts with round doors and plough their fields in circles, do not experience the Müller-Lyer illusion as strongly as we do.
two Devil's	32. Conventions for representing three dimensions on a _____-dimensional surface, apparently account for our inability to reproduce the "impossible" object sometimes called the "(Devil's) tuning fork".
relative size	33. According to Berkeley, "We cannot sense distance in and of itself," but must construct it from a set of cues, such as the _____ of an object.

lens
accommodation

disparity

ears

binaural

Perspective

closer

opposite

same
parallax

expansion

ecological

radio set

schemata
computer

stable

evolutionary

computational

decomposition

frequencies

two
primary features

localizes
outside
awareness

34. When we look at objects at different distances, contractions of the ciliary muscles cause the width of the _____ to change. This change is called ocular _____.

35. Binocular _____ refers to the fact that the left and right eyes receive a slightly different view of any given stimulus.

36. The difference in location of the two _____ also provides us with distance information. Since sound is composed of physical pressure waves, the wave can strike the two ears at different points in its cycle, producing _____ disparity.

37. _____ is the external distance cue illustrated by the tendency for parallel lines to appear to converge on the horizon.

38. In the absence of other cues, the brighter of two objects will be judged to be _____.

39. When you look out the widow of a moving car, stationary objects close outside the car appear to move in the _____ direction. Some objects in the far distance seem to move in the _____ direction. This difference in movement is called motion _____.

40. Optical _____ refers to the fact that as we approach a scene, objects close to us appear to approach us faster than do those far away.

41. The _____ approach emphasizes the relevance of external information in perception. Proponents of this theory compare the perceiver to a _____; they both tune into the environment and pick up information they are built to receive.

42. The constructivist approach emphasizes the role of _____ in perception. This view likens the perceiver to a _____ making judgments and decisions about the external world according to past experience or programs.

43. The constructivist approach assumes that we must invent a _____ world anew, each moment, and that this invention is the product of trial and error. This view ignores _____ history, which causes an organism to select important information in the environment.

44. David Marr began to develop a "_____" approach to visual perception. He tried to assess the specific process of _____ into elements that the nervous system can deal with, and how these elements are later assembled, or composed into perceptions.

45. Some confirmation of Marr's theory has been found in studies of how the nervous system responds to different _____ of stimulation.

46. Recent research by Treisman has demonstrated that object perception may proceed in _____ stages. First our visual system detects certain _____ in the patterns of light in our visual field. Then the visual system identifies the objects composed of the primary features and _____ them in space. The first stage takes place _____ of awareness while the second stage requires _____.

SELF-QUIZ

MULTIPLE-CHOICE ITEMS

1. Which of the following is *not* true about perception?
   a. It is a passive process.
   b. It is an organizing process.
   c. It results in the experience of meaningful patterns.
   d. It simplifies sensory input.

2. Perception begins with
   a. selection.
   b. reception.
   c. computation.
   d. creation.

3. Two characteristics of the environment that we perceive have been studied by ecological psychologists. They are
   a. assimilation and accommodation.
   b. reception and selection.
   c. affordance and invariance.
   d. organization and interpretation.

4. Once stimuli are organized into a _____, it becomes difficult to see them again as separate and disorganized.
   a. gestalt
   b. figure
   c. shape
   d. percept

5. When elements are close together they tend to be perceived as
   a. an ambiguous figure.
   b. a unit.
   c. differing in relative brightness.
   d. differing in relative size.

6. The organism-environment transaction approach of Ames and his colleagues focuses on how _____ affect our perception.
   a. assumptions
   b. invariances
   c. Gestalt organizing principles
   d. affordances

7. _____ refers to the way we interpret incoming information to match our existing schemata.
   a. Perceptual transactioning
   b. The transactional cycle
   c. Assimilation
   d. Accommodation

8. Which of the following is *not* among the established perceptual constancies?
   a. brightness
   b. loudness

c. size
   d. shape
9. Many of the perceptual illusions work because they cause us to misapply the rules that govern
   a. size
   b. accommodation
   c. assimilation
   d. constancy
10. The optical image on the retina is upside down from the way it actually exists and from what we perceive. All we need to be able to adapt to the external world is
    a. consistent information.
    b. for the image to be inverted.
    c. special glasses.
    d. contrast.
11. The sensory replacement device designed by Collins and his colleagues to help blind people perceive the world, relies on "televised" _____ images.
    a. kinesthetic
    b. neurological
    c. tactile
    d. auditory
12. People from different cultures may not be fooled by the same optical tricks because they do not share the same
    a. abilities.
    b. accommodations.
    c. assimilations.
    d. assumptions.
13. Which of the following is *not* among the internal cues to distance?
    a. binocular disparity
    b. binaural disparity
    c. perceptual organization
    d. ocular accommodation
14. Binocular disparity refers to the fact that each eye
    a. receives slightly different information about an object in the environment.
    b. accommodates differently to objects of different shape.
    c. accommodates differently to distance cues.
    d. processes information at a different rate depending upon the location of the stimulus.
15. Which of the following is (are) among the major movement cues to distance?
    a. texture gradient
    b. interposition
    c. optical expansion
    d. perspective

16. Evolution is most distinctly characteristic of which of the following approaches to the study of perception?
    a. cognitive
    b. Gestalt
    c. constructivist
    d. ecological
17. Which of the following is *not* among the progressive stages of internal analysis described in Marr's computational approach to visual perception?
    a. raw primal sketch
    b. full primal sketch
    c. two-dimensional sketch
    d. algorithmic sketch
18. Some confirmation of Marr's theory of perception has been found in studies of the way the nervous system responds to different _____ of stimulation.
    a. sources
    b. amplitudes
    c. frequencies
    d. intensities

TRUE-FALSE ITEMS

1. T F Our experience of the world is far simpler than the external world itself.
2. T F The mind's fusion and coordination of separate stimuli into something meaningful is known as percept interpretation.
3. T F The German world "gestalt" roughly translates to "stimulus."
4. T F Hastorf's research showed that our judgments of how far away a thing is depends on how big we assume it to be.
5. T F Research by Bruner and Goodman found that when shown a coin, children from poor homes saw it as smaller than did richer children.
6. T F Accommodation is the process by which we interpret incoming information to match our existing schemata.
7. T F We experience great change when sensory information reaching us changes radically.
8. T F Perceptual constancy is the capacity through which we perceive objects to be the same size and shape regardless of our vantage point.
9. T F The Ponzo illusion is due to our being misled by the rules of perspective that normally help us to judge size and distance.
10. T F The optical image on our retina is upside-down from what we actually "see."
11. T F It took Ivo Kohler's subjects anywhere from 6 months to 1 year to adapt in even a marginally satisfactory way to the distorting lenses they wore.
12. T F After his sight was restored by means of a corneal transplant, the 52-year old man who had been blind from birth had no idea what a lathe was until he closed his eyes and smelled it.
13. T F Pygmies of the Congo tend to have a very strongly developed, highly acute concept of size constancy.

14. T F The tactile sensory replacement (TSR) project has devised a machine that uses sound patterns to allow blind individuals to recognize objects in front of them.
15. T F The information received because of binocular disparity decreases the closer we get to the object we are looking at.
16. T F Texture gradient is a stationary cue to the distance of an object.
17. T F According to the ecological approach, the information for color vision is present directly at the receptors.
18. T F The ecological view does not account well for the fact that the same stimulus is can mean different things to different people.
19. T F Marr's theory is a computational approach to visual perception.
20. T F Marr's theory has important implications for "cracking the neural codes" of human experience.
21. T F According to Treisman, perception is a two-stage process. In the first stage, our visual system identifies the objects composed of the primary features and localizes them in space. Then the visual system can detect certain primary features in the patterns of light in the visual field.
22. T F The world is experienced as stable only because of the way the brain is organized.
23. T F The process of organization and simplification of the world begins at the sensory nerve cell.
24. T F Sensory information is both decomposed and composed in the brain.

ANSWER KEY TO SELF-QUIZ

MULTIPLE-CHOICE ITEMS

1. a 2. b 3. c 4. d 5. b 6. a 7. c 8. b 9. d 10. a 11. c 12. d 13. c 14. a 15. c 16. d 17. d 18. c

TRUE-FALSE ITEMS

1. T 2. F 3. F 4. T 5. F 6. F 7. F 8. T 9. T 10. T 11. F 12. F 13. F 14. F 15. F 16. T 17. T 18. T 19. T 20. T 21. F 22. T 23. T 24. T

THINKING ABOUT THE PSYCHOLOGY OF YOUR OWN EXPERIENCE

1. The split between sensation and perception can sometimes be experienced at the level of the self. Choose a recent event that had an impact on how you feel about yourself and:

   a. Write out an objective description of what happened. Refer only to things that could be seen, heard, or otherwise observed directly by anyone present.

   b. What conclusions might an observer have reached about the event based only on the objective circumstances?

   c. Write an explanation of how you interpreted all that happened, and how this interpretation had an impact on your feelings about yourself.

   d. How might the event, as you described it, have been interpreted differently from the way you experienced it?

2. We do not often realize how automatic our normal perceptions and actions are. Take a moment to notice all those items you normally "screen out" of your perception. For example, as you look down at the page, can you see the tip of your nose? Can you feel your tongue in your mouth? Now look up, can you see those little floating things in your eye? Can you feel your chest rise and fall as you breath? Are you hungry? Your body is very busy isn't it, yet a few moments ago, you had screened out most of these sensations. This is just one example of the way we simplify the world in order to perceive.

7
CONSCIOUSNESS AND THE NATURE OF THE MIND

GENERAL STUDY QUESTIONS

After reading Chapter 7, you should be able to answer the following questions.
1. What is the essential criterion of whether we are conscious of something or not?

2. What are some of the differences between conscious processes and unconscious processes?

3. How do routine behaviors become "automatized?"

4. The brain gives which events fast access to consciousness?

5. What are the four levels of awareness?

6. The delay between a stimulus and the attainment of neuronal adequacy may provide time for what? Why is it important?

7. What are the four categories of daydreams? Why might daydreaming be good for you?

8. What are the two distinct kinds of sleep? How are they defined?

9. What are the four stages of sleep? A sleep walker is in what stage of sleep?

10. What happens to people after two or three days without sleep?

11. What three things determine the kind of dreams people have?

12. According to Freud, what purpose do dreams serve? What two levels of dream content did Freud distinguish?

13. How does the activation-synthesis model explain dreams?

14. What are lucid dreams?

15. What is the aim of meditation? What are the two forms of meditation discussed and how do they differ?

16. What does de-automatization have to do with meditation?

17. William James delineated four characteristics of mystical or religious experience. What are they?

18. How do drugs work?

19. What are psychedelics and how do they work?

20. What is the essential characteristic of the hypnotic state?

21. Hypnotically susceptible people share what characteristics?

22. What is the hidden observer?

OUTLINE OF KEY TERMS AND CONCEPTS

Conscious and unconscious processing
  Unconscious processors
  Conscious processes
  Attention
  Automatization
Functions of consciousness
  Levels of awareness
    Conscious awareness
    Subconscious awareness
    Preconscious
      Blindsight
    Unconscious
    Unconscious motivation
  Are we aware of what we do?
    Primary evoked response
    Neuronal adequacy
  Self-awareness
Variations in consciousness
  Daydreaming categories
    Self-recriminating
    Well-controlled and thoughtful
    Autistic
    Neurotic or self-conscious
Sleep
  Two kinds
  Stages of sleep
    Stage 1
      Hypnagogic dreams
    Stage 2
      Sleep spindles
    Delta sleep (stages 3 and 4)
    REM sleep
  Circadian rhythms

Functions of sleep
  Sleep deprivation
  Sleep disorders
    Insomnia
    Arousal disorders
      Night terrors
      Sleeptalking
      Sleepwalking
Dreaming
  Freud's theory
  Activation-synthesis model
  Dream recall
  Lucid dreaming
Deliberate alterations of consciousness
  Sensory deprivation and isolation
  Subliminal perception
  Meditation
    Concentrative meditation
    Opening-up meditation
    Effects of meditation
  Teaching stories
  Religious experiences
    James's four characteristics
      Unity or oneness
      Sense of realness
      Ineffability
      Vividness and richness
  Consciousness-altering drugs
    How drugs work
    Psychedelics (hallucinogens)
    Marijuana
    Methoxylated amphetamines
    Anesthetics

PCP and ketamine
Nitrous oxide and ether
Hypnosis
Hypnotic susceptibility

Trance logic
Posthypnotic suggestions
Hidden observer
Hypnotic analgesia

COMPLETION ITEMS

consciousness

1. The part of the mind where different decisions cross is _____, which exists on several levels.

modules
module

2. The mind contains dozens of independent, unconscious processors—or _____—that operate automatically and in parallel. Each _____ specializes in doing only one thing, and it does it rapidly, efficiently, and effortlessly.

Conscious

3. _____ processes, in contrast, occur one at a time, take effort, and are relatively inefficient.

attend

4. If something unexpected suddenly happens, we automatically _____ to it.

5. The reason that only new and important information gets into consciousness is that well-learned actions and patterns of events become

automatized
priority system

_____.

6. In consciousness, the _____ of the brain is administered.

awareness

7. When something is in _____ it means that we are keeping track of it.

aware

8. We may be _____ of something without being conscious of it.

subconsciousness

9. This state of awareness below consciousness is _____ awareness.

subliminal perception

10. Stimuli too weak to be consciously recognized can still have a measurable impact on the mind through _____.

neuronal adequacy

filter

11. According to research by Libet, the delay required between a stimulus and the attainment of _____ may provide a time in which perceptions could be modified or excluded from consciousness. This could provide a _____ to prevent too much information from entering consciousness.

retroactive

12. The ability of a subject to veto an intention to act after the unconscious process has begun indicates that we may have some _____ control of our behavior.

Daydreams

13. _____ usually occur when outside events are boring, automatized, or unchanging. Those that are prompted by the question, "What should I have done or said," are referred to as

self-recriminating

_____ ones.

physiological

14. The differences in mental activity during sleep depend largely upon differences in the _____ state of the sleeper.

two
REM—Rapid Eye Movement

15. There are _____ distinct kinds of sleep. These are quiet sleep and active or _____ sleep.

EEG
eye movement

delta
walking/talking

muscle tension

circadian

sleepiness
function quite well

microsleeps

psychosis
increases

insomnia

symptom

wish fulfillment

latent

synthesis

information

conscious

lucid

hallucinations

stimulation

oneself
concentrative

16. In addition to the electroencephalograph _____, researchers use indications of _____ and muscle tension as clues to the stage of sleep a subject is experiencing.

17. The deepest stage of sleep is reached when the proportion of _____ wave activity in the EEG exceeds at least 20 percent. Sleep _____ occur during delta sleep.

18. During REM sleep, the brain, breathing, heart rate, and cerebral blood flow are all excited, but the sleeper's _____ drops to nothing.

19. The daily fluctuation in biological functioning experienced by human beings is known as the _____ rhythm.

20. Complete sleep deprivation has its most profound effect on the feeling of _____. After one to three sleepless nights, people usually _____.

21. After two or three days without sleep, people start to show _____ on their EEG.

22. Twenty years ago it was thought that depriving a person of REM sleep would lead to _____ but this was an exaggeration. REM sleep deprivation probably _____ the excitability of the central nervous system.

23. The most common sleep disorder is _____. Rather than being a disease in itself, insomnia is usually a _____.

24. Freud's influential _____ model of dreaming held that dreams were disguised symbols of primitive, unacceptable needs and desires welling up from the unconscious.

25. According to Freud, the _____ content of a dream is the hypothetical underlying dream thought that gives rise to the surface or manifest content of the dream.

26. According to the activation _____ theory, dreams are a conscious interpretation of information. If this theory is correct, then the experience of dreams can be understood as a product of the nature of the mental operating system when the brain is generating its own "raw" _____.

27. Research indicates that at times we can be fully _____ in our dreams while we remain soundly asleep. LaBerge and co-workers devised a method for testing claims for _____ dreaming that relied on correspondence between the pattern of dream gaze changes and actual eye movements.

28. In early experiments in sensory deprivation, people reported unusual experiences, temporal disorientation, _____, and extreme pathology. When people are put into such situations, they immediately tend to seek _____.

29. The aim of meditation is to increase one's knowledge of _____ and one's place in the world. The important factor in common to all techniques of _____ meditation is that the same information is cycled through the nervous system over and over again. The purpose of "heightening" consciousness in this

CHAPTER 7 / CONSCIOUSNESS AND THE NATURE OF THE MIND

de-automatize

interpretation

actual

teaching

ideas

religious

artificial mysticism

mind-manifesting

hallucinogens

sensory input

more

less

Anesthetics

PCP

ketamine

hallucinatory

consciousness

role playing

hypnotically susceptible

imaginative involvement

observer

suggestion

immune

way is to restructure schemata and thus _____ one's response to the world.

30. The so-called opening-up exercises emphasize the difference between information that reaches consciousness and the _____ of that information. In philosophical and religious traditions, these are intended to dissociate one's "models" of the outside world from the _____ outside world.

31. Another method for upsetting routine and for deepening consciousness is the so-called _____ stories, which are narratives containing paradoxes and unusual events. They are said to contain specially chosen patterns of events that encourage openness to new _____.

32. Many meditation and spiritual exercises result in what are called _____ experiences. According to William James, one characteristic of the mystical experience is "unity"—which refers to the idea that experience becomes comprehensive rather than fragmented, and relationships are seen between things normally regarded as separate.

33. Psychoactive drugs serve many roles to the people who use them, from pure escapism and pleasure seeking to what William James called "_____".

34. The word psychedelic in Greek means "_____". Psychedelic drugs are also called _____ because they tend to induce perceptual distortions, enhancements, and elaboration.

35. The psychedelics inhibit the modulations of _____ by an area of the reticular activating system. As a result, the brain becomes much _____ sensitive and _____ selective to sensory input, and the normal pattern recognition functions of the brain start to work overtime.

36. _____ are drugs whose primary medical purpose is the induction of a state of decreased consciousness in which the experience of pain is blocked. Unlike barbiturates _____ and _____ stimulate activity in the central nervous system. The combination of decreased sensory input with brain activation works to create the _____ experience of users of these drugs.

37. Some researchers believe hypnosis is a distinct state of _____, whereas others believe it is simply an extreme case of _____.

38. Those who enter the hypnotic state easily are called _____. These people share several characteristics; among them is the capacity for _____.

39. Demonstrations of the "hidden _____," such as the one reported by Hilgard, indicate that experiences below consciousness may enter consciousness through hypnosis.

40. There are many remarkable examples of ways in which the body can be altered in profound ways by hypnosis and _____. Such an approach, which effectively cures warts, most probably works by either activating the body's _____ system or by altering the blood flow to these growths, or both.

SELF-QUIZ
MULTIPLE-CHOICE ITEMS

1. The essential criterion of whether we are conscious of something or not is whether
    a. we can see it.
    b. we can feel it.
    c. we can describe it.
    d. we can categorize it.
2. The ability to accomplish familiar actions without thinking is a result of our ability to
    a. attend to them.
    b. know what we are doing.
    c. concentrate.
    d. automatize them.
3. _____ memories are stored knowledge of the world.
    a. Subliminal
    b. Foreconscious
    c. Representational
    d. Episodic
4. The delay between the occurrence of events and the brain's response may mean that
    a. we may react to things we are not even conscious of.
    b. it is easy to forget most of what happens.
    c. it is difficult to learn new tasks.
    d. it is easy to learn new tasks.
5. Which of the following *is not* among the daydream categories outlined by Singer?
    a. self-recriminating
    b. autistic
    c. psychotic or delusional
    d. neurotic or self-conscious
6. The state of consciousness we enter just before sleep is called
    a. hypnopomic.
    b. hypnogogic.
    c. nonconscious.
    d. preconscious.
7. During which of the following stages of sleep do sleep spindles and K-complexes make their appearance?
    a. stage one
    b. stage two
    c. stage three
    d. stage four

8. Successive REM periods throughout a night's sleep
   a. increase in length and the interval between them decreases.
   b. decrease in length and the interval between them increases.
   c. are decreasingly likely to be dream periods.
   d. are decreasingly likely to be dream periods the person remembers.
9. Prolonged sleep deprivation is *most likely* to make you
   a. sleepy.
   b. crazy.
   c. cranky.
   d. paranoid.
10. Which of the following sleep behaviors *is not* classified as an arousal disorder?
    a. insomnia
    b. sleep walking
    c. sleep talking
    d. night terrors
11. According to the activation synthesis model, dreams are
    a. objectively meaningful.
    b. subjectively meaningful.
    c. a result of what we expect to find in the world.
    d. the result of random signals bombarding the cortex.
12. LaBerge's research on lucid dreaming demonstrated striking physiological correlation for a variety of described behaviors, including all of the following *except*
    a. time estimation.
    b. breathing.
    c. sexual activity.
    d. problem solving.
13. Which of the following is the *aim* of meditation in spiritual practices?
    a. knowledge of oneself and one's place in the world.
    b. to reduce sensation and forget the world.
    c. the development of tolerance for lack of sensation.
    d. greater appreciation for the world.
14. Opening-up exercises are referred to as "mindfulness" in
    a. Zen.
    b. Yoga.
    c. Sufism.
    d. Dianetics.
15. William James used the expression _____ to describe the fact that mystical or religious experiences are impossible to communicate.
    a. "vividness and richness"
    b. "sense of realness"
    c. "ineffability"
    d. "ephemeral"

16. The psychological effect of any drug results from
    a. the mental set of the user.
    b. the setting in which the drug is used.
    c. the expectations of the drug user.
    d. all of the above
17. Which of the following *is not* true about hypnosis?
    a. Hypnosis cannot be used to make a person do something contrary to their ethical or moral principles.
    b. Hypnotically susceptible people have a high capacity for imagination.
    c. Hypnosis is physiologically not sleep.
    d. One essential characteristic of the hypnotic state is hypersuggestibility.
18. _____ has/have been treated successfully by redirecting blood flow to the hands.
    a. Peptic ulcers
    b. Duodenal ulcers
    c. Migraine headaches
    d. Warts

TRUE-FALSE ITEMS

1. T F Conscious processes occur one at a time, take effort, and are relatively inefficient.
2. T F Consciousness tends to be nonselective in the information on which it focuses.
3. T F We are conscious of a great deal more than we are aware of.
4. T F Preconscious memories become conscious only when the situations stimulates them.
5. T F We may react to many things we are not conscious of.
6. T F The phenomenon of blindsight indicates that people, at some preconscious level, can perceive and act on information that they do not know they are seeing.
7. T F Seeing a horse fly across the classroom is an example of a daydream of the type Singer describes as "psychotic."
8. T F The two stages of sleep are REM sleep and non-REM sleep.
9. T F Generally, the cycle of sleep stages is repeated about four or five times during the night.
10. T F REM sleep periods last an average of ten seconds or less.
11. T F The major cause of jet lag is lack of sleep.
12. T F The activation-synthesis theory assumes that the same mental operating system is at work during both wakefulness and sleep.
13. T F The so-called teaching stories are built around paradoxes and unusual events.
14. T F Meditation is effective because it meets the human sensory system's need for unchanging stimulation.
15. T F Psychoactive drugs work by affecting normally occurring physiological processes in the brain.
16. T F Little is known about how marijuana works to alter consciousness.

17. T F The most commonly experienced effect of PCP (and ketamine) is the perception of an alteration of body image.
18. T F Some researchers believe that hypnosis is simply an extreme case of role playing.
19. T F Research has shown that although hypnosis may be useful for inducing analgesia during some types of surgical procedures, it has little or no effectiveness as a healing technique.
20. T F While consciousness is the crossroads of the mind, it exists on only one level.

ANSWER KEY TO SELF-QUIZ

MULTIPLE-CHOICE ITEMS

1. c 2. d 3. c 4. a 5. c 6. b 7. b 8. a 9. a 10. a 11. d 12. d
13. a 14. b 15. c 16. d 17. a 18. d

TRUE-FALSE ITEMS

1. T 2. F 3. F 4. T 5. T 6. T 7. F 8. T 9. T 10. F 11. F 12. T
13. T 14. F 15. T 16. T 17. T 18. T 19. F 20. F

THINKING ABOUT THE PSYCHOLOGY OF YOUR OWN EXPERIENCE

1. We now know that there are many things we respond to that are outside of conscious awareness. Some people believe that extrasensory perception (ESP) is simply an extension of this idea and that ESP is a learnable skill. What do you think?
   - Take a deck of playing cards and a friend to a quiet place.
   - One person should act as "transmitter" the other as "receiver."
   - The "transmitter" should take one card at a time, concentrate on it, and try to communicate it to the "receiver."
   - The receiver then guesses aloud which card it is.
   - The receiver must make a guess.
   - The transmitter says whether the guess is correct or not.
   - If the guess is incorrect, the transmitter reveals the card.
   - Proceed through the entire deck.
   - Keep a record of the "hits" and "misses."
   - Repeat the process.
   - Is the hit rate better than chance (50/50)?
   - Does the hit rate improve on successive trials?
   - Is one of you better at it than the other?

It is through procedures very much like this one that students of parapsychology test for individual differences in the capacity for extrasensory perception and the ability to develop paranormal abilities. What do you think?

2. Are dreams meaningful?

Try to keep a record of your dreams. Some people remember many dreams while others claim they never dream. Put a paper and pencil by your bed when you go to sleep and when you awaken, try to recall the dream and quickly make notes on it. If you can't remember many dreams try setting an alarm for six hours after you go to bed. (REM sleep periods increase in length and become more frequent the longer you have been asleep. Since dreaming is associated with REM you are more likely to catch yourself dreaming later in the night.)

Using your notes as a guide, answer the following questions:

- What was the story of the dream?
- Who was in the dream?
- Where did the dream take place?
- Was the dream realistic or "fantastic?"
- Can you recall any events or thoughts of the previous day that "explain" the content of the dream?
- If you have recorded dreams from more than one night, is there a connection between them or are they individual dreams?
- Does the dream have any meaning beyond the story?

Compare notes with a friend. Do you think dreams have special meaning or are they simply random firing in the brain that we then try to fashion into a meaningful story? Does it matter?

8
THE BASICS OF LEARNING

GENERAL STUDY QUESTIONS

After reading Chapter 8, you should be able to answer the following questions.

1. What is learning?

2. What is "the bond that connects all experience?"

3. Pavlov found that respondent conditioning can occur only under a certain condition. What is it?

4. What are the two kinds of respondent conditioning?

5. Whether or not a neutral stimulus becomes a conditioned stimulus depends on what?

6. What is extinction?

7. What is the difference between respondent conditioning and instrumental (or operant) conditioning? What is the law of effect?

8. What are the two ways to motivate a donkey and what do they have to do with operant conditioning?

9. What is the difference between negative reinforcement and punishment?

10. How do you change behavior through operant conditioning? What is Premack's principle?

11. Under what conditions does punishment *not* work?

12. What are the two broad categories of reinforcers?

13. When is the best time to administer reinforcement?

14. What are the two possible patterns of reinforcement?

15. Give an example of each of the four schedules of reinforcement. Which one is most resistant to extinction?

16. What are the essential similarities between respondent and operant conditioning? What is the difference between them?

17. What is behaviorism?

18. In learning through insight, what is it that is learned? What are the mental operations that form the basis of insight?

19. What is a cognitive map?

20. What is latent learning?

21. What are the four processes involved in observational learning?

22. The controversy surrounding the difference between the cognitive and behavioral approaches to learning centered around what basic question?

23. How do learning theorists rephrase the question, "Are some things easier to learn than others?"

24. What does instinctive drift have to do with the continuum of preparedness?

25. What is the "sauce bearnaise phenomenon" and what does it have to do with human preparedness for learning?

OUTLINE OF KEY TERMS AND CONCEPTS

Classical or respondent conditioning
   Association
      British empiricists
   Conditions of conditioning
      Stimulus significance
      Orienting reflex
      Appetitive conditioning
   Timing and frequency of stimuli
      Recency
         Simultaneous
         Delay
         Trace
         Backward
         Temporal
      Frequency
   Extinction
   Generalization and discrimination
      Transfer
      Watson and Raynor's experiment
         Albert
      Razran's work
      Impossible discriminations
   Applications of respondent conditioning
      Overcoming fears
      Counterconditioning
Instrumental or operant conditioning
   Law of effect
      Thorndike's work
         Instrumental conditioning
   Operant conditioning
      B. F. Skinner's work
         The Skinner box

Operant level of response
Operant strength of response
Reinforcement and punishment
　Positive reinforcement
　Negative reinforcement
　Punishment
　Characteristics of reinforcers
　　Timing
　　Frequency
　　Recency
　Relativity of reinforcement
　　Premack's principle
　Primary reinforcers
　Conditional reinforcers
　Physiological reinforcement
　　Electrical stimulation
　　　Olds and Milner's work
　Schedules of reinforcement
　　Continuous reinforcement
　　Partial reinforcement
　　　Fixed interval (FI)
　　　Variable interval (VI)
　　　　Superstitious behavior
　　　Fixed ratio (FR)
　　　Variable ratio (VR)
　Practical applications of operant conditioning
　　Teaching machines
　Respondent and operant conditioning compared
　　Similarities
　　　Learned associations
　　Differences
　　　Involuntary versus voluntary responses
Cognitive learning
　Insight
　　Kohler's work
　Latent learning
　　Tolman's work
　Cognitive map
　Learning how to learn
　Making things fun to learn
　　Challenge
　　Fantasy
　　Control
　　Interpersonal motivation
　Observational learning
　　Bandura's work
　　Modeling
　　　Four processes
　　　　Attention
　　　　Retention
　　　　Production
　　　　Motivation
　　Imitation
　　　Rosekrans and Hartup's work
　　　　Observing violence on television
　　　　Aggressive behaviors
　　Abstract modeling
　　　Creative thinking
What we are prepared to learn
　Behavioral repertoire
　Assumption of equivalence of associability
　Continuum of preparedness
　　Seligman's work
　　Response difference
　　　Breland and Breland's work
　　　Species-specific defense reactions
　　Stimulus difference
　　　Garcia and Koelling's study
　　Human preparedness
　　　Seligman's "sauce bearnaise phenomenon"
Learning theory and modern day behavior
　Skinner's observations
　　Feedback between actions and consequences
　Evolutionary perspective

COMPLETION ITEMS

experience
associate

1. Learning is, essentially, a process by which we change our thinking or behavior as a result of _____. We learn things because we _____ some aspects of our experience with other aspects.

knowledge

2. Associations form the basis of our _____ of the world; they underlie our ability to know what events occur together, how events are linked to actions, and how actions are linked to each other.

orienting reflex

3. The _____ occurs in response to any stimulus that is consciously perceived as novel or unexpected. Pavlov found that only stimuli that initially elicit an orienting reflex can become successfully associated with neutral stimuli.

appetitive

aversive

4. In _____ conditioning, the organism will instinctively approach the unconditioned stimuli. Shock, pain, and loud noises are stimuli that an organism will instinctively try to avoid and are therefore used in _____ conditioning.

5. Whether or not a neutral stimulus becomes a conditioned stimulus (CS) depends on when and how often it is paired with an

unconditioned stimulus - UCS

_____.

simultaneous

trace

delay

backward

temporal

delay

6. In _____ conditioning, the CS and UCS are presented at the same time. In _____ conditioning, the CS is presented, but is discontinued before the UCS is presented. In the _____ arrangement, the CS is presented and continues until the UCS is presented. In _____ conditioning, the CS is presented after the UCS. And in _____ conditioning, the UCS is simply presented at regular intervals. Of these various arrangements, _____ conditioning is the most effective, and backward is the least effective.

7. If, after a CR has been acquired, the CS is presented repeatedly *without* the UCS, the CR gradually decreases through a process called

extinction

_____.

Generalization

8. _____ refers to the fact that once a CR has been associated with a specific CS, stimuli similar to the original CS may also elicit that CR. Razran demonstrated this principle in an experiment on

semantic

_____ conditioning in which changes in subjects responses were noted to certain words and their homonyms and synonyms.

Effect

9. The Law of _____ refers to the idea that organisms act in such a way as to seek pleasure and avoid pain.

instrumental

10. B. F. Skinner renamed _____ conditioning "operant" conditioning because it involves conditioning the organism's *operations* or actions.

11. The number of times a rat presses the bar in a Skinner box *before* it is conditioned is called the _____ level of that response.

operant

Reinforcement

12. _____ is something that strengthens the possibility that a certain response will occur.

13. When something pleasant is given to an animal after it makes a desired response, this is called _____ reinforcement. In

positive

negative

_____ reinforcement, something unpleasant is taken away from the animal after it makes a desired response. Punishment is the opposite of reinforcement in that it is a consequence that

decreases

_____ the likelihood that a response will recur.

14. The termination of an electric shock to an animal's feet every time it presses a lever in a Skinner box is an example of _____ rein-

negative

relative

forcement. Reinforcements also tend to be _____— that is, $100 is a lot of money to a poor man, but not very much at all to a rich man.

reinforce	15. Premack's principle states that a more favored behavior can be used to _____ a less favored one. Primary reinforcers, such as food, water, and relief from pain, are inherently reinforcing—they need no training.
conditioned	16. Money is probably the most common _____ reinforcer in human life.
preceded	17. Olds and Milner found that animals tended to repeat actions that immediately _____ the delivery of electrical stimulation to certain locations in their brains.
delay	18. Grice found that the shorter the _____ between response and reinforcement, the faster rats learned.
Continuous partial	19. _____ reinforcement means that reinforcement occurs every time a correct response is made. In _____ reinforcement, reinforcement does not always follow the occurrence of the response being trained.
fixed	20. In a _____ interval schedule, reinforcement is presented at regular intervals after the occurrence of the correct response. "Superstitious" behavior often develops when organisms are put in a
variable	_____ interval schedule of reinforcement.
extinction	21. A response conditioned by continuous reinforcement tends to be acquired faster but also undergoes _____ more rapidly than one that is conditioned on a schedule of partial reinforcement.
involuntary	22. Respondent conditioning involves _____ responses in the organism elicited by stimuli; operant conditioning involves voluntary ones emitted by the organism, with these responses then being followed
reinforcing	by _____ stimuli.
superstition	23. When a behavior is accidentally associated with reinforcement, a _____ may be the result.
insight	24. Studies in which chimps show that they can use a short stick to reach a longer stick, which they then use to reach a piece of fruit outside their cage, demonstrate that problem solving may involve some kind of _____ into the solution.
	25. Tolman believed that organisms learn not only by responding to simple stimuli, but by developing a set of expectations about the relationship of elements in the environment, which he referred to as a "cognitive
map	_____."
latent	26. There is evidence that learning can occur without being manifested in performance improvement; such _____ learning amounts to a change in ability not yet demonstrated by performance.
goals	27. Most highly motivating activities such as games and scientific research have multiple levels of _____ for different people at different times.
similar	28. Practice with learning a task will often lead to improved performance on _____ tasks.
cognitive behaviorist	29. The _____ approach to learning emphasizes that the learner is an active part of the process. The _____ approach to learning emphasizes the measurement of observable responses.

schemata modeling	30. In observational learning, what the observing organism acquires is an organized set of associations or _____ that direct behavior. They are learned through the process of _____; watching others perform and then, eventually, performing in the same way.
observational Attentional	31. Four processes are involved in _____ learning. _____ processes determine the perception and exploration of the modeled behavior. Motivational processes determine whether or not the observationally acquired behaviors will actually be
performed	_____.
rewarded	32. In general, we are more likely to imitate behaviors we have seen _____ than to imitate those we have seen punished.
aggressively	33. In a study by Rosekrans and Hartup, children tended to behave more _____ after watching a videotape in which adults behaved violently.
familiar	33. Creative thinking is largely a matter of combining _____ elements in a new way.
repertoire	34. The set of "built-in" abilities with which an organism comes into the world is called its behavioral _____.
associability prepared	35. Seligman questioned the assumption of equivalence of _____ and suggested that organisms are more _____ to associate some events than others.
instinctive	36. The Brelands used the term "_____ drift" to refer to the difficulties they observed in training animals to perform certain acts.
"bright-noisy" water nausea	37. The rats in Garcia and Koelling's experiment were apparently "prepared" to associate foot shock with external events _____ but not with _____, an internal event.
aversion	38. An acquired taste _____, such as suggested by the *sauce bearnaise phenomenon* described by Seligman, exemplifies the kind of prepared learning human beings share with other species.
feedback	39. As B. F. Skinner sees it, current society has eroded the normal _____ between actions and consequences.
mismatch	40. Some of the problems in today's world are due to a _____ between human adaptations to an ancient world and the modern world human beings have made for themselves.

SELF-QUIZ
MULTIPLE-CHOICE ITEMS

1. Which of the following is used in appetitive conditioning?
   a. shock
   b. snakes
   c. food
   d. noise

2. The salivary reflex when food is placed into a dog's mouth is a(n)
   a. CR.
   b. CS.
   c. UCS.
   d. UCR.
3. _____ is the most effective temporal arrangement for conditioned stimulus (CS) and unconditioned stimulus (UCS).
   a. Delay
   b. Trace
   c. Backward
   d. Simultaneous
4. What happens to a conditioned response if a the bell signal continues to sound but no food is presented?
   a. the conditioned response increases suddenly
   b. the conditioned response increases gradually
   c. the conditioned response decreases suddenly
   d. the conditioned response decreases gradually
5. A child who was once bitten by a poodle becomes afraid of boxers, collies, and German shepherds. This is called _____.
   a. stimulus discrimination
   b. semantic conditioning
   c. stimulus generalization
   d. semantic generalization
6. If you win at the racetrack, you are likely to bet again. If you burn your hand, you are unlikely to do it again. These behaviors are predicted by
   a. knowing the operant strength of the behaviors.
   b. knowing the operant level of the behaviors.
   c. the law of effect.
   d. the law of behavior.
7. Which of the following is not a characteristic of operant conditioning?
   a. It involves feedback.
   b. The response precedes the reinforcement.
   c. The response is emitted voluntarily.
   d. Skinner called it respondent conditioning.
8. Negative reinforcement and punishment
   a. are synonyms.
   b. have similar consequences.
   c. have opposite consequences.
   d. The consequences depend on the situation.
9. Which of the following is a secondary reinforcer?
   a. sex
   b. food
   c. money
   d. comfort

10. A _____ schedule of reinforcement is illustrated by a situation wherein a rat is given a food pellet every fifth time it presses a lever.
    a. fixed interval
    b. fixed ratio
    c. continuous reinforcement
    d. variable ratio

11. The schedule of reinforcement that sometimes fosters superstitious behavior is the _____ schedule.
    a. fixed interval
    b. variable interval
    c. fixed ratio
    d. variable ratio

12. Which of the following is *not* a similarity between respondent and operant conditioning?
    a. Reinforcement is required for learning to occur.
    b. stimulus generalization occurs
    c. discrimination occurs
    d. They involve involuntary responses.

13. With insight learning, what is learned are _____.
    a. rules
    b. responses
    c. relationships
    d. associations

14. Kohler's experimental observations of the way a chimp used a short stick to get a long stick and then pulled fruit toward his cage, demonstrate
    a. the effects of variable interval reinforcement.
    b. variable ratio reinforcement.
    c. insight.
    d. spontaneous recovery of a CR.

15. Which of the following is not among the four processes of observational learning?
    a. attentional
    b. retention
    c. rehearsal
    d. motivational

16. The bitter controversy between proponents of the cognitive approach and the behavioral approach to learning centered on which of the following questions?
    a. Could psychologists study anything other than external, observable responses?
    b. Do thoughts really explain behavior?
    c. Does behavior necessarily follow thought?
    d. What is the connection between the brain and the mind?

17. The "sauce bearnaise phenomenon" would predict that
    a. eating rich food while ill is not a good idea.
    b. eating twinkies before becoming seasick would cause you to dislike twinkies in the future.
    c. eating rich food before becoming seasick would cause you to dislike boat trips.
    d. eating rich food while in a boat trip will cause you to become seasick.
18. As Skinner sees it, a major problem in "Daily Life in the Western World" has to do with the fact that
    a. respondent conditioning techniques have been exploited for selfish capitalistic goals.
    b. actions are not clearly associated with their consequences.
    c. actions are too closely associated with their consequences.
    d. technological advances are still too vastly lagging behind the capabilities of the evolving human brain.

TRUE-FALSE ITEMS

1. T F The idea that certain kinds of knowledge are innately built into the organism is more congruent with the empiricist than with the cognitive approach to the study of learning.
2. T F The basis of conditioning, association, is an idea that originated with the British empiricists in the seventeenth century.
3. T F Electric shock is a common UCS in appetitive conditioning.
4. T F In temporal conditioning the CS is presented after the UCS.
5. T F Counterconditioning is a method of conditioning that helps people overcome their fears by training a person to form a new association.
6. T F Instrumental conditioning tends to follow the Law of Effect.
7. T F The cessation of a painfully loud noise each time a rat presses a lever in a Skinner Box is an example of positive reinforcement.
8. T F Negative reinforcement is another way of describing punishment.
9. T F According to the Premack principle, a more favored behavior can be used to reinforce a less-favored behavior by linking them.
10. T F If you want to train an animal to make a response that, once established, would persist even though no reinforcement were provided, a variable ratio schedule would be more effective than continuous reinforcement.
11. T F Respondent conditioning involves involuntary responses elicited by stimuli.
12. T F Since performance is the ultimate test of learning, if an organism doesn't demonstrate what it knows then it hasn't learned.
13. T F The results of Tolman's research on rats trained to find food on a cross-shaped maze showed that, animals learned the task faster if they needed to make their turn responses to the same side of their body (the right side) on every trial.
14. T F Creative thinking is largely a matter of combining familiar elements in a new way.
15. T F What an organism learns in operant conditioning is an association between its actions and their effects on the environment.
16. T F The behavior that results from observational learning is called imitation.

17. T F The results of Rosekrans and Hartup's study indicated that simply observing a videotape of an adult behaving aggressively toward a Bobo doll, had little or no effect on children's immediately subsequent behaviors.
18. T F Abstract modeling has to do with the way observers generate and test hypotheses about the rules guiding performance of models.
19. T F The Brelands' observations of what they called instinctive drift contradict the idea of species differences in behavioral repertoire.
20. T F According to the text, the world which human beings have made for themselves is far different from the world to which the human brain is adapted.

ANSWER KEY TO SELF-QUIZ

MULTIPLE-CHOICE ITEMS

1. c 2. d 3. a 4. d 5. c 6. c 7. d 8. a 9. c 10. b 11. b 12. d
13. c 14. c 15. c 16. a 17. b 18. b

TRUE-FALSE ITEMS

1. F 2. F 3. F 4. F 5. T 6. T 7. F 8. F 9. T 10. T 11. T 12. F
13. F 14. T 15. T 16. T 17. F 18. T 19. F 20. T

THINKING ABOUT THE PSYCHOLOGY OF YOUR OWN EXPERIENCE

1. Do you pick up pennies you spy on the street? Do you have certain articles of clothing that you are sure to wear when taking exams? Do you eat only certain foods before important events? Many performers and ball players have just such superstitions. According to behaviorists, superstitions are the result of associations we make between events that are not really related or are not related in the way we think they are. Perhaps that smelly old Mickey Mouse sweatshirt didn't really help you ace your algebra final. But just in case, you wear it to all your finals the following semester.

Think of any superstitions you have formed and try to trace their origin—what behavior did they reward originally? Ask your friends about their superstitions.

2. When you get on an elevator, where do you stand? Which way do you face? If there are other people already on the elevator when you enter, where do you stand then? Which way do you face? Who told you to do that? Most of us haven't had elevator etiquette lessons but know to stand facing the door, as far away from the others as possible. How did we learn to do this? By watching what others do. This is what observational learning theorists call modeling. It provides a basic element of the socialization process. We learn what is the appropriate thing to do by watching what others do and noting what happens as a result.

Next time you are someplace where families gather, watch them. A park on a holiday is a good place to watch fathers and sons and mothers and daughters. How are they dressed? What kind of equipment do they have? Who is in charge of the food. If it is a barbecue, who is actually cooking the food? Who is doing and who is helping? Watch to see how much actual "instruction" is going on and how much is simply "demonstrating." Think back to your own childhood and try to isolate how much of what you know about being male and being female came as a result of just such interactions.

9
REMEMBERING AND FORGETTING

GENERAL STUDY QUESTIONS

After reading Chapter 9, you should be able to answer the following questions.

1. What are the three important principles of memory?

2. What is declarative memory?

3. Give examples of the two types of declarative memory.

4. What is procedural memory?

5. How is memory organized?

6. The recall of a specific event depends on what?

7. What are the two types of retrieval? Which is easier?

8. What is the storage capacity of short term memory?

9. What are engrams and why are scientists looking for them?

10. What is the single-process hypothesis?

11. Ebbinghaus's curve describes what?

12. Interference can be either proactive or retroactive. Give an example of each.

13. What two general factors influence interference?

14. Give an example of a flashbulb memory.

15. According to Hermann and Neisser, what eight characteristics distinguish individual memories?

16. According to results of Mishkin's work, which parts of the brain appear to be associated with memory?

17. What does context have to do with memory?

18. Memory of duration depends on what factors?

19. What is the effect of schemata on memory?

20. What is chunking?

21. According to Craik and Tulving, what determines the likelihood of being able to recall a word?

22. What is the deepest level of processing a word? How can you deepen the level of processing?

23. What is the major criticism of the levels of processing approach to memory?

24. Why do we remember meaningful events?

25. What are four ways to improve your memory?

OUTLINE OF KEY TERMS AND CONCEPTS

Some principles of memory
   Association
   Simplicity
   Meaningfulness
Functions of memory
   Declarative memory
     Episodic
       Experiences
     Semantic
       Language
       Word meanings and use
       Rules for inference
   Procedural memory
     Schemata for routine actions
Memory organizes and makes past experience accessible
   Organization
     Associated events
   Accessibility
     Storehouse
Process of memory
   Memory cycle
     Perceptual encoding
     Retention
     Retrieval
       Recognition
       Recall
   Memory system
     Short-term memory
     Long-term memory
   Alternative interpretations of memory cycle and system
     Memory changes with experience
       Estes' theory
     Memory changes like a radio dial
       Adaptation
     Memory is a single and continuous process
   How we forget and what we remember
     Factors of forgetting
       Ebbinghaus's work
         Nonsense syllables
         Forgetting curve
       Decay of memory
       Interference
         Proactive

            A-B-B
        Retroactive
            C-D-C
        Primacy
        Recency
    Memory for life experiences
        Memory for recent real-world events
            Linton's work
            Personal meaning
        Memory for distant events
            Gradual and continuous
        Flashbulb memories
            Emotionally arousing
            Life markers
    Recognition of pictures and odors
    Individual differences in memory
        Inventory of memory experiences
            Rote memory
            Absentmindedness
            Names
            People
            Conversation
            Errands
            Retrieval
            Place
Memory and the brain
    Brain damage
    Amnesia
    The brain's storage of information
        Mishkin's work

Meaningfulness and organization in memory
    Importance of context
    Experience of time
        Duration
        Memory storage space and time
    Information is organized into meaningful units
        Effect of schemata on memory
            Bartlett's work
        Chunking and coding
    Reconstructive nature of remembering
        Loftus's work
            Tomato versus orange
            Eyewitness testimony
    Levels of processing
        Craik and Tulving's work
            Semantic qualities of words
                Structural
                Phonemic
                Semantic
        Relating information to yourself
    Why do we remember meaningful events better?
        Many associations
    Great feats of memory
        Chunking in chess
        Russian mnemonist
Improving memory
    Change encoding
    Relate information to yourself
    Mnemonics
    Method of loci

COMPLETION ITEMS

associated

1. William James stated that "The more other facts a fact is _____ with in the mind, the better possession of it our memory retains." This idea has carried over to modern psychology, wherein it has been established that the more we associate an event with something we already know, the better we tend to

remember

_____ it.

selects
simpler

2. Memory _____ and simplifies reality. Thus, memories are much _____ than actual experience.

means
familiar

3. Perhaps the most important criterion for remembrance is what an event _____ to us. Since we remember meaningful details, we often overlook _____ details of everyday life.

Declarative

4. _____ memory is our mental record of information that we use to recall events, to think, and to communicate. Our individual experiences are recorded in our _____ memory, which is a sort of continuing "autobiographical reference."

episodic

semantic, Semantic	5. The knowledge of languages, including the shape of letters, the sounds of language, and the meaning of words constitutes _____ memory. _____ memory also contains the rules for everyday inferences.
Procedural	6. _____ memory contains the automatized schemata for performing routine actions, whether they are simple, like throwing a ball, or complex, like driving a car. Procedural memory, unlike
declarative	_____ memory, is not subject to verbalization; it's easier done than said.
associated	7. Memory is organized around relating _____ events to each other. Perhaps the most important function of memory is that it is
organized	_____ in such a way as to make information accessible.
cycle	8. The memory _____ describes the press by which we experience something, retain it, and later retrieve it.
system	9. The memory _____ includes the different divisions of memory, from momentary visual impressions to lifelong retention of important moments in our lives.
perceived	10. Recall depends on three prior processes. First, the event must be sensed, transduced into neural language, and _____. Second, the information must be stored or retained. Finally, the stored information must be brought into consciousness through a process referred to as
retrieval	_____.
Recognition	11. _____ is the ability to correctly identify an object or
Recall	event. _____ is the ability to summon up stored information in the absence of the actual object or event.
short-term	12. Information that is retained temporarily, for only a few seconds, is stored in _____ memory. The storage capacity of short-term
seven	memory is about _____ items.
long-term	13. Both episodic and representational memory are stored in _____ memory.
experience	14. Cognitive psychologist William Estes suggests that "Human memory does not, in a literal sense, store anything; it simply changes as a function of _____."
continuous	15. From the standpoint of the theory that memory is a single and _____ process, each repetition of an event causes an increase in the strength of association of that event, thereby increasing the probability that it will be remembered later on. In this view, short- and long-term memory are regarded as extreme ends of a
single	_____ process.
nonsense	16. In his pioneering studies of memory, Ebbinghaus tried to eliminate the possible confounding effects of subjects' personal experiences on their ability to recall information by using _____ syllables as the stimulus items in his research. He found that the rate of
forgetting	_____ followed a predictable pattern.
slept	17. In Jenkins and Dallenbach's classic experiments, subjects who _____ after they learned lists of nonsense syllables retained more of what they learned than did those who stayed awake. The

decay	results of this study thus suggested that the _____ of memory is not just a matter of time, but that the particular events that occur in time are also a potentially significant factor.
Proactive Retroactive	18. _____ interference occurs when previous knowledge disrupts present memory. _____ interference occurs when old memories are disrupted by newly acquired information.
longer similar	19. Two general factors in interference are the _____ the interval between two events, the less interference, and the more _____ the items, the more interference.
primacy effects recency effect	20. Psychologists use the term "_____" to refer to our enhanced recall for the beginnings of events. The expression "_____" refers to our enhanced recall for the endings of events.
forgetting	21. Marigold Linton, in studying memories for her own life events, found her rate of _____ to be much less rapid than was that reported by Ebbinghaus in his nonsense syllable research.
faces names	22. In a study by Bahrick, Bahrick, & Wattlinger, recognition for the _____ of former classmates was found to remain at over 90 percent for intervals of up to 34 years. Recognition of the _____ of those classmates, however, was found to be not nearly as durable over time.
flashbulb	23. The phenomenon of "_____ memory" explains why you are likely to recall vividly your own circumstances when you saw or heard about the space shuttle *Challenger* explosion.
odors	24. The results of research in which saturated cotton balls were used as stimuli indicate that although _____ may not be recognized as well as pictures at first, the decline in recognition seems to be practically nonexistent.
Memory rote retrieval	25. Hermann and Neisser developed a questionnaire called the Inventory of _____ Experiences, which asks respondents how often they remember and forget different kinds of things. Their analysis of the responses reveals eight characteristics that distinguish individual memories: _____ memory, absentmindedness, names, people, conversation, errands, _____, and place.
brain limbic hippocampus	26. Different forms of damage to the _____ can affect both the storage and retrieval of memory. Epileptic seizures often overstimulate and damage the _____ system. If the particular area known as the _____ is affected, either by epilepsy or subsequent surgery, there are profound effects on memory.
Amnesia	27. _____ is the general term for deficits in learning and memory that occur abruptly.
sensory infero-temporal cortex	28. Mishkin's work suggests that memories are actually stored in the higher level pressing areas of _____ systems. One of these areas is the _____, part of the visual system which has cells that respond to complex shapes, rather than the simple line-detection cells common in the primary visual cortex.

101

COMPLETION ITEMS

29. Of all the information we receive and of all the experiences we have, the things we remember are those that are the most _____ to us. Meaningful and nonmeaningful events are distinguished by the strength of their _____ with other items in memory.

meaningful
association

30. The main function of _____ is to provide a way of organizing information *beforehand*, thereby making it more memorable.

context

31. The more we remember of a given situation, the _____ it seems. _____ experience seems to be based on how much we remember and how that memory is organized.

longer
Time
repertoire

32. In his 1932 book, Bartlett demonstrated the important effects of a person's existing knowledge structure on memory, using the method of _____ reproduction. According to Bartlett, unfamiliar features "invariably suffer transformation in the direction of the _____."

serial

familiar

33. We tend to organize the individual things we perceive and remember into units of memory called _____ by using a code of some sort.

chunks

34. In a study by Carmichael and associates, subjects' drawn reproductions of an _____ doodle were very much influenced by the verbal label that had been applied to that doodle. Related to this observation, subjects in a more recent study were more likely to report having seen broken glass in a film depicting an automobile accident if the world "smashed" was used in querying them as to what they saw.

ambiguous

35. Craik and Tulving found that the recognition and recall of a word tend to increase according to the _____ at which that word is processed. The results of their study indicated that _____ processing tends to produce a higher amount of recall than phonemic, and phonemic a higher level than processing at the _____ level.

depth

semantic

structural

36. The hypothesis of levels of processing has been criticized as a _____ explanation of memory. A possibly simpler explanation is that the memory for an event depends on the number of _____ it evokes.

circular

associations

37. The meaningfulness of an event is a function of the number of _____ it evokes.

associations

38. Techniques for improving memory are generally oriented to changing the way information is _____ in memory so that it becomes more accessible. The self is the most efficient _____ for remembering.

organized

context

39. The more ways in which information is _____, the better it will be retained.

encoded

40. The most famous case of memorization is that of the person known as S., the _____ studied by the Russian psychologist Luria. Apparently, the extraordinary feats of memory were largely attributable to the encoding of information with as many _____ associations as possible.

mnemonist

meaningful

SELF-QUIZ
MULTIPLE-CHOICE ITEMS

1. William James' conceptualization of memory presupposes that the more an event is associated with something already known, the
   a. greater the proactive inhibition.
   b. greater the retroactive inhibition.
   c. better it is remembered.
   d. more difficult it is to remember.

2. Which of the following is *not* true about remembering?
   a. Memory involves associations.
   b. Memories are much more complicated than actual experience.
   c. We remember meaningful events.
   d. We remember only the meaningful details.

3. Semantic memory involves all of the following *except*
   a. Contains the automatized schemata for performing routine actions.
   b. Stores our knowledge of the world independent of context in time.
   c. Stores our knowledge of the world independent of context in space.
   d. Contains rules for every day inference.

4. Memory is organized around
   a. more complex events.
   b. the self.
   c. associated events.
   d. each other.

5. The memory cycle description of memory includes
   a. experiencing the event.
   b. retention of the event.
   c. retrieval of the event.
   d. all of the above.

6. The storage capacity of short-term memory is about _____ items.
   a. three
   b. five
   c. seven
   d. ten

7. An engram is
   a. a memory trace in the brain.
   b. a measure of memory capacity.
   c. the machine that measures memory capacity.
   d. a lesion in the brain.

8. From the standpoint of the single process hypothesis, short- and long-term memory are regarded as
   a. measures of perceptual processing.
   b. differentially affected by proactive inhibition.
   c. extremes of the same process.
   d. separate mechanisms.

9. In Jenkins and Dallenbach's study, subjects who slept after a memorization task _____ than did those who stayed awake.
   a. retained far more
   b. retained far less
   c. reported finding the material more interesting
   d. reported finding the material less interesting

10. In the study reported by Bahrick, Bahrick, and Wittlinger, which of the following characteristics of their classmates were high school graduates found to remember best?
    a. their names
    b. their faces
    c. whether or not they were good students
    d. how popular they were

11. In comparison to pictures, research has indicated that odors are
    a. more easily recognized.
    b. not as easily recognized.
    c. not as easily associated with other stimuli.
    d. none of the above.

12. Amnesia can result from damage
    a. to the hippocampus.
    b. to the frontal lobe.
    c. due to electroconvulsive shock.
    d. all of the above.

13. Mishkin's work suggests that memories are stored
    a. in the limbic system.
    b. in the higher level processing areas of the sensory system.
    c. in the hippocampus.
    d. in the amygdala.

14. The exercise involving the story about Columbus's voyage to America is used in your text to illustrate how _____ may effect memory.
    a. retroactive interference
    b. boredom
    c. recency
    d. context

15. The individual items of human memory are organized into _____ by means of a code.
    a. chunks
    b. experiences
    c. loci
    d. mnemonemes

16. Which of the following is *not* among the four "semantic qualities" investigated by Craik and Tulving in their study of the various "levels" at which words are processes in human memory?
    a. structural
    b. functional
    c. phonemic
    d. semantic

17. One dominant view in psychology, which began with the British empiricists and continues among many current researchers, is that the mind is best described as
    a. a computer.
    b. a filing cabinet.
    c. switchboard.
    d. a network of associations.
18. Which of the following is *not* among the methods for improving your memory discussed in the text?
    a. changing encoding
    b. changing context
    c. relating information to yourself
    d. using mnemonics

TRUE-FALSE ITEMS

1. T F William James argued that the more other facts with which a given fact is associated, the less likely we are to remember it.
2. T F You would use your episodic memory to answer the question, "What were you doing at noon on the first of August, last year."
3. T F The shapes of letters and the meaning of words constitute part of your procedural memory.
4. T F It is easier to recognize something than it is to recall it.
5. T F The storage capacity of short-term memory is about seven items.
6. T F Both episodic and representational memory are stored in long-term memory.
7. T F Ebbinghaus discovered that the rate of forgetting follows a predictable pattern.
8. T F In Jenkins and Dallenbach's study, subjects who slept after memorization of a task, showed more anxiety about recall of that task than did subjects who stayed awake between the original learning and the recall test.
9. T F The interference of new information with previous memories is known as retroactive interference.
10. T F The longer the interval separating two events in memory, the less they are likely to interfere with one another.
11. T F We remember the beginning of an event better than the middle and ending of an event.
12. T F One explanation for "flashbulb memories" is that they are often events that we use as reference points in our life.
13. T F Odor recognition seems to decline in memory more rapidly than does the recognition of visually portrayed material.
14. T F There is apparently only one form of amnesia, and it is due to a dysfunction in one particular brain mechanism.
15. T F Bartlett used the method of serial reproduction to study the effects of a person's existing knowledge structure on memory.
16. T F Psychological research on memory has shown that we tend to remember best those things that "don't fit" with what we already know.

17. T F Research by Loftus and her colleagues has tended to support the idea that eyewitness testimony is unaffected by the particular words used in questioning observers about the events witnessed.
18. T F Craik and Tulving's research has indicated that recognition and recall of words are about the same, regardless of the "depth" at which they are processed.
19. T F Research has shown that people remember best words they can relate to themselves.
20. T F The more ways information is encoded, the more difficult it is to remember.

ANSWER KEY TO SELF-QUIZ

MULTIPLE-CHOICE ITEMS

1. c 2. b 3. a 4. c 5. d 6. c 7. a 8. c 9. a 10. b 11. b 12. d
13. b 14. d 15. a 16. b 17. d 18. b

TRUE-FALSE ITEMS

1. F 2. T 3. F 4. T 5. T 6. T 7. T 8. F 9. T 10. T 11. F 12. T
13. F 14. F 15. T 16. F 17. F 18. F 19. T 20. F

THINKING ABOUT THE PSYCHOLOGY OF YOUR OWN EXPERIENCE

1. This chapter points out the *individuality* of human memory. One way to illustrate this for yourself is to watch a movie with a friend. Then both of you write out a brief summary of the film and a brief evaluative review of it. After you finish writing, exchange summaries and reviews and read what the other has written. Consider the following questions.

- In what ways are your summaries *similar*?
- In what ways are your summaries *different*.

How do you account for these similarities and differences using the principles of remembering and forgetting (for example, organization, perceptual encoding, personalization, the reconstructive nature of memory and so on)?

What do the results of this exercise suggest to you about the difficulties of communication between people?

2. According to Brown and Kulik (1977), flashbulb memories are dramatic, life-altering, or life-threatening events. Sometimes these events are public events shared by others, such as the *Challenger* disaster, other times these are private events such as an automobile accident or news of the death of a friend. Make a list of your own flashbulb memories and then ask as many people of different ages as you can to name their own flashbulb memories.

- What kinds of private events are similar?
- What public events are named by most people?

There are two explanations offered in the text for flashbulb memories. Which of the two do you think accounts best for what you found?

10 THINKING AND LANGUAGE

GENERAL STUDY QUESTIONS

After reading Chapter 10, you should be able to answer the following questions.

1. What is a category and what is the primary function of categorization?

2. How do natural categories and artificial categories differ?

3. What is a prototype? Give an example.

4. In what way is our tendency to overgeneralize adaptive?

5. What are heuristics? What is the trade-off in the use of heuristics?

6. Give an example of each of the three types of heuristics.

7. What is psychological accounting?

8. What is the difference between a problem and a decision?

9. What are the four basic elements in decision making? What is this way of thinking about decisions called?

10. What are the three systematic biases that prevent impartiality in certain kinds of judgments? Give an example of each.

11. Hypothesis testing is used to solve what kind of problem?

12. Most problems have three basic elements. What are they?

13. What are the two most important steps in solving a problem?

14. What is the difference between using algorithms and using heuristics to solve problems?

15. Creative problem solving involves what four steps?

16. When is a sound considered a phoneme? When do phonemes take on meaning?

17. What is the difference between grammar and syntax?

18. What is transformational grammar? What is the difference between deep structure and surface structure?

19. What is the cooperativeness principle? What are the four conversational maxims that speakers usually obey when they speak?

20. What is the diluted version of Whorf's hypothesis?

21. Define artificial intelligence. What are the two goals of artificial intelligence inquiry?

22. What is the "Turing test" and what is it used for?

23. What are two major differences in processing between the human brain and the computer?

24. Describe a simple neural network model.

25. What are the two primary functions a desk must serve?

OUTLINE OF KEY TERMS AND CONCEPTS

Classification into categories
    Function of categories
        Simplify
        Reflect structure of the world
    Natural and artificial categories
        Natural categories
            Color
        Artificial categories
            Man-made objects
        Cultural relativity of categories
    Characteristics of categories
        Basic level
        Typicality and prototypes
            Best examples
            Rosch's work
    Generalization and overgeneralization
        Saves effort
        Protects against danger in changing circumstances
    Heuristics in categorization
        Simplifying strategies
        Rules of thumb that guide decision making
        Representativeness
            Concrete or vivid events overpower other evidence
        Availability
            Ease of recall
        Comparison
            Anchoring
            Changing standards of comparison
Decision making and judgment
    Elements of decision making—evaluating:
        Alternatives
        Possible outcomes
        Preferences among outcomes
        Probabilities that choice will lead to outcome
    Biases in decision making
        Availability
            Biased by ease of recall
            Tversky and Kahneman's work
        Representativeness
            Prototypical example
        Vivid information

- Overpowers statistical information
- How powerful are general heuristics?
  - Use heuristics to explore possible solutions
  - Try first solutions that worked in the past

Problem solving
- Solving simple problems
  - Trial and error
  - Hypothesis testing
    - Krechevsky's work
- Problem-solving strategies
  - Elements
    - Initial state
    - Operations
    - Goal
  - Sequence of problem solving
    - Understand the problem
    - Planning a solution
    - Carrying out the plan
    - Checking the results
  - Problem representation
    - Visual representation
    - Mathematical representation
  - Algorithms
    - Generate and test strategy
      - Searching the test space
  - Heuristics in problem solving
    - Hill-climbing
    - Means-end analysis
      - Break problem into sub-goals
    - Insight
      - "Aha"
      - Kohler's work
- Studying problem solving
  - Protocol analysis
  - Problem of "set"
  - Luchin's work

Creativity
- Generation and evaluation
  - Creativity and natural selection
- Process of creation
  - Preparation
  - Generation
  - Evaluation
  - Implementation

Language
- Elements of language
  - Speech acts
    - Declarative sentence
    - Question
    - Imperative
  - Phonemes
    - Sounds of language
  - Morphemes
    - Units of meaning
  - Grammar and Syntax
    - Study of rules of language
    - How words are arranged to convey meaning
  - Deep and surface structure
    - Transformational grammar
      - Transforms deep structure (or meaning) into surface structure (expression in words.)
  - Meaning in language
    - Active processing
    - Context
      - Warren and Warren's work
  - Conversational maxims
    - Cooperative principle
    - Four maxims
      - Quantity
      - Quality
      - Relation
      - Manner
- Language and thought
  - Whorf's hypothesis
    - Rosch's work
  - Revision of Whorf's hypothesis
- Computers and the mind
  - Goals of artificial intelligence
    - Commercial application
    - Insights about how people think, reason, communicate, and solve problems.
      - Natural languages
      - Artificial languages
  - Similarities between the computer and the mind
    - Symbol-processing
    - The Turing test
  - Differences between the computer and the mind
    - Sequential calculations
    - Analog versus digital processing
    - Serial versus parallel processing
  - Neural network models of thinking and language
    - Simple neural network model
    - Learning in neural networks

COMPLETION ITEMS

simplification

Classification
simplify

remember
equivalent
mental model

natural

black
white

basic level

prototypes

Overgeneralization
overgeneralize

Heuristics

Representativeness

vivid

availability

standard

anchored

accounting

smaller

comparison
cutoff

1. Thinking involves _____: we select a bit of information and base our decisions on it.

2. _____ is a major simplifying factor in mental life. The primary function of categorizing is to _____; to give the most information with the least effort.

3. A category is a grouping of objects or concepts that can be considered _____ in an important dimension. Categories are not random and arbitrary; rather, they are part of a _____ that reflects events and occurrences in the world.

4. In addition to _____ categories, such as those we have developed for dealing with colors, there are artificial categories that refer to the attributes of constructed objects, like chairs or buildings.

5. The research by Berlin and Kay indicated that if a language has only two color terms, they will be _____ and _____.

6. Those categories in terms of which we most naturally divide the world are referred to as _____ categories.

7. Categories are organized around best examples or _____, which are those examples that most typify a particular category.

8. _____ accents the most recent information, even at the cost of ignoring past knowledge. Our tendency to _____ is adaptive; it helps protect against dangers associated with changing circumstances.

9. _____ are simplifying strategies used to make judgments and solve problems.

10. _____ is the judgment that an object is typical of its category. However, using this heuristic can lead to mistakes of overgeneralization: for example, we often judge concrete or _____ examples of a category as representative when they are not.

11. The _____ heuristic is used when we are asked to guess the frequency or probability of events.

12. Once a _____ has been used in trying to solve a problem, a person is less likely to change or adjust, even if compelling new data are present or common sense would dictate a change. In such circumstances, the person is said to be _____ in his or her strategy.

13. Kahneman and Tversky use the term "psychological _____" to describe the fact that we often apply different standards of comparison to different situations. Their research showed that people are less likely to drive 20 minutes to save $5 on the purchase of an item when the savings represent a _____ proportion of the total.

14. The way we categorize things can effect _____. We seem to possess _____ points for our categories—a fact that is often taken into account by retailers in decisions as to how to price the things they sell.

15. The four basic elements in every decision are a set of __alternatives__ from which to choose; a set of possible __outcomes__; the decision maker's __preferences__ regarding the different outcomes; and the decision maker's judgments of the __probabilities__ that a particular choice will lead to a particular outcome.

16. Heuristics provide "shortcuts" that are often useful for increasing the efficiency of decision making, but they may also lead to systematic __biases__ in certain kinds of judgments.

17. When people are asked to judge the relative frequency of different causes of death they overestimate the frequency of well-__publicized__ causes, such as homicide and underestimate the frequency of less remarkable ones, such as diabetes. This demonstrates that people's judgments are biased by how easily they can __recall__ specific examples.

18. Trial and __error__ is the most basic problem-solving strategy. However, David Krechevsky found that rats, required to run through a maze with four choice points, did not treat the situation in a trial-and-error way, but rather seemed to deal with the task by testing __hypotheses__.

19. It is useful to think of problems as having the following three elements: the initial __state__ or starting point of the problem, a set of __operations__ or actions that the problem-solver can use to change the state of the problem, and a __goal__ or description of the states that would be solutions to the problem.

20. Once a problem is identified and its solution begun, there are four basic steps: __understanding__ the problem, planning a __solution__, carrying out the __plan__, and checking the __results__.

21. The way a person thinks about or __represents__ a problem may make it either more difficult or easier to solve.

22. Strategies known as __algorithms__ are those that, if followed exactly, will lead eventually to the solution of a problem.

23. Looking at many alternative actions in terms of a generate-and-test strategy is called __searching__ the test space.

24. When the heuristic known as "hill-climbing" is used, operations are applied so that the state of the problem is brought more in line with the __goal__ state.

25. The heuristic known as means-__end__ analysis involves working backward from the goal of a problem through the kinds of operations required to achieve that goal.

26. "Aha, that's it!" is the feeling associated with the experience psychologists refer to as "insight," when all the component elements of a problem seem to suddenly come together in a way that leads to the solution. Wolfgang Kohler demonstrated that this experience can occur even in animals, as evidenced in his experiment in which chimpanzees eventually got hold of bananas, which were deliberately placed out of their reach, by stacking __boxes__ on top of one another to form a platform from which they could reach the goal objects more easily.

successful

set

random

natural

preparation

evaluation

acts

phonemes

different

morphemes

Grammar
syntax

deep
surface

cooperative

quantity

quality
relation

manner

language

influences

artificial

natural

27. One important problem with thinking in general, and in problem solving in particular, is that people tend to repeat actions that have been _____ for them in other circumstances. The Luchins water jar problem is a classic demonstration of how such a _____ can interfere with effective thinking.

28. Campbell has suggested that ideas are generated at _____ in creative thinking, with those that are useful or adaptive being retained or selected. From this viewpoint then, creativity is considered a process similar to _____ selection.

29. Creativity involves four essential processes: _____, which involves immersion in the subject and often an especially intense period just before the solution is reached; generation of ideas; _____ of those ideas, which involves an assessment of their worth; and implementation, or actually carrying out those ideas.

30. The different forms of language are called speech _____. A declarative sentence conveys specific information, a question is a request for information, and an imperative conveys a command.

31. The sounds of a language are called _____. One way to isolate these is to say a word and systematically change one of the sounds until the word changes into a _____ word. Phonemes are combined to produce the units of meaning referred to as _____.

32. _____ is the study of the specific rules of language; how words are arranged to convey meaning is called _____.

33. From the standpoint of his theory, Chomsky distinguishes between the underlying network of thought conveyed in a sentence called _____ structure and the actual sentence in which that underlying thought is carried, called _____ structure.

34. Communication between two speakers generally follows what is called the _____ principle, which refers to the fact that each speaker tries to understand *why* the other said what he or she said.

35. Following this principle, there are four basic "conversational maxims" that speakers usually obey when they are in communication with each other: _____, which refers to the tendency to try to make what we say as informative as required, but no more so; _____ or the attempt to be as truthful as we can in conversation; _____, which describes the attempt to make our contributions relevant to the conversation; and _____, or the attempt to be clear and orderly.

36. According to the hypothesis proposed by Benjamin Whorf, it is _____ that determines the structure of thinking. A qualified version of Whorf's hypothesis would be that language _____ but does not determine thought.

37. The field of _____ intelligence deals with attempts to get computers to do intelligent things and to do them in the same way that people do them. The problem of getting computers to understand _____ languages (such as English and French) has turned out to be much more difficult than researchers initially expected.

Turing 38. _____ tests involve having a person communicate with two other "people," one of whom is actually a computer.

digital 39. Almost all computers used today are _____—which means that their basic processing occurs in terms of exact categories. Information processing in the human brain, in contrast, seems to depend

analog at least in part on what are called _____ properties of the behavior of neurons.

nodes 40. The basic idea of neural network models is that "_____" are connected to each other in a network and are "activated" by stimulation from the other nodes they are connected with. At a very general level,

neurons this resembles the way _____ in the brain activate
neurons other _____ via their synaptic connections.

SELF-QUIZ
MULTIPLE-CHOICE ITEMS

1. Using the adjective "red" to describe a sunset, an apple, and a tomato exemplifies _____ in human thinking.
   a. maladaptive overgeneralization
   b. category incongruence
   c. classification
   d. structural antecedence

2. Berlin and Kay's research has indicated that if a language has only three color terms, they will be
   a. black, white, and red.
   b. red, blue, and yellow.
   c. red, yellow, and green.
   d. black, green, and red.

3. _____ level categories are those that seem to be the level at which we most naturally divide the world.
   a. Prototype
   b. Basic
   c. Attribute
   d. Substance

4. Which of the following is/are *not* true about the tendency toward overgeneralization in human thinking?
   a. It is most advantageous in a stable situation.
   b. It simplifies.
   c. It allows us to adapt quickly to changes in the world.
   d. None of the above are true.

5. Which of the following is *not* a heuristic?
   a. representativness
   b. symmetry
   c. availability
   d. comparison

6. The use of the heuristic known as _____ is apparently what accounts for the subjects in Kahneman and Tversky's experiment guessing incorrectly that there are more English words beginning with K than there are words in which K is the third letter.
   a. symmetry
   b. comparison
   c. availability
   d. representativeness

7. The tendency for a problem-solving standard to be maintained without being changed or adjusted, even if compelling new data are present or common sense dictates such a change, reflects what is called _____ effects in human thinking.
   a. cognitive structuring
   b. liability
   c. primacy
   d. anchoring

8. Which, if any, of the following is/are among the basic elements to be considered in every decision?
   a. the alternatives from which one has to choose
   b. possible outcomes
   c. the decision maker's preferences for alternative outcomes
   d. all of the above

9. According to the effect availability has on decision making, when people are asked to judge the relative frequency of different causes of death, they are most likely to overestimate the frequency of which of the following?
   a. diabetes
   b. asthma
   c. emphysema
   d. cancer

10. Trivial problems, such as how to open a jar, are best solved through the use of
    a. heuristics
    b. means-end analysis
    c. algorithms
    d. trial-and-error

11. The process of solving a problem includes all of the following basic steps *except*
    a. finding the problem
    b. understanding the problem
    c. planning a solution
    d. checking the results

12. Which of the following problem solving strategies is used most by computers?
    a. heuristics
    b. algorithms
    c. insight
    d. hypothesis testing

13. The results of Luchins' research using the water jar problems demonstrates the effects of _____ in human thinking.
    a. insight
    b. protocol analysis
    c. set
    d. trial-and-error
14. All of the following are part of the creative process *except*
    a. preparation
    b. selection
    c. generation
    d. implementation
15. The individual sounds of a language are called
    a. phonemes
    b. morphemes
    c. syntax
    d. surface structure
16. When we listen and read, attending selectively and filling in the gaps, we are
    a. using heuristics
    b. using algorithms
    c. processing actively
    d. transforming grammar
17. Which of the following is *not* true about modern computers?
    a. They process meaningful symbols.
    b. They pass the "Turing test" quite convincingly.
    c. Their basic processing occurs in terms of exact categories.
    d. Analog processing is more characteristic of the human brain than it is of computer operations.
18. Which model of the brain suggests that processing may not be sequential but simultaneous?
    a. heuristic processing model
    b. algorithmic processing model
    c. analog model
    d. neural network model

TRUE-FALSE ITEMS

1. T F The tendency toward classification in human thinking is a major simplifying factor in mental life.
2. T F A table is a natural category because people have no trouble agreeing on what it is.
3. T F Our tendency to overgeneralize is adaptive in that it helps protect against dangers associated with changing circumstances.
4. T F Our preference for "round numbers" and multiples of 10 exemplifies our use of prototypes and categories.
5. T F The heuristic of representativeness is one effective means of avoiding mistakes of overgeneralization.

6. T F In human thinking, the standard of comparison shifts constantly.
7. T F Tversky and Kahneman's research has indicated that the decision of whether or not to drive 20 minutes to save $5 on some purchase is independent of the total amount of the expenditure.
8. T F Current information tends to be given less weight than long-established information in decision making.
9. T F The human mental system tends to ignore large daily dangers—even life-threatening ones.
10. T F The human mental system tends to ignore short-term scarcity.
11. T F Heuristics probably result in more efficient decision making overall.
12. T F Trial and error is the most basic problem-solving strategy.
13. T F Algorithms guarantee that a solution will be found to a problem if the problem solver persists.
14. T F Protocol analysis is a "thinking aloud" technique.
15. T F Phonemes are as meaningless as individual letters.
16. T F From the standpoint of Chomsky's transformational grammar approach, it is assumed that the grammar of language is learned primarily by operant conditioning.
17. T F Deep structure is the underlying network of thought conveyed in a sentence.
18. T F Computers have essentially unlimited language-understanding capabilities.
19. T F No computer program today is close to being able to pass even the most general form of the Turing test.
20. T F People are much better than modern computers at learning new concepts.

ANSWER KEY TO SELF-QUIZ

MULTIPLE-CHOICE ITEMS

1. c 2. a 3. b 4. a 5. b 6. c 7. d 8. d 9. d 10. d 11. a 12. b 13. c 14. b 15. a 16. c 17. b 18. d

TRUE-FALSE ITEMS

1. T 2. F 3. T 4. T 5. F 6. T 7. F 8. T 9. T 10. F 11. T 12. T 13. T 14. T 15. T 16. F 17. T 18. F 19. T 20. T

THINKING ABOUT THE PSYCHOLOGY OF YOUR OWN EXPERIENCE

1. One of the most important decisions we make in life is the career, vocation, or profession we choose for ourselves. Even if you have already settled on a career path, use the following exercise in decision analysis to evaluate your choice. If you haven't yet chosen a career, this might help you to narrow your options.

Step 1: Define a set of alternative careers, vocations, or professions from which to choose. Of the following, which are most important to you.

   a. How well do the alternatives you have considered meet your needs and/or aspirations with regard to:

1. The job market demand for the services and/or goods you could provide
2. Income and standard of living
3. Prestige as it is associated in this society with what we do for a living
4. The stimulation value, novelty, and meaningfulness of the work you do.

b. To what extent is your own unique pattern of aptitudes, abilities, and interests, realistically suited to the kind of training, education, and/or experience required to attain the positions you have identified?

Step 2: What do you see as the probable outcomes, in terms of your own life experience, of each of the alternatives you have identified?

Step 3: Rank the alternatives in the order of your personal preference for each of them.

Step 4: Evaluate each of the alternatives in terms of the considerations suggested in 1a and 1b. (Use a 10 point scale with 1 being very low and 10 being very high.)

Step 5: Do a means-end analysis of the alternative you ranked as the one you most prefer. Starting with your first choice career, work backward from that long-range goal, outline briefly the subgoals you see as leading to it. Having done this, you will have written a behavioral program of operations for getting yourself from where you are now to the career goal to which you aspire.

2. People learning a language come to understand word meaning through context. Sometimes children will invent a word they need and members of the family will adopt the child's word. One child may go out to play wearing his shoes and "rah rahs." Another child waves to his father who is taking off at the airport in a "meme." Often, family nicknames come into being this way. See if you can get your friends to pickup a nonsense word of your own invention. All you have to do is decide on the word—say a new name for your backpack or your car—and use it consistently without explanation.

11
THE MEASUREMENT OF INTELLIGENCE

GENERAL STUDY QUESTIONS

After reading Chapter 11, you should be able to answer the following questions.

1. Who devised the first tests of intelligence and what were they designed to measure?

2. What was Alfred Binet's test devised for?

3. What three strategies did Binet and his associates use to define and measure intelligence?

4. What is an intelligent quotient (IQ)? How is it derived?

5. The Wechsler tests of intelligence had what advantage over the Binet tests? How many scores does it yield?

6. What does your IQ predict?

7. IQs are best used for what?

8. What is the difference between fluid abilities and crystallized abilities?

9. Guilford organizes the different mental factors into what three categories?

10. How do psychologists try to determine whether intelligence is inherited?

11. What portion of intelligence do psychologists now believe is possibly inherited?

12. The claim that certain races are genetically inferior in intelligence rests on what three erroneous assumptions?

13. What does the text suggest is the most productive use of the concept of IQ?

14. What environmental factors increase IQ scores?

15. Which type of preschool experiences show the greatest long-term gain in IQ?

16. How did the "toy demonstrator" program work?

17. What is instrumental enrichment (IE)? What four IE concepts help to improve intelligence?

18. Sternberg's triarchic theory of intelligence is comprised of what three parts?

19. How does Sternberg define intelligence?

20. What are the six "frames of mine" proposed by Gardner?

OUTLINE OF KEY TERMS AND CONCEPTS

Galton's tests
  Head size
  Sensory acuity
Binet: The beginnings of modern intelligence testing
  Binet's assignment
    Predicting school success
      Using actions teachers regard as intelligent
      Ability to rank students
      Chronological age–mental age link
  Mass testing
    Single score as measure of intelligence
Modern intelligence testing
  Intelligence quotient (IQ)
    Stanford-Binet test
      IQ: Mental age/Chronological age x 100
      Deviation IQ
    The Wechsler tests
      WAIS-R
      WISC-R
      Verbal and performance
    Stability and validity
      Sorting children for school
  Testing for general versus specific intelligence
    The search for general intelligence
      Spearman's g
    The search for specific intellectual abilities
      Cattell's work
        Fluid abilities
        Crystallized abilities
      Guilford's work
        Independent abilities
          Contents
          Operations
          Products
Distribution of intelligence
  Inheritance of IQ and intelligence
    Relative roles of genetics and environment
      Adoption studies
  Problems with studying heredity and IQ
    Adoptions not random
    Fraudulent studies
  Racial differences in IQ
    All ethnic groups new to US subject to argument
  Misconceptions about race and IQ
    IQ represents a fixed capacity
    Racial differences are important
    Difference in intellect between blacks and whites is due entirely to heredity
  Investigations of racial differences and IQ
    Scarr's work
    Effect of early experiences and nutrition
    Effect of large families
    Intelligence not adequately defined
Enhancing intelligence
  Influence of nutrition
    Brain structure and intelligence
    Nutrition and brain development
  Stimulation in early experience
    Orphanage studies
Programs to develop intelligence
  General enrichment
    Preschool environments
    Head start
      Westinghouse report
      Jensen's interpretation
    Toy demonstration program
  Instrumental enrichment (IE)
    Concepts
      Cultural deprivation vs cultural difference
      Making adaptive responses to new situations
      Cognitive modifiability
      Mediated learning experience
Analysis of components of the mind
  Triarchic theory of intelligence—Sternberg
    Information-processing components
      Metacomponents
      Performance components
      Knowledge-acquisition components
    Coping and automatizing
      Three kinds of insight

Selective encoding
Selective combination
Selective comparison
Adaptability
Frames of mind—Gardner
Six kinds of intelligence

Linguistic
Musical
Logical-mathematical
Spatial
Bodily-kinesthetic
Personal

COMPLETION ITEMS

scientific
variations

1. Charles Darwin's, *The Origin of the Species*, began the modern _____ era in biology and related sciences. In psychology, it provoked great interest in the study of _____ in human abilities.

acuity

2. Darwin's cousin, Francis Galton, examined the concepts of head size and sensory _____ as the primary indicators of intelligence.

predict
age

3. In 1904, the French government asked Alfred Binet to devise a test to _____ which children would be least likely to succeed in school. He noted that as children _____ , their intellectual abilities increase. He thus constructed tests to measure cognitive

development

_____.

Mass

4. _____ testing of intelligence began during World War I when psychologists were called upon to develop intelligence tests that could be given to large groups and scored quickly. The quantified scores took on more importance than they had in Binet's original tests.

mental, chronological

5. An IQ score on the Stanford-Binet test is derived by dividing a person's _____ age by his or her _____ age and then multiplying by 100.

performance

6. The advantage of the Wechsler scales over the Binet tests, is that the WISCs test verbal and _____ areas of intelligence.

grades

schooling

7. Research has shown that the higher a child's IQ, the better the _____ she/he tends to get in school. The best use of IQ seems to be close to Binet's original purpose: to identify those children who are most likely to profit from different types of _____.

general

8. Charles Spearman's studies were based on his assumption that a single, _____ intelligence would characterize each individual.

fluid

9. According to Raymond Cattell's approach, _____ abilities are those that involve perception of the world, are genetically based, and are thus independent of culture. Crystallized abilities, in contrast, are those that derive from specific cultural experiences.

independent

10. Guilford and his colleagues conceive of intelligence as being a very large set of _____ abilities, each distinct from the other.

Binet

discriminate

11. The use of _____-type intelligence tests has caused more controversy than any other product of psychology. Much of the time, the standard tests _____ against people whose backgrounds differ from the norm.

genetically	12. The more _____ similar two people are, the more similar they are in IQ. The correlation of IQ of identical twins is higher
together	when they are reared _____ than when they grow up
inherited	apart. There is an _____ component to the elusive qualities we all intelligence. It is the nature of that
inheritance	_____ that is in question.
	13. Problems arise in adoption studies attempting to determine the extent to
determined	which IQ is a biologically _____ trait. For example, adoption agencies go to great lengths to place children in homes that are
compatible	not only stable and middle class, but _____ with that
thinking	of their biological parents.
	14. Sir Cyril Burt had apparently documented a strong association between biological heredity and IQ, but his work was later revealed to be a com-
fraud	plete _____.
	15. In a celebrated article in 1969, Arthur Jensen argued that compensatory education programs that attempt to improve the intelligence of black chil-
innate	dren fail because racial differences in IQ are _____.
genetically	16. The claim that certain races are _____ inferior in intelligence is based on a number of misconceptions. One of these is that IQ represents a fixed capacity rather than one that can be affected by the
environment	_____.
	17. If whites are innately more intelligent than blacks, then blacks having
genes	more "white" _____ should have higher IQs. Scarr's research failed to support this prediction.
IQ	18. There are many other influences on _____ in the
nutrition	United States. Early experiences and _____ have long-
deprivations	lasting effects on intelligence; environmental _____, if continuous, can be devastating to a child.
enrich	19. It is more productive to use the concept of IQ to _____ the environment of children who score lower on intelligence tests. Perhaps we should reconsider Binet's earliest notion: use the IQ to aid children
environment	whose _____ has been deficient, and to identify those with organic deficits.
75	20. Most of the brain's growth—about _____ percent of its weight, occurs outside of the womb. Therefore, certain early experiences can have a strong effect on brain growth, and consequently, on
intelligence, enriched	_____. Rats reared in _____ environments have enlarged brain size, as measured by the depth of the cortex.
	21. Children who attend preschools, such as the Montessori schools, that em-
curiosity	phasize _____ and self-motivation show the greatest long-term gains in IQ.
	22. A major setback to the Head Start program came in 1969 when the
Westinghouse	_____ report claimed it did not work because children in the program showed no improvement in IQ as compared with non-Head Start children. However, children in Head Start programs, on the average, get better grades and score higher on
achievement	_____ tests.

COMPLETION ITEMS

mother

enrichment
content

structure

mediated

meaning

metacomponents

knowledge

novelty

automatize

adaptation

single

mind

independent
cognitive

23. The success of Phyllis Levenstein's "toy demonstrators" program testifies to the fact that improving _____-child interaction is an important intervention in increasing the child's intelligence.

24. Reuven Feuerstein, developer of the instrumental _____ approach, points out that cultural differences can lead to a deficiency in the _____ of intelligence, whereas cultural deprivation can lead to a deficiency in the _____ of the mind.

25. Another critical point on Feuerstein's approach is that interaction with people in their environment gives children _____ learning experiences. This refers to the idea that other people, usually parents or siblings, interpret experience and give _____ to events.

26. From the standpoint of Sternberg's triarchic theory of intelligence, the _____ are "executive" or higher order processes, such as planning or evaluating that are responsible for working out task strategy. Thus, it is the _____ acquisition components that help us learn new things.

27. The ability to deal with _____ and the ability to cope in extraordinary situations are also a measure of intelligence. Sternberg proposes that the extent of an individual's ability to _____ information processing is a measure of intelligence.

28. According to Sternberg's theory, intelligence is defined as mental activity involved in purposive _____ to the shaping of and selection of real-world environments relevant to one's life.

29. Intelligence is not a _____ function: it comprises a wide array of cognitive and other skills. We ought to define these skills and learn how best to assess and train them, not combine them into a single but possibly meaningless number.

30. Howard Gardner postulates six major "frames of _____." He believes that the many mental activities of human beings are separate and potentially _____ abilities. This theory is important for psychologists because it is the first modern _____ approach that has broadened the concept of IQ.

SELF-QUIZ

MULTIPLE-CHOICE ITEMS

1. Which of the following was *not* among the kinds of abilities measured in Galton's tests of intelligence?
    a. reaction times in response to sound
    b. verbal reasoning
    c. speed in naming colors
    d. judgment of points on the skin

2. Alfred Binet devised a test to
   a. measure intelligence.
   b. predict how well a child would do in life.
   c. predict how well a child would do in school.
   d. select gifted children for special schools.
3. IQs on the Stanford-Binet test are calculated by which of the following procedures?
   a. CA/MA x 100
   b. MA/CA x 100
   c. MA x 100/CA
   d. CA x 100/MA
4. Which of the following is *not* among the "crystallized abilities" as they are conceptualized in Cattell's theory of intelligence?
   a. perceptions of the world
   b. vocabulary
   c. mathematics
   d. social reasoning
5. Which of the following is *not* among the categories of independent abilities described in the conceptualization of intelligence offered by Guilford and his colleagues?
   a. contents
   b. operations
   c. products
   d. processes
6. Psychological research has indicated the greatest similarity in IQ in which of the following cases?
   a. identical twins reared apart
   b. identical twins reared together
   c. fraternal twins reared together
   d. sisters reared together
7. *Not* among the important factors that influence IQ differences between people are
   a. genes.
   b. nutrition.
   c. culture.
   d. All of the above are important influences on IQ differences between people.
8. The greatest long-term gains in intelligence seem to be achieved by children who attend preschools that emphasize
   a. basic skill learning.
   b. conventional instructional techniques.
   c. both a and b.
   d. curiosity and self-motivation.

9. The success of the "toy demonstrators" program is probably due to the fact that many intellectual skills important in school depend on
    a. perceptual-motor coordination.
    b. predominantly "right-brain" learning.
    c. language.
    d. emotional maturity.
10. The aim of Feuerstein's instrumental enrichment approach is to measure the individual's
    a. current level of achievement.
    b. verbal and performance intelligence.
    c. learning ability.
    d. reasoning skills.
11. From the standpoint of Sternberg's triarchic theory of intelligence, mental operations such as those involved in planning or evaluating a task strategy would most likely be described as functions of the
    a. metacomponents.
    b. protocomponents.
    c. cognitive schema components.
    d. performance components.
12. From the standpoint of Sternberg's theory of intelligence, which of the following is *not* among the types of "insight" involved in the ability to deal with novelty and cope with extraordinary situations?
    a. selective encoding
    b. selective combination
    c. selective comparison
    d. selective discrimination
13. According to Sternberg's triarchic theory, intelligence is mental activity involved in _____ adaptation.
    a. conceptual
    b. structured
    c. purposive
    d. discriminative
14. Which of the following is not among the six major "frames of mind" postulated by Howard Gardner's theory of intelligence?
    a. perceptual-motor
    b. linguistic
    c. logical-mathematical
    d. musical
15. Howard Gardner's theory of intelligence is important for psychologists because it is the first modern _____ approach that has broadened the concept of IQ.
    a. perceptual
    b. cognitive
    c. linguistic
    d. neurophysiological

TRUE-FALSE ITEMS

1. T F Galton's tests of intelligence emphasized measures of verbal ability.
2. T F Binet's first tests of intelligence were developed for use in the selection and placement of recruits in the French Army.
3. T F A person with a score of 132 on the current version of the Stanford-Binet would place two standard deviations above the norm.
4. T F A review of data on intelligence cited in your text reveals essentially no relationship between IQ and the grades children get in school.
5. T F According to Cattell's theory, fluid abilities are genetically based and independent of culture.
6. T F Cyril Burt's work proved that differences between races in IQ are genetically based.
7. T F According to the text, a productive use of the concept of IQ would be to enrich the environment of children who score lower in intelligence tests.
8. T F IQ is not a fixed capacity.
9. T F Children who have attended preschool typically show an initial increase in IQ, followed by a decline to the norm at around second grade.
10. T F Three years after the program ended, children who had "toy demonstrators" visit their homes showed no difference in IQ scores as compared to a comparable group of children not visited.
11. T F From the standpoint of Feuerstein's instrumental enrichment approach, deficiencies in the structure of the mind are more like to result from cultural deprivation.
12. T F Binet-type tests of intelligence are tests of current achievement.
13. T F Sternberg has proposed that the extent of an individual's ability to automatize information processing is a measure of intelligence.
14. T F Howard Gardner's "frames of mind" theory is based on the assumption that intelligence is a single, general capacity.

ANSWER KEY TO SELF-QUIZ

MULTIPLE-CHOICE ITEMS

1. b 2. c 3. b 4. d 5. d 6. b 7. d 8. d 9. c 10. c 11. a 12. b 13. b 14. a 15. b

TRUE-FALSE ITEMS

1. T 2. F 3. T 4. F 5. T 6. F 7. T 8. T 9. T 10. F 11. F 12. T 13. T 14. F

THINKING ABOUT THE PSYCHOLOGY OF YOUR OWN EXPERIENCE

1. All of us categorize other people simply and easily—"blond" or "tall" are good concrete examples. But when we try to categorize people along more subtle dimensions like "smart," we may run into trouble. The problem is that different people and different cultures have varying concepts of what smart is.

Consider the differences in mental abilities that are suggested in the chapter. Ask yourself: What do I judge as intelligent? Is it only what the academic world encourages? Is it reading books and learning; is it looking at a broken machine and knowing how to fix it; is it being able to sell Big Macs to a vegetarian?

- What do you consider intelligence?
- How did you come by this conceptualization?
- Would your ideas about intelligence be different if you had grown up in another culture?

2. Life achievements and personal fulfillment, of course, depend on many other factors besides abilities, such as motivational and emotional characteristics. Nonetheless, much frustration and unhappiness could be avoided of only it were possible to set goals that are realistically suited to our abilities and potential.

By writing answers to the following questions, you may sort out some of these factors as they pertain to you. First, describe your own patterns of abilities by making a list of your strengths and on a separate page make a list of your weaknesses. Include factors from all the different ways of looking at intelligence discussed in the chapter. Then consider the following:

- Was there ever a time in your life when any of the abilities you have listed as "strengths" were "weaknesses," or vice versa? An example of this would be if you were thought to be too impulsive in one situation but found that your ability to think and act quickly was an asset in another.
- How is anything you are doing now in life directed to either building upon your strengths or minimizing your weaknesses in abilities? (Are you taking math?)
- How does your current career plan tend to fit the "ability profile" you have described for yourself here? (Are you too gregarious to be a writer?)
- Find someone who does what you want to do in life. (You may be surprised how willing even very successful people are to answer questions about their work.)
- Ask that person what personal factors are important for success in that career "in the real world."
- Compare that with what you have been told in school about career requirements in your chosen field.
- Finally, compare what you learned from the professional and with the list of your own attributes.

PART IV

...

THE WORLD OF THE SELF

12
EMOTIONS AND HAPPINESS

GENERAL STUDY QUESTIONS

After reading Chapter 12, you should be able to answer the following questions.

1. In what way do emotions simplify an organism's experience?

2. Give four reasons why we have emotions.

3. In what way can emotions serve as schemata?

4. What is a social releaser?

5. When verbal behavior and nonverbal behavior don't match, which do we consider more valid? Why?

6. What are three reasons given for women's superior skills at decoding nonverbal behavior?

7. What are the eight primary emotions suggested by Plutchik?

8. These emotions vary on what three dimensions?

9. What is the difference between feelings and emotions?

10. What is affect?

11. What is temperament?

12. What is the primary organ of human social communication? What is second?

13. How do we differentiate between fear and anger?

14. What are the three types of signals provided by the face?

15. How long do most facial expressions of emotion last?

16. Most of the reactions involved in emotions involve what?

17. What two major divisions of the brain are responsible for many emotional reactions? Which part of the brain controls pleasure? Which part of the brain controls emergency reactions?

18. Why is the *Mona Lisa's* smile so ambiguous?

19. What is appraisal and what are its three basic dimensions?

20. Describe the emotion cycle.

21. What is the cognitive appraisal theory of emotion?

22. What are some of the consequences of frustration?

23. According to Robert Zajonc, which comes first, thinking or feeling?

24. What is the difference between fear and anxiety?

25. How do strong emotional reactions seemingly by-pass consciousness?

OUTLINE OF KEY TERMS AND CONCEPTS

What emotions are and do
   Automatic
   Involuntary
Function of emotions
   "Movement"
   Arousal
   Organization
     Serve as schemata
   Directing and sustaining actions
   Communication
     Social releasers
Gender differences in nonverbal behavior
   Consider nonverbal behavior more valid
     Encoding
     Decoding
       Women better at decoding
     Touch
       Men allowed more space
       Men touch women more than women touch men
     Suggested explanations
       Men are more powerful
       Women are more attentive and polite
       Different hemispheric specialization
Basic emotions
   Plutchik's theory
     Joy
     Acceptance
     Fear
     Surprise
     Sadness
     Disgust
     Anger
     Anticipation
       Vary along three dimensions
         Intensity
         Similarity
         Polarity
       Emotion wheel
   Descriptive terms
     Affect
     Emotions
     Feelings
     Moods
     Temperament
Are emotions universal?
   Darwin's observation

Displayed by face
Emotional expression in infants
  Progressive differentiation
  Attachment
How we experience emotions
  Autonomic nervous system
  Interpret physical reactions
  Activation of emergency reaction
    Emergency reactions
      Fight or flight
    Sympathetic nervous system
  Patterns of activation
    Controlling facial expressions and emotion
      Poses of face
    Individual characteristic emotional response
  Emotions and the brain
    Limbic system
      Stimulation of pleasure center
    Cortex
      Emergency reaction
    Left hemisphere
      Verbal content
    Right hemisphere
      Tone and gesture
    Asymmetry of facial expressions
Knowing what we feel
  Appraisal and reappraisal
    Evaluation
    Potency
    Activity
  Interpretation of emotions
    Cognitive appraisal theory
      Interpretation of physiological state
      Arousal common in different emotions
        Interpretation of unexplained arousal
  Consequences of frustration
    Frustration-aggression hypothesis
    Conflict
      Internal conflicting demands
      External conflicting demands
      Internal demands conflict with external ones
Feeling and thinking
  Zajonc's hypothesis
    Preferences and inferences
  Fear and anxiety
    Fear: immediate and specific
    Anxiety: ambiguous situation
      Side effects of antianxiety drugs
  How fear bypasses consciousness
    Respond emotionally before thinking
The pursuit of happiness
  Happiness is relative
    Wealth doesn't predict happiness
  Small pleasures

COMPLETION ITEMS

automatic
simplify

1. Emotions have an _____ and involuntary quality that set them apart from thinking and reasoning. They _____ an organism's experience by preparing it for action.

signal

sustain

2. Emotions move us into action; they _____ that something important is happening. Emotions not only initiate and direct action, but _____ and engage it.

organizing

schemata

3. Emotions can serve as schemata and aid in _____ consciousness. When an event enters consciousness, all associated _____ actuate as well.

perception
angry

4. Feeling in consciousness influences _____. When you are angry, you see others as _____, even if they are not.

adaptive

5. A "sweet tooth" has _____ value because natural sweet fruits are nutritious and unlikely to be poisonous.

releasers

6. "Social _____" are signals and gestures by means of which animals communicate information about probable behavior to each other.

nonverbal	7.	We communicate a great deal through our _____ behavior. If a person's _____ and nonverbal behavior don't match, we tend to consider the _____ behavior more valid.
verbal		
nonverbal		
face	8.	Women are somewhat better than men at decoding nonverbal cues, particularly those expressed by the _____. In other words, women outperform men at inferring the _____ state of a target person by his or her facial expression.
emotional		
happy	9.	Men who smile a lot are described as _____, affiliative, and sociable. Women who smile a lot are described as _____ and uncomfortable.
anxious		
colors	10.	In Plutchik's theory, emotions are compared to _____. Plutchik thus postulates eight primary emotions, which are assumed to vary on the dimensions of intensity, similarity, and _____.
polarity		
Affect	11.	_____ refers to the feeling dimension of life. _____ are the subjective experience of emotions. _____ is a predisposition to specific emotional reactions in certain situations.
Feelings		
Temperament		
facial	12.	Charles Darwin observed that all peoples of the world express grief by contracting the _____ muscles in the same way. Emotional expression develops naturally in a predictable _____. Like motor skills, it begins as _____ and disorganized and gradually becomes more refined and precise.
sequence		
undifferentiated		
autonomic	13.	Emotional reactions involve the _____ nervous system. That we differentiate emotions means that we must _____ our physical reactions.
interpret		
face	14.	There is more brain area devoted to control of the _____ than to any other surface of the body. Expression of the emotion of _____ usually involves a response of getting away from or getting rid of something offensive.
disgust		
arousal	15.	The strongest physiological effect of emotion is _____. Emotions turn on the body's emergency reaction, allowing us to prepare for immediate action such as the "_____-or-flight" response. Most of the reactions involved in the activating mechanisms are of the _____ nervous system.
fight		
sympathetic		
facial	16.	Ekman asked people to assume different _____ expressions, such as raising the eyebrows and lowering the lips. When they did, they _____ the emotions they were expressing.
felt		
limbic	17.	The _____ system of the brain is largely responsible for many emotional reactions. Stimulation of the pleasure center in the _____ yields intense awareness of pleasure.
hypothalamus		
verbal	18.	The left hemisphere of the brain responds to the _____ content of emotional expression and the right to tone and gesture. The left seems to involve _____ emotions such as happiness and the right _____ ones such as anger.
positive		
negative		

COMPLETION ITEMS

Appraisal

evaluation

potency

cognitive

arousal

feedback

interpretation

sexual

ambiguous

Frustration

aggressive

internal

external

inferences

Fear

Anxiety

REM

separately

limbic

emotional bypasses

think

19. _____ is the understanding of the meaning of an event. There are three basic dimensions in this process. The first is _____, which concerns whether the situation is good or bad, benign or threatening. The second is _____: Is it alive or dead, strong or weak, fast or slow? The third is activity: Is it active or passive?

20. The _____ appraisal theory of emotion states that interpretation of the physiological state leads to different emotional experiences. One factor that may cause confusion in our lives is that _____ is common to quite different emotions.

21. One approach to test this theory is to provide experimental subjects with false _____ on the internal state itself. If emotional experience depends upon _____, then false information should also have an effect on experience.

22. In the wobbly bridge study, the arousal caused by crossing a dangerous bridge was misinterpreted as _____ excitement upon seeing an attractive woman. Activation, especially in contrived or _____ situations, is subject to misinterpretation.

23. _____ is a normal reaction to the stress that results when a desired outcome is thwarted or delayed.

24. At one time psychologists thought that all frustrations increase the probability of _____ behavior, and that all aggression was due to frustration.

25. Combat stress, which includes a need to survive along with a need to be respected by others, is an example of _____ conflicting demand.

26. A child with one parent who demands excellence in athletics and a second parent who wants the child to become a musician is a victim of _____ conflicting demands.

27. Robert Zajonc has expressed his belief that feelings come before thinking in his phrase, "Preferences need no _____."

28. _____ is an immediate and specific emotional reaction to a specific threatening stimulus.

29. _____ is the more general reaction that occurs in higher animals and human beings that develops in response to the anticipation that something harmful may occur in the future.

30. Drugs such as alcohol, barbiturates, and Valium may help a person to function but interfere with complex learning and inhibit _____ sleep.

31. Emotions can be routed specially and _____ to the brain. They form the ground plan of the brain, in the _____ system.

32. LeDoux and his collaborators have begun to establish routings, primarily in the amygdala of the limbic system of what are called "_____." Thus, we can respond emotionally before we can _____ of what we're doing—a response mechanism that is very useful in emergencies.

CHAPTER 12 / EMOTIONS AND HAPPINESS

increases
money

33. In our culture, once we are over a minimal standard of wealth, then _____ in wealth don't seem to matter as much as we think. The bottom line is, if we want _____ to make us happy, then we'll have to be poor.

happiness

34. According to research conducted by Diener, _____ springs from how much of the time a person spends feeling good, not from the momentary peaks of ecstasy.

35. Simple pleasures—hours spent walking on a sunny day, gardening, running with the dog, chopping wood - are more allied with happiness

strong feelings

than are _____.

SELF-QUIZ
MULTIPLE-CHOICE ITEMS

1. The word "emotion" is rooted in the Latin word for
   a. anger.
   b. passion.
   c. energy.
   d. movement.

2. Which of the following is *not* an explanation offered to explain the observation that women are better than men at decoding nonverbal communication?
   a. Women are in a subordinate position to men in this society.
   b. Women are more attentive and polite.
   c. Differences between women and men in hemispheric specialization.
   d. Women smile more and this make others to relax and become "leakier."

3. Pure emotions are
   a. rarely experienced.
   b. experienced as flatness of affect.
   c. defined by psychologists as the basic elements of temperament.
   d. defined by psychologists as moods.

4. Which of the following is *not* among the "primary" emotions as outlined in Plutchik's theory?
   a. joy
   b. acceptance
   c. anticipation
   d. love

5. Which of the following is *not* one of the three dimensions along which primary emotions vary, according to Plutchik's theory?
   a. intensity
   b. duration
   c. similarity
   d. polarity

6. _____ is the most permanent and characteristic aspect of emotional life.
   a. Affect
   b. Feeling
   c. Temperament
   d. Emotion
7. Research has revealed that smiling in infants
   a. does not occur.
   b. reflects a different pattern of underlying emotions than in sighted infants.
   c. shows the same pattern of development as in sighted infants.
   d. remains undifferentiated until about the age of two or three years.
8. Which of the following is *not* among the three types of signals provided by the face?
   a. static
   b. phasic
   c. slow
   d. rapid
9. Which of the following is not among the physiological changes most typically associated with emotional activation?
   a. increased blood flow to the muscles
   b. increase in the secretion of norepinephrine
   c. increase in skin resistance
   d. increase in gastric motility
10. The only specific pattern of bodily reaction that consistently relates to emotional expression among people is
    a. facial expression.
    b. the pupillary constriction response.
    c. the degree of increase in skin resistance.
    d. the degree in parasympathetic ANS activity.
11. The "pleasure center" in the brain is located in the
    a. frontal lobes.
    b. hypothalamus.
    c. left hemisphere.
    d. right hemisphere.
12. The right hemisphere of the brain is apparently specialized for response to the _____ of emotional response.
    a. most positive aspects
    b. the feeling of happiness
    c. tone and gesture aspects
    d. verbal content
13. A basic emotional reaction such as fear is probably_____.
    a. learned
    b. voluntary
    c. innate
    d. none of the above

14. Which of the following is *not* among the basic dimensions of our "appraisal" of events we experience?
    a. evaluation
    b. potency
    c. activity
    d. polarity
15. In support of the cognitive appraisal theory, the emotional reaction experienced by subjects injected with epinephrine was found to be affected by
    a. the amount of drug they were given.
    b. how they interpreted the arousal that was so induced.
    c. their age.
    d. their degree of social maturity.
16. Conflicting demands that lead to threat or frustration are
    a. internal only.
    b. external only.
    c. both internal and external.
    d. dependent on level of arousal.
17. An important emotion resulting from stress is
    a. frustration.
    b. anger.
    c. anxiety.
    d. depression.
18. We seem to gauge happiness by
    a. how much money we make.
    b. how satisfying our work is.
    c. comparing our own experiences.
    d. comparing ourselves with others.

TRUE-FALSE ITEMS

1. T F Most human emotions are common to other animals.
2. T F According to Tompkin's analysis, the human appetite for sweet-tasting foods is primarily responsible for the increasing incidence of diabetes in adolescents and young adults in this society.
3. T F Emotions not only initiate and direct action but sustain it.
4. T F "Social releasers" are nonverbal cues, like standing far away or frowning, that get us out of uncomfortable social situations.
5. T F Plutchik's theory uses the analogy of colors to explain emotions.
6. T F Jealousy is a feeling but not an emotion.
7. T F In human beings, emotions are primarily displayed by the face.
8. T F Eibl-Eibesfeld's research has shown that children born blind tend not to display the basic facial expressions in appropriate situations.
9. T F Most of the "reactions" involved in emotions are due to the activating mechanism of the sympathetic nervous system.
10. T F It is rare for a facial expression of emotion to last more than 5 to 10 seconds.
11. T F It is possible to control different emotions using only simple poses of the face.

12. T F The right hemisphere of the brain responds to the verbal content of emotion and the left to the tone and gesture.
13. T F We seem to express emotions more on the right than the left side of our face.
14. T F Results of the experiment in which subjects were injected with epinephrine supported the view that emotional experience is due to physiological arousal.
15. T F Frustration is a normal reaction to stress.
16. T F The kind of stress a soldier experiences in a combat situation is an example of external conflicting demands.
17. T F Fear is an immediate and specific emotional reaction to a specific threatening stimulus.
18. T F Although they may affect REM sleep, antianxiety drugs do not seem to interfere with complex learning.
19. T F It is possible for us to control fears of loud noises, heights, or other dangers, even though we "know" they're dangerous,
20. T F Research by Diener and his colleagues found that it wasn't how positive people felt but how often people felt positive that determined happiness.

ANSWER KEY TO SELF-QUIZ

MULTIPLE-CHOICE ITEMS

1. d 2. d 3. a 4. d 5. b 6. c 7. c 8. b 9. c 10. a 11. b 12. c 13. c 14. d 15. b 16. c 17. c 18. c

TRUE-FALSE ITEMS

1. T 2. F 3. T 4. T 5. T 6. T 7. T 8. F 9. T 10. T 11. T 12. F 13. F 14. F 15. T 16. F 17. T 18. F 19. F 20. T

THINKING ABOUT THE PSYCHOLOGY OF YOUR OWN EXPERIENCE

1. The theory and research presented in Chapter 12 suggest that our health may be powerfully affected by the way we manage the expression of emotion in our lives. This exercise is designed to stimulate your thinking about your own style of emotional response.

Write out descriptions of the most recent incidents in your life in which you remember experiencing each of the following "primary" emotions:

- joy
- acceptance
- fear
- surprise
- sadness
- disgust
- anger
- anticipation

For each incident, pay particular attention to the following questions:

a. What led up to the event?
b. What *thoughts* occurred to you throughout the course of the event?
c. What *bodily feelings* did you experience as the event unfolded? How, if at all, did you *ventilate* any of these feelings?

d. What did you do in the situation? How did your *actions* fit with what you were thinking or feeling?

   e. Did you surprise yourself in the situation? That is, could you have predicted your response if you had been told about the situation in advance?

2. We don't often consider carefully what it takes to make us happy, and we don't often ask others about their happiness. Consider the following questions:

   a. What would it take to make you truly happy?

   b. Is the answer to this question the same as it would have been five years ago?

Make a list of the times and circumstances which you recall as having made you happy. Ask a friend to compare his or her list with you.

- Are the kinds of things on this list similar to the kinds of things you expect would make you happy in the future?

Next, ask someone at least twenty years older than you what times and circumstances have made him or her happy. Then ask this person what it would take to make him or her happy now.

- Are any of the things mentioned by this person on your list of happiness-makers?

If possible, ask someone at least forty years older than you the same questions.

- What are the similarities and differences you found on these lists of things that make people, or might make people happy?

13
NEEDS AND GOALS

GENERAL STUDY QUESTIONS

After reading Chapter 13, you should be able to answer the following questions.

1. What are the two different types of motives? Give an example of each.

2. What are drives and what do they do?

3. Do humans have instincts?

4. What is creative adaptation?

5. What is prepotence?

6. The primary motivation for all organisms is what?

7. What is homeostasis and how does it operate?

8. How does the body warm and cool itself?

9. List three benefits of sauna bathing.

10. What happens if there is no fluid intake, such as occurs in sleep?

11. What are antigens and why are they important to us?

12. What do lymphocytes do for us?

13. How do we know we are hungry?

14. What does the hypothalamus have to do with whether you gain weight or not from overeating?

15. What causes obesity?

16. Why is it so hard to lose weight? What is the "what-the-hell-effect"?

17. According to Syme, "When I was young and felt bad, my grandmother used to tell me, 'Go out and play with your friends'" Why is this good advice?

18. Goals serve what function?

19. What is competence and what is its reward?

20. What are some of the factors that contribute to need for achievement in an individual?

21. What causes boredom? In what kind of cultures is boredom most prevalent?

22. The term self-actualization refers to what?

23. What are seven distinguishing features of self-actualized individuals?

24. In what way are functional autonomy and motivation linked?

25. Why are optimistic beliefs and confidence sometimes more important than the reality of our situation?

OUTLINE OF KEY TERMS AND CONCEPTS

Overview of needs and goals
  Needs
  Drives
    Drive reduction
  Instincts
    Predispositions
  Goals
    Homeostatic adaptation
    Creative adaptation
  Maslow's pyramid of motivation
    Prepotence
Physiological needs
  Keeping stable
    Homeostasis
      Feedback
    Temperature regulation
      Set point
      Thermometer neurons
Getting heat
  Physiological changes
  Pleasure
  Czech study
    Increase beta-endorphins
  Chemical changes in brain
    Increase serotonin
  German study
    Reduce illness
  Burn calories
Thirst
  Fluids
  Electrolytes
  Sympathetic nervous system
    Renin release from kidney
  Anterior hypothalamus
    Antidiuretic hormone (ADH)
    Diabetes insipidus
Hunger
  How do we know we are hungry?
    Gastric factors
      Cannon's balloon experiment
    Metabolic factors
      Blood sugar (glucose)
      Hypothalamus
      Lateral hypothalamus
  How do we know when to stop eating?
    Ventromedial nuclei (VMN)
      Hyperphagia
        Internal mechanisms

- External cues
- Obesity
  - Love of food
    - Adaptive value until recently
  - Temperature and food intake regulation
    - Body as furnace
  - Set point
    - Calorie
    - Hypothalamus
  - Innate factors
    - Some are born to be fat
      - Too many fat cells
      - High set point
  - The losing battle
    - Fat vs. carbohydrate
    - "Brown fat"
    - Difficulty with altering set point
      - Protection against famine
    - Increase exercise
      - Increases heat production
    - Does thin equal healthy?
- Anorexia and its treatment
  - Case of Ellen West
    - Reconditioning treatment
- Resisting disease
  - Mechanisms of immunity
    - Antigens
    - Allergies
    - Autoimmune diseases
    - Natural immunity
      - Inflammatory processes
      - Permeability of capillaries
      - Interferon
      - Lymphocytes
        - T-cells
        - B-cells
        - Microphages
        - Lock-and-key principle
        - Lymphokines
  - The brain and immune system
    - Hypothalamus
    - Thymus
    - Pituitary
      - Norepinephrine
  - Emotions and immunity
    - West Point study
      - Epstein-Barr virus
      - High expectations plus poor academics
    - Other predictors
      - Loneliness
      - Life stress
      - Anxiety
      - Depression
  - Psychoimmunology
    - Positive state of mind
    - Hypnosis study
      - Visualization helps
- Belonging and safety
  - Pain and pleasure
    - Lemniscal system
      - Sudden pain
    - Spinothalamic system
      - Slow pain
  - Belonging
    - Cooperation
    - Health consequences of deprivation
      - Lebanese orphans
      - Symes' findings
        - Health - social network link
    - Maternal care
      - Hormone transfer studies
- Human goals
  - Humans motivated by possibilities
    - Creative adaptation
  - Competence and excellence: esteem
  - Achievement
    - Achievement motivation
      - Culturally relative
    - Characteristics of achievers
      - Need for achievement (nAch)
      - Set realizable goals
      - Not failure avoidant
      - Internally motivated
      - Take risks
      - Independent
      - Value competence in others
      - Like concrete feedback and criticism
      - Prefer activities with definable goals
    - Environmental factors
      - Parental accomplishments and standards
      - Middle and upper income homes
    - Can be learned
      - Key quality - perseverance
  - Knowledge
    - Need sense of organization
    - Need curiosity and exploration

Avoiding boredom
   Set-point for information, stimulation, change
  Destabilizing challenges
   Life changes
  Age and need for stimulation
   Seek stimulation and reduce complexity
Curious for life
  Need to explore natural scenes
Optimal level of arousal
   Inverted-U curve
    Performance deficits if underaroused or overaroused
Self-actualization
  Maslow's work
   Distinguishing characteristics
  Transcendence
   Meaning of life
   Religious experience
  The motives combined
   Functional autonomy
Building confidence
  Optimistic beliefs
  Confidence
   Importance of perceived control
   Critical to health
    Set realistic goals
  Importance of optimism
   Pollyanna was right

COMPLETION ITEMS

motivates
1. People act in very different ways depending on what _____ them.

Needs
Drives
2. _____ are specific deficits that any animal must satisfy, such as hunger and thirst. _____ are physiologically based goads to behavior: they literally move us to action.

instinct
3. An _____ is a behavior typical of every member of a species, and it appears, without learning, on the first occasion the appropriate situation occurs.

goal
4. A _____ is a desired outcome that has not yet occurred.

prepotence
5. What distinguishes the different levels of Maslow's hierarchy is _____, which refers to the relative strength of different needs.

survival
stable
6. The primary motivation for all animals is _____. The entire mental system and brain adapts continuously to keep the body _____ in a changing world.

Homeostasis
hypothalamus
7. _____ is a built-in mechanism to keep the body in a constant state. In human beings, the set point body temperature of 98.6 F is maintained by thermometer neurons in the _____ of the brain.

body temperature, expends
8. Sweating is an active physiological response to help lower _____. It _____ a considerable number of calories; a person can burn up 300 to 800 calories during a sauna.

brain
hormones
serotonin
9. The feeling of relaxation following a sauna may also be due to other chemical changes in the _____. The heat may deplete our body stores of stress _____. Saunas also increase _____, a powerful hormone associated with relaxation and sleep.

Fluids

75

water
renin
thirst

antidiuretic

stomach

VMN
hyperphagia

internal

lymphocytes

macrophages

viruses

hypothalamus

mononucleosis

Metabolism

fat

calorie
set

adipocites, carbohydrates

decreased

overweight

10. _____ are essential: every cell of the body is bathed in them. They have the appropriate mineral concentration of sea water, and they constitute _____ percent of our body weight.

11. Pressure receptors in blood vessels detect even the smallest reduction in the _____ content of the blood. This leads to the release of _____, an enzyme produced by the kidney, that activates the sensation of _____.

12. The anterior hypothalamus produces _____ (ADH), a hormone that signals the kidneys to divert water in the urine to the bloodstream when you are thirsty.

13. On the basis of a study in which he cajoled his research assistant into swallowing a balloon, Cannon proposed that _____ contractions were the primary signal of hunger.

14. Destruction of the ventromedial nuclei _____ of the hypothalamus results in _____ or extreme overeating. Obese people and rats with VMN lesions have lost _____ mechanisms or cues that control eating.

15. Antigens are "foreign" cells or large molecules that originate outside the body. Acquired immunity works through a type of white blood cell known as _____. Large scavenger cells that ingest and destroy antigens and attack tumors and virus-infected cells are called _____.

16. Some _____, such as herpes simplex, are always present in the body, but become active only when something goes wrong with the immune system.

17. Removal of certain areas of the _____ leads to suppression of the immune system.

18. Kasl's research indicated that West Point cadets who wanted a military career but were doing poorly academically were the ones most likely to develop symptoms of infectious _____.

19. _____ is the process in which food is burned to make heat to keep the body warm and provide energy. When there is more fuel than can be burned, it is stored as _____ to be used when needed.

20. A _____ is a measure of heat production. The "_____ point" is the body weight around which the brain attempts to maintain homeostasis.

21. Fatness is related to the number and size of the body's fat cells, called _____. Since the calories from _____ have to be metabolized before they are deposited as fat in the body, they lead to less fat deposits than calories from fats which are deposited directly in the tissues.

22. To maintain weight loss, food intake must be continually _____ as a diet goes along, since our caloric needs decrease at lower weights.

23. Research by Reuben Andres has shown that people who are average weight or slightly _____ for their ages are the healthiest.

Anorexia

reinforced

lemniscal

spinothalamic

social

belonging

health

extensive

invention

creative

Competence

standard

moderately

competence

stable

ill

understimulated

concentration

Curiosity

information

stimulation

middle

mind

growth

actualized

Transcendence

purpose

24. _____ nervosa patients can be successfully treated by reconditioning procedures in which successive movements associated with eating are _____.

25. The _____ system quickly transmits sudden pain information. The _____ system transmits slow pain information, such as that of an old back problem.

26. Human beings are _____ animals. Recent evidence suggests that when people are deprived of _____ to a group, they may suffer health consequences.

27. In an extensive study of the effect of social networks on _____, Syme and others found that healthy people have a more _____ network of friends than those less healthy.

28. Human beings are motivated not only by biological deficits, but by the _____ of possibilities. Goals all serve the function of _____ adaptation.

29. _____ is how well we can carry out an intended action.

30. David McClelland defines the drive for achievement as "competition" with a _____ of excellence." People with a high level of n-Ach tend to set _____ high, realizable goals for themselves, to be more internally motivated than low achievers, and to be more likely to associate with others on the basis of their _____ than on the basis of friendship.

31. The external world, so chaotic and changing, becomes _____, simplified, and seemingly coherent in the mind. When this sense of coherence is disrupted, the person is more likely to become _____.

32. We must deal both with the destabilizing challenges of life changes and with the destabilizing that can result when the brain is _____. When people are not stimulated, they rapidly become disorganized, lose their intellectual ability, _____, and coordination.

33. _____ increases mental activity by conveying more stimulation from the outside environment.

34. We are motivated to regulate the amount of _____ we received within our own set of range just as we regulate temperature and weight. The brain apparently has a need for a certain amount of _____ and information to maintain its organization.

35. The optimum level of arousal is in the _____ of an organism's response range.

36. Abraham Maslow believed that all people naturally tend toward _____ and health unless obstructed from doing so. One of the characteristics that he found distinguishes self-_____ individuals is an unconventional morality of what is right and wrong.

37. _____ refers to going beyond an ordinary understanding of life. The foremost objective of religious activity is to attain a direct knowledge of how the world is organized and the _____ of human life.

autonomy

38. The concept of functional _____ refers to the tendency for an often repeated action to become a motive in its own right.

optimistic

39. The _____ beliefs and confidence we have are sometimes more important than the reality of our situation.

future health

40. A person's confidence in his or her own health turns out to be one of the best predictors of _____.

SELF-QUIZ
MULTIPLE-CHOICE ITEMS

1. The concept of drive reduction accounts well for behaviors associated with
   a. very basic needs.
   b. curiosity.
   c. exploratory activity.
   d. all of the above.

2. Maslow developed a _____ conceptualization of human motivation.
   a. linear
   b. curvilinear
   c. hierarchical
   d. neurophysiological

3. In Maslow's theory of motivation, "prepotence" refers to the relative _____ of different needs.
   a. immaturity-maturity
   b. importance
   c. strength
   d. organization

4. Homeostasis operates by the process of
   a. schemata regulation.
   b. hormone depletion.
   c. feedback.
   d. metabolism.

5. The "set point" for body temperature in human beings is maintained by "thermometer" neurons in the
   a. pituitary.
   b. thyroid.
   c. hypothalamus.
   d. occipital lobe.

6. _____, produced by the kidney, is an enzyme involved in the activation of thirst sensations.
   a. Fibrin
   b. Actosin
   c. Mitosin
   d. Renin

7. Rats whose lateral hypothalamus has been destroyed tend to
   a. develop diabetes.
   b. urinate and drink excessively.
   c. stop eating.
   d. become hyperphagic.
8. Which of the following is *most likely* to occur as a result of VMN lesion?
   a. an increase in circulating insulin
   b. the animal will eat so excessively as to cause its own death
   c. the animal will eat so as to maintain a lower body weight
   d. increase burning of fatty acids
9. After indulging in a heavy meal at night, the person with _____ is the most likely to "sweat out" the excess calories overnight.
   a. a VMN lesion
   b. a lot of "brown fat"
   c. the least amount of "brown fat"
   d. hyperphagia
10. Both the immune and nervous system
    a. regulate the body.
    b. receive and transmit excitatory signals.
    c. learn and remember.
    d. all of the above.
11. _____ are large scavenger cells that ingest and destroy antigens.
    a. Macrophages
    b. Neprosines
    c. Troposines
    d. Bactophores
12. The results of a study by Kasl showed that West Point cadets were most likely to develop symptoms of infectious mononucleosis if they
    a. wanted a military career.
    b. were doing poorly academically.
    c. both a and b.
    d. never really did want a military career.
13. Posthypnotic suggestion for subjects to _____, has been found to be effective in actually increasing the number of lymphocytes in easily hypnotized people.
    a. see themselves as physically large and very strong
    b. relax deeply
    c. decrease their own blood pressure
    d. visualize their white blood cells as powerful sharks
14. Exercise
    a. increases a person's appetite.
    b. actually inhibits weight loss in obese people.
    c. increases heat production after a meal.
    d. decreases heat production after a meal.

15. The case of anorexia nervosa discussed in the text was treated effectively by means of
    a. conditioning therapy.
    b. hypnosis.
    c. megavitamin therapy.
    d. drugs which intensified the patient's appetite.
16. According to the text, a key quality of achievers is
    a. intelligence.
    b. social status.
    c. perseverance.
    d. the circumstance.
17. Each of us has an optimum level of arousal which is _____ of the range of possible responses.
    a. at the high end
    b. at the low end
    c. in the middle
    d. none of the above
18. Which of the following is not among the traits that Abraham Maslow found to be characteristic of self-actualized people?
    a. creativity and inventiveness
    b. objectivity and detachment
    c. high tolerance of ambiguity
    d. ego-centeredness

TRUE-FALSE ITEMS

1. T F Drives are psychologically-based goads to behavior.
2. T F An instinct is an unlearned behavior typical of every member of a species.
3. T F The creation of goals is unique to human motivation.
4. T F The needs for esteem, knowledge, and the like are much more equivalent to one another than Maslow presumed.
5. T F Mental processes maintain a constancy of the perceived world, and homeostasis maintains a constancy in our internal, physiological world.
6. T F Homeostasis operates by the process of feedback.
7. T F The only effective way to quench thirst is to place water directly into the stomach.
8. T F The absence of ADH leads to an increase of 10 to 15 times the normal amount of urine and almost constant thirst and drinking.
9. T F Macrophages are "foreign" cells or large molecules of origin outside the body that intrude into the body and stimulate the immune system responses to defend against them.
10. T F Stomach contractions stop when sugar is injected into the bloodstream, even though the stomach is empty.
11. T F Losing and gaining weight it simply a matter of regulating calorie intake.

12. T F Obese people have more fat cells than do people of normal weight.
13. T F In order to lose weight, food intake must be continually decreased as the diet continues.
14. T F Recent research has shown that people who are underweight for their age are the healthiest.
15. T F Syme and other researchers have found that healthy people tend to be "loners" and have less need for an extensive social network than do unhealthy people.
16. T F People with a high level of the need to achieve have been found to motivate themselves by setting extremely high, difficult to attain goals.
17. T F According to the n-shaped curve hypothesis, the optimum level of arousal is at the low end of an organism's response range.
18. T F The foremost objective of religious activity is to attain a direct knowledge of how the world is organized and the purpose of human life.
19. T F Functional autonomy refers to the fact that any action which is repeated often enough eventually loses its motivational value.
20. T F Pollyanna was probably right.

ANSWER KEY TO SELF-QUIZ

MULTIPLE-CHOICE ITEMS

1. a   2. c   3. c   4. c   5. c   6. d   7. d   8. a   9. b   10. d   11. a   12. c
13. d   14. c   15. a   16. c   17. c   18. d

TRUE-FALSE ITEMS

1. F   2. T   3. T   4. T   5. T   6. T   7. F   8. T   9. F   10. T   11. F   12. T
13. T   14. F   15. F   16. F   17. F   18. T   19. F   20. T

THINKING ABOUT THE PSYCHOLOGY OF YOUR OWN EXPERIENCE

1. The concept of achievement motivation is one that has been studied extensively by American psychologists. In this culture, a person's achievement orientation can be a powerful organizing force in his or her life. In fact, it borders on being a "personality style" that is often crucially involved in determining the direction and quality of our lives. But this personality style develops out of the culture in which we are imbedded as we grow up.

Consider why you are in college and how you came to attend the school you are attending. Think about your own life and the expectations, often unstated, that were held by your parents about achievement. Specifically:

- In high school, was it expected that you would function at the top of your class in school or was passing your classes sufficient?
- Were certain colleges considered "out of reach" or "not good enough?" On what basis were these judgments made?
- Was academic achievement or athletic achievement encouraged?
- Was it assumed that you would train for work using your mind or did your family value the ability to make things work?
- How was success defined: paycheck, fame, social status, large network of friends, "self-actualization"?

So you can see that the concept of achievement is not clear-cut. What kind of achievement are you willing to work hard for?

2. The link between optimism and health was described in the chapter. Fill out the Life Orientation Test developed by Carver and Scheirer (1987) found on page 463 of the text.

- What is your score? (Recall that subjects who scored 20 and over were found to have fewer health symptoms that subjects who scored below 20.)
- If you score below 20, play Pollyanna for a few days. See if you can think positively and only say positive things. Don't verbalize complaints. Like the studies where the physical act of smiling put people in a good mood, expressing a positive attitude may also work to improve your attitude. (This works because the feedback from others in the environment will be more positive.)
- If playing Pollyanna doesn't work, take Syme's grandmother's advice and go out and play with your friends. That will make you feel better about

14
PERSONALITY

GENERAL STUDY QUESTIONS

After reading Chapter 14, you should be able to answer the following questions.

1. What is personality?

2. What are three kinds of parapraxes?

3. Psychoanalysis is based on what two fundamental hypotheses? Give an give an example of each.

4. What is the pleasure principle? What are the two major drives?

5. Give an example of cathexis.

6. List the psychosexual stages of development.

7. According to Freud, what are the three parts of the personality? What kind of thought is associated with two of them?

8. What is the primary symptom of neurosis?

9. Which of Freud's followers were known as "ego-psychologists?" Why?

10. How does Erikson's theory differ from Freud's?

11. How does Jung's concept of the unconscious differ from that of Freud? What is the collective unconscious?

12. What is being analyzed in psychoanalysis? What three methods are used discover material to be analyzed?

13. The use of projective tests rests on what assumption?

14. What is the difference between a temperament, a trait, and a type?

15. Buss and Plomin report three stable aspects of personality. Give an example of each.

16. Are people consistent? What four things contribute to our belief that they are?

17. What are the three principles of action identification theory?

18. What makes an objective personality test, objective? Give an example of an objective personality test.

19. What is the "third force" in psychology. What is its central concept?

20. Carl Rogers divided the personality into four parts. What are they?

21. What are conditions of worth and what do they have to do with "congruence?"

22. What are self-schemata?

23. What is reciprocal determinism?

24. According to Erikson, how do we create an identity?

25. According to socioanalytic theory, what is the task of psychotherapy? Why?

OUTLINE OF KEY TERMS AND CONCEPTS

What is personality?
  Basic questions
    What is nature of human nature?
    What accounts most for behavior, person or situation?
  Why study personality?
    Curiosity about self and others
    Help people
Sigmund Freud
  Grand theory
    Began as neurologist
    Treat hysteria with hypnosis
    Need insight not catharsis
  Fundamental ideas
    Psychic determinism
    Consciousness is rule not exception
  Dynamics of personality
    Drives
      Eros
      Thanatos
    Libido
    Cathexis
  Human development
    Psychosexual stages
      Oral
      Anal
      Phallic
        Oedipus complex
        Electra complex
      Latency
      Genital
  Structure of personality
    Id
      Pleasure principle
      Primary process thought
    Ego

                Reality principle
                Secondary process thought
            Superego
        Civilization and neurosis
            Unconscious conflicts
            Anxiety
        Theory is difficult to test
    Neo-Freudians
        Ego-psychologists
        Emphasize social interactions
        Alfred Adler
            Individual psychology
        Harry Stack Sullivan
        Karen Horney
        Erich Fromm
    Erik Erikson
        Expanded on Freud
            Goal to become integrated human being
            Development throughout lifespan
                Psycho*social* stages
    Carl Jung
        Analytical psychology
            Development throughout lifespan
                Individuation
            Ego
                Shadow
            Personal unconscious
            Collective unconscious
                Archetypes
    Exploring personality: Making the unconscious conscious
        Psychoanalysis
            Free association
            Dream analysis
            Interpretation of faulty actions (Freudian slips)
        Word association test
        Projective techniques
            Rorschach ink blot test
            Thematic apperception test
        Case study
    Temperament, traits, and types
        Categorizing people
            Greeks - "humors"
                melancholic
                choleric
                sanguine
                phlegmatic
            Sheldon's somatotypes
                mesomorph
                ectomorph
                endomorph
        Temperament
            Buss and Plomin's dimensions
                emotionality
                activity level
                sociability
            Eysenck—superfactors
                extraversion-introversion
                instability-stability
                psychoticism-superego functioning
        Traits
            Allport
                Cardinal traits
                Secondary traits
            Cattell
                16 Personality factors
        Types
        Are traits and types useful?
        Are people consistent?
            Consistent and inconsistent people
            High and low self-monitors
            Implicit personality theories
                Person schemata
    Action identification
        Hierarchy of ways to think about action
        Three principles
            Identification chosen helps to maintain action
            Tend to identify at highest possible level
            Drop to lower level, can't maintain high
    Measuring personality
        Objective tests
        MMPI
        SCII
    The self
        Humanistic psychology
            Maslow
            Rogers
                Three parts to personality
                    Organism
                    Experiential field
                    Self
                        Organismic valuing process
                    Incongruence
                    Conditions of worth
        Self as a set of ideas
            Self-schemata
        Investigating the self

Q-sort
Life narratives
The person and the environment
Social learning theory
Reciprocal determinism
Creating identity
Erikson
Socioanalytic theory
Balance
Need for status
Need for structure and order
Lead to individual mix of
Sociability
Conformity
Becoming optimistic
Explaining events
Global or specific cause
Internal or external cause
Stable or unstable cause
Optimism—health

COMPLETION ITEMS

stable

situations

hypotheses
psychic determinism

iceberg

meaningful

sex
Eros
pleasurable
libido

cathexis

psychosexual
erogenous
pleasure
phallic

sexual
Oedipus complex

superego, pleasure principle

reality principle
id

1. Personality consists of the unique and _____ qualities, including thoughts, feelings, and actions, that characterize an individual over time and across _____.

2. Psychoanalysis is based on two fundamental _____. First is the principle of _____, which is the idea that no behavior happens by chance.

3. Freud likened consciousness to an _____ with only a small part observable and accessible. Not only is a thought or an action _____, but the reason for it is to be found in the past which we have forgotten.

4. In the final version of his theory, Freud suggested that there are two major drives, _____ and aggression. Freud sometimes referred to the sexual drive as _____. By this he meant not just a drive for sex, but for all _____ experience.

5. Freud offered the term _____ for the psychic energy associated with the sexual drive. When psychic energy becomes invested in the mental representations of a person or an object it is called _____.

6. According to Freud, human development proceeds through a series of _____ stages. Each of the five stages is named for an _____ zone, which is a part of the body that, when stimulated, produces _____.

7. At about age 3 the child enters the _____ stage, in which the genitals are the focus of pleasure. Freud believed that during this stage, the child's love for the opposite-sex parent takes on a _____ element. In boys, this is called the _____.

8. Freud divided the personality into the id, the ego, and the _____. The _____ guides the id, but the id cannot act directly in the outside world to gain pleasure and avoid pain.

9. The ego is guided by the _____. It comes into existence to gratify the wishes of the _____.

secondary	10. The ego is characterized by _____ process thought which is rational, and is responsible for the ego's capacity to delay action until the proper time to satisfy the id's wishes.
Neuroses	11. _____ are unconscious conflicts between the desires of the id and the demands of the superego. They often occur as a result of _____ experiences in early childhood. The primary symptom of a neurosis is _____.
traumatic	
anxiety	
	12. The conception of an unconscious defense system is generally thought to be a _____ description of many mental processes. But, even after almost a century, the theory remains _____ in scientific proof.
useful	
lacking	
ego	13. One group of neo-Freudians was called _____ psychologists because they expanded the role of the ego. In their view, rather than simply trying to keep the peace, the ego is responsible for such behaviors as exploration and _____.
mastery	
interpersonal	14. One of the neo-Freudians, Harry Stack Sullivan, defined personality in terms of _____ interactions. He believed that our personality is defined by the way we _____ ourselves and are perceived by others.
perceive	
independently	15. Erikson believes that the ego develops _____ rather than derives from the id. In addition to defending the personality, the ego is responsible for maintaining a sense of _____.
identity	
opposites	16. Jung formed his own school of thought called analytical psychology, which is based on the principle of _____. Jung believed that _____ energy is created by tension between opposites within the personality.
psychic	
unconscious	17. Jung believed that the _____ is even more vast and complex than Freud suggested. The _____ unconscious consists of memories that have been forgotten, or suppressed.
personal	
collective, inherited	18. The _____ unconscious is the _____ foundation of personality, the experience common to all persons, and is not dependent on an individual's experience.
archetypes	19. The collective unconscious consists of _____, which are the inherited predispositions to have certain experiences.
exploring the unconscious, free association	20. Psychoanalysis was first regarded as a technique for _____. It begins with _____ during which the patient is told to relax and simply say whatever comes to mind.
Projective	21. _____ techniques induce the subject to project needs and conflicts onto ambiguous stimuli. These techniques rest on the same assumption as psychoanalysis, that is, that the unconscious must be approached _____.
indirectly	
Temperament	22. _____ is a genetic predisposition to respond to specific events in a specific way. It is a _____ of behavior.
style	
	23. Traits are the general and enduring qualities that exist within us and underlie our thoughts, feelings, and actions over time and across
situations	_____.

COMPLETION ITEMS

type
absolute

predictable

same

consistent
underestimate
shapes

standardized

motives

self
third force

organism
organismic valuing process

self-concept

incongruence
set of ideas

interactions

Q-sort

meaning
stability

longitudinal study

life narrative

identity

learned
Bandura

reciprocal determinism

24. A _____ is a cluster of related traits. With types, an individual is usually described in _____ rather than relative terms.

25. By thinking in terms of traits that influence behavior, most of us believe that other people are more _____ than they really are. Researchers have found that people are consistent over time in the _____ situations, but not in different situations.

26. There are a number of reasons for our belief that people are _____ across situations. For example, we have a tendency to _____ the influence of the situation a person is in. Second, our own behavior _____ the behavior of those around us.

27. Objective personality tests such as the MMPI are objective in the sense that they are _____ and can be scored by a computer. While the tests themselves may be objective, the people who take them have a variety of _____ when they fill in those bubbles.

28. The _____ is a central concept in humanistic psychology. This branch of psychology is known as the "_____" in psychology, the other two being psychoanalysis and behaviorism.

29. Carl Rogers divided the personality into the _____, the experiential field, and the self. By using our _____, we evaluate experience according to whether it helps or hinders our self-actualization.

30. Sometimes in order to receive positive regard from the world, we change our behavior in ways not consistent with our _____. This implies a discrepancy between the actual self and the ideal self, which Rogers called _____.

31. To cognitive psychologists, the self is a _____ we have about ourselves. We gather an array of information by monitoring our thoughts and feelings as well as from _____ with others.

32. _____ is a method of ranking statements according to how relevant they are to you. With this method, the person who sorts the items is the one to assigns _____ or weight to an item.

33. In order to document personality _____ over time, researchers must follow lives over time. One method is the _____, in which a group of subjects is studied over many years.

34. With personal history or _____ we create a story about ourselves that integrates our thoughts, feelings, and memories. It is a way we have of making sense of our lives and constructing our _____.

35. Social learning theory emphasizes that most behavior is _____ rather than instinctually determined. According to _____ we learn by watching others be rewarded or punished, not simply by being rewarded or punished ourselves.

36. The idea that the environment has an impact on our thoughts, feelings, and actions while we, in turn, shape the environment is called _____.

expectations

elicits

status and success

sociability

stable
affect everything
Optimism

control

37. We can create situations through our _____ and the behavior of others is interpreted in light of the expectations we have of them. If you believe someone to be attractive, you are more likely to behave in a flirtatious manner, which in turn _____ warm, friendly behavior from that person.

38. According to socioanalytic theory, each of us balances a need for _____ with a need for structure and order in the social environment. Each of us has within us a unique mix of _____ and conformity that influences the way we are able to seek status while trying to remain acceptable to the group.

39. When bad events occur, pessimists explain the causes in _____, global, internal terms. ("It's going to last forever, its going to _____ I do, and it's all my fault!").

40. _____, in psychological terms, is the tendency to seek out, to remember, and to expect pleasurable experiences. An optimistic person faces the future and faces difficulties as a challenge and believes that he or she can _____ the environment.

SELF-QUIZ

MULTIPLE-CHOICE ITEMS

1. Freud's description of personality in terms of the iceberg metaphor, refers to the
   a. conscious and unconscious.
   b. relationships between id and superego.
   c. relationships between parents an children.
   d. conflicts between the individual and society.

2. Which of the following is *not* among the methods used in psychoanalysis to gain access to the unconscious?
   a. hypnosis
   b. parapraxes (Freudian slips)
   c. dreams
   d. free association

3. The term Freud offered for the psychic energy associated with the sexual drive was
   a. drive.
   b. cathexis.
   c. libido.
   d. catharsis.

4. According to psychoanalytic theory, the _____ is the reservoir of psychic energy
   a. libido
   b. id
   c. ego
   d. superego

5. During which stage of psychosexual development does the child develop a conscience?
   a. oral
   b. anal
   c. phallic
   d. latency
6. Which part of the personality is governed by secondary process thought?
   a. id
   b. ego
   c. superego
   d. unconscious
7. The primary symptom of neurosis is
   a. forgetfulness.
   b. dreams.
   c. defensiveness.
   d. anxiety.
8. Which of the following is *not* among the factors that were emphasized more strongly in the neo-Freudian theories than in Freud's classic psychoanalytic approach?
   a. the importance of inherited biological instincts
   b. higher mental functions
   c. social influences
   d. the role of ego and conscious processes
9. If you meet a man who is cold and rejecting, Jung would suggest that
   a. you should give him unconditional positive regard.
   b. you should examine his childhood for clues to his personality.
   c. the opposing warmth is buried in his unconscious.
   d. you should reward any warmth he demonstrates.
10. In psychoanalysis, what is being analyzed?
    a. childhood memories
    b. the way the ego defends the personality
    c. the way the id tries to get what it wants
    d. symptoms
11. Classifying a person according to a sign of the zodiac is an example of a
    a. temperament.
    b. trait.
    c. type.
    d. none of the above.
12. Which of the following is *not* one of the dimensions of temperament according to Buss and Plomin?
    a. emotionality
    b. sociability
    c. neuroticism
    d. activity level

13. Are people consistent?
    a. People are consistent across time and over situations.
    b. People are consistent across time but not in different situations.
    c. People are consistent in different situations but not across time.
    d. People are consistent across time in the same situations, but not in different situations.
14. The format for most personality tests is
    a. objective
    b. projective
    c. subjective
    d. none of the above
15. Which of the following is *not* a part of the personality according to Carl Rogers?
    a. Organism
    b. Ego
    c. Self
    d. Experiential field
16. According to socioanalytic theory, what is the natural unit of social behavior?
    a. reciprocal determinism
    b. the ego ideal
    c. the role
    d. drive
17. Which of the following pattern of explanations for bad events characterizes the pessimist?
    a. stable, global, internal
    b. unstable, global, internal
    c. stable, specific, external
    d. unstable, specific, external.

TRUE-FALSE ITEMS

1. T F In psychoanalytic theory, the principle of psychic determinism is the idea that no behavior happens by chance.
2. T F The psychological investment in the mental representation of a person or an object is called catharsis.
3. T F In developmental order, the psychosexual stages are oral, anal, genital, latency, phallic.
4. T F According to Freud, the ego is the last part of the personality to develop.
5. T F In psychoanalytic theory, the primary symptom of neurosis is anxiety.
6. T F Research evidence on the effectiveness of psychoanalysis as a therapy provides little evidence that it is effective.
7. T F The psychologists known as neo-Freudians de-emphasized determinism while emphasizing higher mental functions along with social influence.
8. T F As in Freud's psychoanalytic theory, Jung's analytical psychology emphasizes the idea that sexuality is the primary motivator of human behavior.

9. T F According to Jung's theory of individual psychology, the developmental process includes dismantling the persona and reconciling the opposites within the personality.
10. T F Jung agreed with Freud that dreams are meaningful.
11. T F A trait is a genetic predisposition to respond to specific events in specific ways.
12. T F Most people are consistent over time in the same situations, but not in different situations.
13. T F High self-monitors tend to use their own internalized standards as the primary guidelines for their behaviors and to be relatively unconcerned about how they appear to others.
14. T F The most widely used personality test is the Minnesota Multiphasic Personality Inventory (MMPI).
15. T F Humanistic psychologists criticize psychoanalysis because it is based on emotionally disordered people.
16. T F According to Carl Roger's theory, conditions of worth are messages from others that provide guidelines to be used to achieve actualization.
17. T F With the method known as personal history or life narrative, the subject is required to recount the facts of his or her life with as much accuracy as possible.
18. T F The idea that the environment has an impact on our thoughts, feelings, and actions while we, in turn, shape the environment is called reciprocal determinism.
19. T F According the Robert Hogan's socioanalytic theory, the task of psychotherapy is one of training in social skills.
20. T F Taking personal responsibility when bad events occur helps to maintain an optimistic frame of mind.

ANSWER KEY TO SELF-QUIZ

MULTIPLE-CHOICE ITEMS

1. a 2. a 3. c 4. b 5. c 6. b 7. d 8. a 9. c 10. b 11. c 12. c 13. d 14. a 15. b 16. c 17. a

TRUE-FALSE ITEMS

1. T 2. F 3. F 4. F 5. T 6. T 7. T 8. F 9. T 10. T 11. F 12. T 13. F 14. T 15. T 16. F 17. F 18. T 19. T 20. F

THINKING ABOUT THE PSYCHOLOGY OF YOUR OWN EXPERIENCE

1. Is your behavior consistent? Are you always honest? Do you always tell the truth? Always? What determines how you behave?

As you read in the chapter, situational factors can play a powerful role in determining behavior. Describe at least two examples of how social circumstances affected the expression of the following dimensions of your personality.

- your speech style and/or mannerisms
- your expressed political or religious views
- your motivation to achieve
- your attitude toward a person of the opposite sex

Now list two examples of times when these expressions of your personality we *not* affected by social circumstances.

- Which examples was it easier to come up with?
- Based on what you read in the chapter, why might this be the case. (Hint, review the section on self-monitoring.)

2. How do you classify people?
   - Smart/not smart?
   - Good looking/not good looking?
   - Nice/not nice?
   - Fun/boring
   - Competent/not competent?
   - Friendly/aloof?

We know we aren't supposed to categorize people but we all do it; it is built into the way we think. But each of us favors different dimensions and the way we classify others may say more about us than it does about them.

One way to find out how you classify is to think about the last time you introduced two of your friends who didn't know each other. What did you say to each of them about the other? Did you describe accomplishments? Did you comment on clothing? Did you tell of an experience you had shared? Does this say something about the others or about you? How would each of these people "classify" you?

Ask others what dimensions they use to classify people. Or better yet, listen carefully while they talk and you may be able to pick up their classification dimensions. Are these classification schemes traits, types, or temperament?

15
PSYCHOLOGICAL DISORDERS

GENERAL STUDY QUESTIONS

After reading Chapter 15, you should be able to answer the following questions.

1. What are psychological disorders? How are they defined?

2. What are psychoses?

3. Describe three characteristics common to most psychological disorders.

4. Why are psychologists interested in probands and concordance rates?

5. What is the *DSM-III-R*?

6. How are fear and anxiety linked?

7. Describe three anxiety disorders.

8. What makes fear a phobia? What are the most common phobias?

9. What is post-traumatic stress disorder? What are some of the symptoms of this disorder?

10. What is the difference between an obsession and a compulsion?

11. What is the difference between somatization disorder and hypochondriasis?

12. What is a personality disorder? What makes it a disorder? Why is treatment rarely successful?

13. There is evidence for genetic factors contributing to which personality disorder?

14. What must happen before the *DSM-III-R* will classify a person was having a drug disorder? What is the most common addiction?

15. What is the "biggest drug problem in the Western world today?"

16. What are the two different kinds of depression?

17. What has to happen before a clinician would diagnose a person as depressed?

18. Is there a genetic component to depression? How do we know?

19. When is schizophrenia diagnosed?

20. Describe the four types of schizophrenia.

21. What is the dopamine hypothesis?

22. What are the four most common age related disorders?

23. How does mental retardation differ from other diagnostic categories?

24. Why is obesity no longer considered an eating disorder?

25. What are organic mental disorders?

OUTLINE OF KEY TERMS AND CONCEPTS

Importance of being normal
   Psychological disorders
      Exaggeration of normal processes
         Deviant and maladaptive
   Psychoses
      Out of touch with reality
Overview of psychological disorders
   Characteristics
      Loss of control
      Unhappiness or distress
      Isolation from others
   Causes
      Biological
         Genetics
            Proband
            Concordance rates
            Population genetics
         Sensory impairment
      Psychological
      Social-situational causes
Classification of disorders
   DSM-III-R
Anxiety disorders
   Fear and anxiety
   Causes of anxiety disorders
      Inherited vulnerability
   Generalized anxiety disorder
   Panic disorder
   Phobic disorders: the fears
      Zoophobia
      Acrophobia
      Agoraphobia
      School phobia
   Post traumatic stress syndrome
      Precipitating event causes severe distress
      Characteristics
         Persistent reexperiencing of the event through intrusive thoughts and nightmares
         Difficulty concentrating
         Hypervigilance
         Sleeplessness
         Flashes of anger alternating with emotional numbness
         Feelings of detachment from friends
      Two-factor learning theory explanation
         Both respondent and operant conditioning
   Obsessive-compulsive disorders
      Uncontrollability of
         Thought—obsession
         Behavior—compulsion
Somatoform disorders
   Somatization disorder

- Complaints without physical basis for symptoms
- Hypochondriasis
  - Patient belief that her or she is suffering from specific disease
- Conversion disorder
  - Loss of physical function without medical basis
  - Patient doesn't seem to care
- Causes
  - Behavior rewarded in past

Personality disorders
- Do not want treatment
- Types
  - Paranoid
  - Schizoid
  - Histrionic
  - Narcissistic
  - Borderline
  - Avoidant
  - Dependent
  - Compulsive
  - Passive-aggressive
  - Antisocial
- Antisocial behavior: sociopathic personality
  - Case of Dan F.
  - Causes
    - Biological factors
      - Decreased emotional response
      - Studies measuring autonomic system
        - Less activation to shock
        - Extreme calm
    - Genetic factors
      - Children of criminal fathers
      - Wadsworth study

Substance use disorders
- Dependence
- Abuse
- Incidence
  - 16 percent have alcohol problems
- Causes
  - Biology plus environment
- Narcotics (opiates)
- Depressants
  - Alcohol
  - Barbiturates
- Stimulants
  - Caffeine
  - Nicotine
  - Amphetamines

Mood disorders
- Depression
  - Two kinds
    - Unipolar
    - Bipolar
      - Mania
  - Every day for two weeks
    - Loss of interest and pleasure
    - Appetite disturbance
    - Sleep disturbance
    - Psychomotor disturbance
    - Decrease in energy level
    - Sense of worthlessness
    - Difficulty in concentrating
    - Thoughts about death
    - Miscellaneous associated symptoms
- Seasonal affective disorder (SAD)
  - Amount of sunlight reaching brain
  - Treatment by high intensity light
- Manic episodes
  - Mirror image of depression
  - Euphoria and expansiveness—no specific cause
- Incidence of mood disorders
  - 0.4 - 1.2 percent of population
- Causes of mood disorders
  - Endogenous factors
    - Predisposition to bipolar depression
      - Transmitted as dominant gene
  - Exogenous factors
    - Stress
  - Personality characteristics
    - Successful
    - Hard-working
- Interesting finding about realism
  - Depressed people are more realistic
- Suicide
  - Risk with depression
  - Growing among young adults

Multiple personality
- Small number of cases
- Traumatic childhood experiences

Schizophrenia
- Deterioration in mental abilities
- Characteristics
  - Disturbances in content of thought delusions
  - Disturbances in form of thought
  - Perception hallucinations
  - Affect

    Blunt
    Flat
    Inappropriate
  Disturbance in sense of self
  Volition
  Relationship to external world
  Psychomotor behavior
  Associated features
Types of schizophrenic disorders
  Hebephrenic
  Paranoid
  Catatonic
  Undifferentiated
Case of Carol North
Causes of schizophrenia
  Genetic factors
    Twin studies
    Biochemical and neurophysiological factors
    Dopamine hypothesis
Age-related psychological disorders
  Childhood autism
    Refrigerator mothers
  Mental retardation
  Eating disorders
    Pica
    Anorexia
    Bulimia
    Cultural influences
  Organic mental disorders
    Dementias
    Alzheimer's
The importance of being normal
  Consequences of diagnostic labels
  Dividing line not easy to determine

COMPLETION ITEMS

extremes

1. Psychological disorders are exaggerations or _____ of the normal patterns of thought, action, emotions, and coping.

detract

deviant

2. Only when unusual thoughts or behavior patterns _____ substantially from our psychological well-being do we consider it a psychological disorder. The thoughts or behavior must be both _____ and maladaptive.

control

distress

3. The fundamental qualities that characterize the experience of a psychological disorder include the following (a) loss of _____ — the feeling that one's emotions and thoughts are beyond one's own competence; (b) unhappiness or _____; and (c) isolation from others, which may involved a physical separation from people and/or a feeling of withdrawal into oneself while in the company of others.

biological

experiences

4. The causal or predisposing factors in the development of psychological disorders include the following: (a) _____ factors, such as a person's genetic inheritance; (b) mental factors, which are those associated with the particular _____ in a person's life; and (c) social-situational factors, whereby specific events may induce an increased susceptibility to the development of a disorder.

Diagnostic and Statistical Manual of Mental Disorders **(DSM)**

5. In the United States, the most widely used classification system is the American Psychiatric Association's _____.

Anxiety

neurotic

neurotic

6. _____ refers to the enduring experience of fear in the absence of a fear-inducing stimulus. Before the 1980 revision of the *DSM-III*, such disorders were classified as "_____ disorders." Although people use the word _____ in everyday speech, psychologists have no useful definition of it.

170

CHAPTER 15 / PSYCHOLOGICAL DISORDERS

generalized	7. People who suffer from what is called _____ anxiety disorder live in constant tension and worry and are often so terrified of making a mistake that they cannot concentrate or make decisions.
sudden onset agoraphobia	8. The cardinal feature of panic disorder is its _____. Panic disorders commonly pair panic with _____ in which a person experiences attacks of panic if he or she thinks about venturing out.
Phobias fear of animals fear of closed spaces, agoraphobia	9. _____ are extreme or unfounded fears. The most common of these include zoophobia _____, claustrophobia _____, and _____ (fear of being alone in public places from which it might be difficult to escape).
Post-traumatic stress disorder (PTSD)	10. _____ is a delayed stress reaction that recurs repeatedly, long after the traumatic event has passed.
obsession compulsive	11. An _____ is a condition wherein a person is preoccupied with one thought that seems to haunt his or her consciousness uncontrollably. In a _____ disorder, the person acts out a particular behavior over and over again, seemingly without being able to control the impulse to do so.
Somatization Hypochondriasis	12. _____ disorder is diagnosed when an individual complains of a physical ailment or pain for which there is no apparent organic or physiological explanation. _____ is similar to somatization disorder but differs in that the person believes he or she suffers from, or may contract a particular disease.
paranoid schizoid narcissistic avoidant sociopathic	13. The following are some of the major types of conditions known as "personality disorders": (a) _____ disorder, characterized by a pervasive and unwarranted suspiciousness and mistrust of people; (b) _____ disorder, wherein there is a defect in the capacity to form social relationships and an absence of warm, tender feelings for other people; (c) _____ disorder, characterized by a grandiose sense of one's own importance and uniqueness; (d) _____ disorder, wherein the person shows a hypersensitivity to potential rejection, humiliation, or shame; and (e) antisocial personality, also called psychopathic or _____ personality, characterized by traits such as superficial charm, lack of a sense of responsibility, and an absence of shame or guilt over one's own antisocial behaviors.
emotional autonomic calm	14. The antisocial personality (ASP) seems to be characterized by a tendency toward decreased _____ irresponsibility, especially to unpleasant stimuli. This hypothesis is supported by studies in which ASPs showed distinctively low levels of _____ system reaction upon receiving an electrical shock. Consistent with this finding, ASPs tend to be characterized by extreme _____, perhaps as a function of a chronically low level of arousal.
impairment	15. Substance use disorder means that there is a consistent pattern of excessive use resulting in _____ of social or occupational functioning.

dependence
Abuse

more
predisposition

cause

Depressants

psychologically

more alert
psychotic

depression

mood

two

pleasure
psychomotor

worthlessness
death
irritability

euphoria
control

endogenous

exogenous

X

exogenous
suicide
increase

sunlight

16. There are two forms of substance use disorder: _____ and abuse. _____ refers to drug use that interferes with the person's ability to function but does not involve physical addiction.

17. If your parents were alcoholics, alcohol very likely dampens your physiological reactions to stress _____ than a person whose parents were not alcoholic. This _____ may play a critical role in the development of alcohol dependence, but no one becomes alcoholic without drinking. In other words, however important genetics are in the development of additions, they do not, in and of themselves, _____ them.

18. _____ lower activity in the brain, thereby reducing physical and cognitive activity. All depressants are _____ addicting and have severe withdrawal symptoms that can lead to death.

19. People use amphetamines to become _____. Heavy amphetamine use can lead to a _____ state much like paranoid schizophrenia, characterized by auditory and visual hallucinations.

20. The clinical syndrome of _____ is much more than a down mood. It is a severe mental disorder that results in an overwhelming sadness that immobilizes and arrests the entire course of life. Depression is classified as a _____ disorder.

21. Before a clinician would diagnose a person's condition as that of depression, at least four of the following symptoms would have to be present every day for _____ weeks: (a) loss of interest in, and an indifference to activities associated with the experience of _____; (b) appetite disturbance; (c) sleep disturbance; (d) _____ disturbance, which refers to some sort of agitation or retardation in action; (e) decrease in energy level; (f) a sense of _____; (g) difficulty in concentrating; (h) preoccupation with thoughts about _____; and miscellaneous associated symptoms such as anxiety, phobias, and _____.

22. In manic episodes, wherein the elevation of mood is commonly felt as pure _____, there is no apparent specific cause, and the mood does not seem to be under the person's _____.

23. The causal factors of both unipolar and bipolar disorder can be divided into factors within the individual—those known as _____ causes and those causes originating outside of the individual called _____.

24. There is some evidence to suggest that a predisposition to bipolar depression may be transmitted as a dominant gene in the _____ chromosome.

25. Stress and other precipitating causes are important as potential _____ factors in the onset of depression.

26. The most serious and tragic outcome of depression is _____. In recent years there has been an enormous _____ in the number of young adults, 15 to 24 years of age, who have attempted suicide.

27. Seasonal affective disorder (SAD) appears directly related to the amount of _____ which reaches the brain. Rosenthal has suc-

full-spectrum		cessfully treated people with this disorder through the use of bright _____ light source for three hours before dawn and three hours after dusk.
Multiple	28.	_____ personality seems to occur in people whose parents were violent, sadistic, and inconsistent in their treatment of them.
Schizophrenia	29.	_____ is considered to be a disease of the central nervous system that affects virtually all cognitive processes and behavior.
disturbance withdrawal	30.	A content of thought delusion is one _____ in schizophrenia. One common delusion is that of thought _____ —the belief that one's thoughts are being stolen from one's mind.
hallucinations psychomotor	31.	Auditory _____ are the most characteristic perceptual disturbances in schizophrenia. Illustrative of _____ disturbances which may also be evidenced in this condition, some schizophrenics maintain a rigid posture for hours, or display, a "waxy flexibility" in their body movements.
1 urban	32.	Psychologists estimate that about _____ percent of all populations suffer from a form of schizophrenic disorder. It is far more likely in _____ than rural areas.
hebephrenia paranoia catatonia undifferentiated	33.	The following are the major types of schizophrenia: (a) _____ which is the form of the disease involving the greatest degrees of personality disintegration and is characterized by extreme disturbance of affect; (b) _____ in which the afflicted person's thinking is dominated by delusions of persecution; (c) _____, which is characterized by strange motor behaviors such as an inclination to maintain an uncomfortable posture for days; and (d) _____, which is a rapidly changing mixture of all or most of the primary symptoms of schizophrenia.
parents siblings 35 to 45	34.	Heston found that 16.6 percent of children reared apart from their schizophrenic _____ developed schizophrenia. The risk of developing this disorder is 5 to 15 times higher in _____ of schizophrenics than in the general population. Along these same lines, if both of a child's parents are schizophrenic, that child runs a _____ percent or more chance of developing the disorder.
dopamine	35.	Support for one hypothesis that focuses on possible biochemical or neurophysiological causes of schizophrenia comes from the observation that the very effective antipsychotic drugs used to help control schizophrenic symptoms work by blocking the neurotransmitter _____ at synapse receptor sites.
social mother brain	36.	The essential feature of childhood autism is the failure to develop _____ relationships. For years, autism was considered a disorder that resulted form interaction with a cold and detached _____. Noting that autism is generally linked to a problem in the mother's pregnancy or to birth complications, most researchers assume that the _____ is damaged in some way during gestation or just after birth.
Obesity	37.	_____ is no longer considered an eating disorder, according to *DSM-III-R*, because it may or may not involve psychological or behavioral problems.

inheritance	38.	There is no evidence for _____ of anorexia or bulemia. Most researchers assume that strong cultural influences are responsible for distorted _____ about perfection and femininity.
beliefs		
Alzheimer's	39.	The symptoms of _____ disease include marked defects in memory and other cognitive processes, including language and perceptual abilities. The cause seems to be linked to abnormalities in the _____ and certain regions of the cerebral cortex.
hippocampus		
labels	40.	Often the _____ that society places on certain behavior can have serious consequences in a person's life. Friends and family may treat them as "disturbed" which can become a _____ judgment.
self-fulfilling		

SELF-QUIZ

MULTIPLE-CHOICE ITEMS

1. The difference between a normal reaction to difficulties and a disordered one is compared in the text to the difference between
   a. day and night.
   b. a brief bout with the flu and a chronic illness.
   c. dictatorship and democracy.
   d. a hot air balloon and an intercontinental ballistic missile.

2. In order for unusual thoughts or behavior patterns to be considered a psychological disorder, they must
   a. be deviant.
   b. be maladaptive.
   c. detract substantially from psychological well-being.
   d. all of the above.

3. Which of the following does *not* characterize most psychological disorders?
   a. loss of control
   b. lack of touch with reality
   c. unhappiness or distress
   d. isolation from others

4. Which of the following is *not* one of the anxiety disorders?
   a. panic disorder
   b. agoraphobia
   c. post-traumatic stress disorder
   d. neurosis

5. The word "phobia" is Greek for
   a. unknown.
   b. hidden.
   c. unconscious.
   d. fear.

6. Acrophobia is an unrealistic fear of
   a. heights.
   b. making decisions.
   c. the unknown.
   d. being alone in public places.
7. Hypochondriasis is classified in *DSM-III-R* as a _____ disorder.
   a. generalized anxiety
   b. personality
   c. somatoform
   d. mood
8. People with personality disorders usually
   a. do not act out their symptoms.
   b. do not want treatment for their disorder.
   c. still relate quite adaptively to their environment.
   d. feel strongly that something is wrong with them.
9. The term "sociopath" is used clinically to refer to a condition known as
   a. neurasthenia.
   b. schizoid personality.
   c. antisocial personality.
   d. passive-aggressive personality.
10. Research evidence has shown that children of fathers who are criminals have _____ than do children of noncriminal fathers.
    a. less complete hemispheric dominance
    b. a higher incidence of generalized anxiety disorders
    c. a less reactive autonomic nervous system
    d. a more reactive autonomic nervous system
11. The *DSM-III-R* criterion for diagnosis of a condition known as substance-use disorder required that the disturbance in behavior caused by the drub must last for at least _____ months.
    a. one
    b. three
    c. six
    d. nine
12. Which of the following is the most common recreational drug in our society?
    a. cocaine
    b. nicotine
    c. alcohol
    d. amphetamines
13. _____ has been referred to as the "common cold of psychological disorders."
    a. Neurosis
    b. Psychosis
    c. Depression
    d. Schizophrenia

14. In bipolar depression, a person suffers from depression and experiences episodes of _____ as well.
    a. schizophrenia
    b. mania
    c. antisocial personality
    d. somatoform disorders

15. Which of the following is not among the exogenous factors contributing to the development of major depressive disorders?
    a. personality predispositions
    b. genetic predispositions
    c. family situation
    d. helplessness

16. Three times as many women as men
    a. use firearms in their suicide attempts.
    b. attempt to kill themselves.
    c. succeed in attempts to kill themselves.
    d. all of the above.

17. The _____ type of schizophrenia is characterized by unusual motor behavior, such as exhibited in the stuporous maintenance of an awkward posture for an extended period of time.
    a. hebephrenic
    b. paranoid
    c. catatonic
    d. undifferentiated

18. Which of the following is *not* considered an eating disorder?
    a. obesity
    b. anorexia
    c. bulemia
    d. pica

TRUE-FALSE ITEMS

1. T F Many psychological disorders are simply extremes of normal patterns of thought, action, and feeling.
2. T F Psychological disorders are defined by their unusual occurrence of deviance from the norm.
3. T F The fact that something runs in families means that it is genetic.
4. T F Fear is a maladaptive emotion.
5. T F In anxiety disorders, there is generally no disturbance of thought processes.
6. T F There is substantial research evidence supporting the view that organic factors contribute to the development of anxiety and somatoform disorders.
7. T F Agoraphobia is the fear of enclosed places.
8. T F An obsession is when a person feels compelled to repeat a certain action over and over.

9. T F Somatoform disorders are those in which the individual complains of a physical ailment of pain for which there is no discernible organic or physiological explanation.
10. T F A person whose major characteristics are those of pervasive and unwarranted suspiciousness and mistrust of people fits most closely the *DSM-III-R* description of a paranoid personality?
11. T F A restricted ability to express warm and tender emotions is a characteristic of the compulsive personality.
12. T F Children of criminal fathers have been found to show less reactive autonomic nervous system responses than do children of non-criminals.
13. T F Nine out of every ten people who try cigarettes become addicted.
14. T F In unipolar depressive disorder, the person suffers from both mania and depression.
15. T F The technique developed by Rosenthal and his colleagues for the treatment of seasonal affective disorder involves having the patient sit directly in front of a bright light.
16. T F All suicides stem from depression.
17. T F Nondepressed people seem to be more realistic in their perceptions of how much people like them than are depressed people.
18. T F Schizophrenia is considered to be a disease of the cerebral cortex that affects virtually all cognitive processes and behavior.
19. T F Personality disintegration is most severe in the form of schizophrenia known as the "hebephrenic" type.
20. T F The essential feature of childhood autism is the failure to learn to speak.

ANSWER KEY TO SELF-QUIZ

MULTIPLE-CHOICE ITEMS

1. b 2. d 3. b 4. d 5. d 6. a 7. c 8. b 9. c 10. c 11. a 12. c 13. c 14. b 15. b 16. b 17. c 18. a

TRUE-FALSE ITEMS

1. T 2. T 3. F 4. F 5. T 6. F 7. F 8. F 9. T 10. T 11. T 12. T 13. T 14. F 15. T 16. F 17. F 18. F 19. T 20. F

THINKING ABOUT THE PSYCHOLOGY OF YOUR OWN EXPERIENCE

1. After reading Chapter 15 did you find yourself "diagnosing" yourself and your friends? This tendency has been called "medical student's illness." This inclination reflects the validity of one of the first issues discussed in the chapter, namely, that there is not any clear discontinuity between behaviors defined as "normal" and behaviors defined as "abnormal." Rather, psychological disorders typically involve exaggerations or extremes of normal patterns of thought, action, emotions, personality, and coping. So it is not surprising for us to find behaviors or experiences associated with a clinical disorder. With this in mind, consider the following (if you haven't already done so):

- Which of the conditions or characteristics you studied in the chapter seemed most similar to your own behavior or experience?
- Which of the conditions or characteristics did you see as descriptive of someone you know and what specific aspects of it fit best with what you know about that person?

2. Since psychological disorders are exaggerations of everyday conditions, how might you use this knowledge to prevent these everyday conditions from becoming a full-blown disorder? Consider a person who is experiencing difficulty in hearing: you now know that this sensory defect might later develop into paranoia. How might you help?

One important general "method" is to try to bring the changes a person experiences into consciousness, for instance, making the person aware that his or her sight is failing. How might knowing the real cause affect a person's tendency to develop a disorder or an exaggeration of a condition?

16
PSYCHOTHERAPIES

GENERAL STUDY QUESTIONS

After reading Chapter 16, you should be able to answer the following questions.

1. What is the difference between a psychiatrist, a clinical psychologist, and a counselor? Which of these is most likely to conduct research?

2. Why did those treating mental illness in the middle ages drill holes in a patient's head?

3. The discovery that syphilis causes general paresis caused what important theoretical breakthrough?

4. Why does a person undergoing psychoanalysis engage in free association? What is resistance?

5. What is transference and why is it important in psychoanalysis? What is catharsis?

6. Psychotherapy based on the behavioristic viewpoint is based on what assumption?

7. What are the two varieties of behavior therapy and what are they based on?

8. What is the underlying assumption of behavior therapy?

9. In what ways is behavior therapy different from psychoanalysis?

10. Describe the three most common reconditioning techniques.

11. What is the main difference between strict behavior therapy and cognitive behavior therapy?

12. What two major assumptions are shared by the two forms of cognitive therapy?

13. According to Beck, what are the four major areas where a person's thought processes make the beliefs self-fulfilling?

14. What are the three phases of stress inoculation therapy?

15. Why do cognitive and behavior therapists refer to consumers of services as "clients" rather than "patients?"

16. Rational-Emotive Therapy (RET) is based on what assumption? What is one criticism of RET?

17. That is the purpose of person-centered therapy? How does it work?

18. What is electroconvulsive therapy and when it is used?

19. What are the four main categories of drugs used in pharmacotherapy?

20. What is the effect of anitpsychotic drugs on schizophrenia?

21. What is the difference between the monoamine oxidase (MAO) inhibitors and the tricyclics in the way they work to alleviate depression?

22. What are the "most prescribed drugs in America?"

23. Drugs are the treatment of choice for what psychological disorders?

24. What are four common "mechanisms of change?"

25. What are two major barriers to the evaluation of psychotherapy?

OUTLINE OF KEY TERMS AND CONCEPTS

Debates about psychotherapy
   Should psychological principles be applied to human problems?
Modern psychotherapists
   Psychiatrist
   Psychoanalyst
   Clinical psychologist
   Psychiatric social worker
History of psychotherapy
   Early approaches
     Medieval times
       Demonic possession
         Trephining
         Torture
     Industrial revolution
       Mental disorder as moral problem
       "Insane" as dangerous nuisances
     Nineteenth century
       Reforms
         Philippe Pinel
         Dorothea Dix
       Insanity as a disease
         Humane treatment
         General paresis
           Mind affected by physical disease
   Classification of disorders
     Diagnostic and Statistical Manual
Psychoanalysis
   Based on Freud's theory
     Unconscious conflict
       Case of "Little Hans"
   Psychoanalytic method
     Free association
     Interpretation of symbolic gestures
     Dream interpretation
     Resistance
     Transference
     Analysis of the transference
   Psychodynamic therapy
     Includes neo-Freudians
     Rely on case study
     Downplay role of research

Behavior therapy
- Disorders due to faulty learning
- Two kinds
  - Based on respondent conditioning
  - Based on operant conditioning
- Assumes:
  - Anxiety is underlying cause of neurotic behavior
  - Behavior is the problem
- Wide range of applications
  - From individuals to community
  - Wide range of disorders
  - Severely disturbed to basically normal
- Methods of behavior therapy
  - Work together with client
  - Discover where and how inappropriate behavior was acquired
  - Role playing
  - Reconditioning techniques
    - Systematic desensitization
      - Counterconditioning
      - Relaxation
  - Flooding
  - Assertiveness training

Cognitive-behavior therapy
- Effects of thought on behavior
- Two assumptions
  - Cognitive processes influence behavior
  - Restructuring cognitive system can change behavior
- Cognitive restructuring therapy
  - Beck
    - Negative beliefs
    - Unrealistic goals
    - Thought processes make beliefs self-fulfilling
      - Absolute thinking
      - Generalizing
      - Magnifying
      - Notice events that confirm negative belief
    - Challenge beliefs
    - Assign tasks
- Stress inoculation therapy
  - Meichenbaum
    - Alter the way people talk to themselves
      - Examine situations and self-statements
      - Acquisition and rehearsal of new statements
      - Application and practice of new statements
- Behavior-cognitive therapy well grounded in research
  - Evaluation as integral part of treatment

Therapy as hypothesis testing
Client not patient

One problem, four treatments
- Case of George
  - Complaints of insomnia
    - Testiness and anxiety
  - Fantasies about Laura
- Behavioral therapy
  - Operationalize complaints
  - Monitoring behavior
  - Relaxation training
- Cognitive therapy
  - Jot down critical events
  - Monitoring thoughts
  - Therapist disputing thoughts
- Family therapy
  - Changes in relationship
  - From emotional reactor to observer
- Psychodynamic therapy
  - Analyzes meaning of:
    - Kind of work George does
    - Reference to self as "testy"
    - Impending fatherhood
  - Obsession to control aggression

Humanistic therapy
- Humans tend toward growth
- Rational-emotive therapy (RET)
  - Albert Ellis
  - Unrealistic beliefs or expectations
    - Interpretation
  - Therapist challenges belief system
    - Inconsistencies between belief and reality
- Person-centered psychotherapy
  - Carl Rogers
    - Client-centered therapy
      - Nondirective
      - Three stages
        - Expression of negative feelings
        - Hope
        - Emergence of positive feelings
- Influenced practice of therapy generally

Biological therapy
- Possible biological factors
  - Somatic complaints
  - Physical disease causes psychological distress
- Electroconvulsive therapy (ECT)
  - Cerletti and Bini

                Create seizures with electric current to brain
                Causes disorientation and memory loss
            Unilateral ECT
                May facilitate release of neurotransmitters
                Used only in severe cases
Pharmacotherapy
    Administering drugs
        Antipsychotic drugs
            Major tranquilizers
            Reduce hallucinations
            Reserpin
                Calming effect
                Serious side effects
            Chlorpomazine
                Thorazine
            Effect on mental hospitals
            Treat but don't cure
            Dopamine hypothesis
        Antidepressants
            Effects on neurotransmitters
                Serotonin and norepinephrine
            MAO inhibitors
            Tricyclics
                Prevent inactivation
                Block re-uptake mechanism
                Many side effects
        Anti-anxiety drugs (minor tranquilizers)
            Mild disorders
            Alcohol, self-prescribed
            Benzodiazepine
                Librium and valium
                Most prescribed drugs in America
            Gray's hypothesis
                Electrical activity in brain
                Block synthesis of norepinephrine and serotonin
Effectiveness of psychotherapy
    Evidence hard to come by
        What does "work" mean
    Early outcome studies
        Psychoanalytic view
            Too complex to study
        Eysenck's work
            Spontaneous remission
    Psychoanalysis
        Most difficult to evaluate
            Few psychoanalysts study outcomes
            Available to few individuals
            Suitable for few disorders
        Behavior-cognitive therapy
            Precise methods
            Desired outcome explicit
            Large literature documenting effectiveness
        Drug therapy
            Results mixed
            In short term, drugs superior
                Treatment of choice for schizophrenia and
                    bipolar affective disorder
                Drugs plus therapy best for major depression
            Problems
                Side effects
                Patient compliance
    Gender differences in depression
        Depression more common in women 2:1
            Not hormonal
            Learned helplessness associated with depression
            Nolen-Hoeksema view
                Different coping styles
                    Men become active and distract themselves
                    Women focus on mood itself which makes
                        it worse
                Suggests intervention strategies
    Meta-analysis of psychotherapy outcome
        Average effect is positive
        Common mechanisms of change
            Therapist variables
                Importance of quality of relationship
                    established with therapist
                Attention
                Benefits of confession
            Placebos: are they for real
                Frank: "placebo is psychotherapy"
                "I shall please"
Scientific future of psychotherapy
    Goals differ according to approach
        Opinion—therapist/client
        Evaluation of observable goals
How to choose a psychotherapist
    Get a referral
    Investigate training
    Ask questions of therapist
    Be open and honest

COMPLETION ITEMS

psychotherapies

premature

Psychiatrists

clinical psychologist

research

general paresis

mind

Diagnosis

therapist

conflicts

anxiety

horses

castration

unconscious

free association

dreams

passively

Transference

insights

catharsis

1. Although all _____ have as their goal the restoration of normal functioning, they vary in method, approach, and assumptions. Many psychologists view psychotherapy as far too _____ in light of our knowledge about psychological problems.

2. _____ are trained as medical doctors with specialization in the treatment of psychological problems. A _____ holds a Ph.D. in psychology. He or she may specialize in a specific psychotherapy and all have received training in _____.

3. A great advance in the treatment of mental disorder was the discovery that the widespread disease syphilis causes _____, a slow, degenerative disease that eventually erodes mental faculties. This breakthrough showed definitively that the _____ could be affected by physical disease.

4. _____ of disorders can assist the therapist in developing a treatment plan based on research with other similarly disordered individuals. This can provide the patient with a sense of relief in knowing what is wrong but it can also cause the _____ to stop looking for new evidence once a diagnosis is made.

5. From the standpoint of Freud's psychoanalytic theory, psychological distress arises from basic _____ of the id and ego. Unconscious wishes and desires cause _____ and fear, so they are repressed and thus forced out of consciousness.

6. The case of "Little Hans" concerned a young boy who was so afraid of _____ that he would not leave the house. Freud interpreted the youngster's problem as due to an underlying fear of _____.

7. Freud believed that a major goal of psychotherapy should be to bring _____ desires to consciousness where they can be analyzed. In his therapeutic practice directed to such objectives, Freud used hypnosis and a technique that he called "_____," wherein the patient is asked to say anything that comes into his mind, regardless of how obscene, unimportant, or silly it may seem.

8. The interpretation of _____ is a cornerstone of Freudian analysis. The Freudian analyst usually listens _____, but occasionally interrupts the patient's free flow of ideas.

9. _____ refers to the way the psychoanalysis patient's conflicting feelings about other people in his or her life are expressed through the relationship with the analyst. Analysis of this aspect of the patient's treatment is intended to provide some _____ into the nature of the patient's conflicts.

10. During the analysis of transference, the patient's recollection of some important event, desire, or fantasy from youth often induces a release of stored up feelings in an intensely emotional experience called a _____, the immediate result of which is a pleasurable feeling of relief.

CHAPTER 16 / PSYCHOTHERAPIES

resolution	11.	The last phase of psychoanalysis involves _____ of the patient's transference.
learning	12.	From the behavioristic standpoint, psychological disorders are regarded as the result of faulty _____. A behaviorist would most likely explain "Little Hans's" symptom pattern in terms of _____.
conditioning		
learning	13.	Behavior therapy and behavior modification refer to treatments that reflect different modes of _____, not different types of therapists. Behavior therapy is based on _____ conditioning, and behavior modification is based on the theory of operant conditioning.
respondent		
behavior	14.	Behavior therapy proceeds from the assumption that the _____ that is causing the person distress is the problem, whereas psychoanalysis assumes that it is only the symptom of an underlying neurosis.
childhood	15.	Unlike psychoanalysis, wherein it is assumed that solving the problems of a person's adult life depends upon solving those of his or her early _____, the aim in behavior therapy is to discover where and how the inappropriate conditioning was acquired. The behavior therapist sometimes uses _____ playing techniques to create hypothetical situations which the client and therapist then act out together.
role		
desensitization	16.	Systematic _____ is a behavior therapy technique based on counterconditioning, wherein the patient is trained to relax in response to anxiety provoking stimuli. Another more intensive technique in which the therapist deliberately presents the client with an anxiety-provoking stimuli is called "_____." Both of these methods are highly effective in treating _____.
flooding		
phobias		
Assertiveness	17.	_____ training is the behavior therapy technique used to teach people that they have a right to their own feelings and opinions.
	18.	The main emphasis in cognitive-behavioral therapies is on the way _____ affect behaviors.
thoughts		
cognitive	19.	Beck's _____ restructuring therapy assumes that psychological disorders result from negative beliefs about events in the world and about oneself. Clients are encouraged to engage in _____ designed to help them confirm or disconfirm their beliefs.
experiments		
interfere	20.	A cognitive restructuring therapist typically assigns the client tasks that are designed to _____ with the "conduct" of the disorder. The client is asked to monitor his or her own thoughts and to question constantly whether or not they are _____.
same		
realistic		
inoculation	21.	Meichenbaum's stress _____ therapy is based on the view that people can be trained to manage stress more effectively by altering the way they talk to themselves.
behavior	22.	Both _____ therapy and cognitive-behavior therapy are firmly grounded in psychological principles and based on empirical research. By and large, proponents of these approaches see _____ as an integral part of treatment.
evaluation		

rational

belief

inconsistencies

person

nondirective

unconditionally

biological

somatic

body

Stress

schizophrenia

Unilateral

brain

depression

Pharmacotherapy

tranquilizers

hallucinations

reserpine

schizophrenia

depression

neurotransmitters

alcohol

addictive

coping

23. A key assumption of Ellis's _____-emotive therapy (RET) is that a person's perceptual interpretations are his or her "world." In contrast to psychoanalysis and behavior therapy, the client in this kind of treatment is confronted directly with his or her _____ system and forced to examine it against reality.

24. In RET, the client's awareness is oriented persistently to the _____ between his or her beliefs and external reality.

25. Roger's _____-centered therapy proceeds from the conviction that psychological disorders are caused by a blocking of the natural inclination toward self-actualization. This approach is also called _____ psychotherapy. The therapists gain the trust of clients by showing that they base concern for the clients on their ability to accept the clients _____.

26. The evidence on possible _____ factors in disorders comes from two sources. First, patients initially feel and experience many disorders as _____ complaints. Second, mood and thought can greatly influence _____ state and vice versa. _____ can cause physical disease, but it is also possible for physical disease to cause psychological distress.

27. The use of electroconvulsive shock therapy (ECT) for the treatment of psychological disorders was begun as a result of an erroneous belief that _____ does not occur in epileptics.

28. _____ ECT, in which the electrical current is passed through only one side of the brain, results in fewer of the disorienting verbal side effects associated with bilateral ECT. Nonetheless, overadministration of ECT may cause significant _____ damage.

29. Today, ECT is used only in the most severe cases of _____ depression) and schizophrenia for which it is the most effective treatment.

30. _____ is the treatment of psychological disorders by the use of drugs.

31. Antipsychotic drugs, which are often called the major _____, are widely used to treat severe disorders such a schizophrenia. They calm the patient and reduce the experience of _____ and delusions. The first such drug used in the United States was _____.

32. Antipsychotic drugs treat _____ but do not cure it.

33. Biochemical abnormalities play an important role in _____. Evidence for this is the effectiveness on drugs used to treat depressive symptoms and the action of these drugs on the _____.

34. The oldest and most widely used antianxiety drug is _____.

35. There is growing concern about the overuse of tranquilizers, first because they are _____, and second because their indiscriminate use may prevent people from developing _____ strategies from within to handle their fears.

CHAPTER 16 / PSYCHOTHERAPIES

psychotherapy remission	36. Eysenck reported a study showing that about two-thirds of a group of neurotic patients recovered or improved to a marked extent whether or not they had received any _____. Eysenck referred to this two-thirds figure as the "spontaneous _____" rate.
mixed superior	37. Results of studies comparing drug treatment to psychotherapy are _____. With certain disorders, there is widespread agreement that drugs are _____ to psychotherapy.
cognitive	38. In their meta-analysis of published studies relevant to the issue of outcomes of psychotherapy, Smith and colleagues found that the _____ approaches seem to be the most effective of all therapies.
client-therapist relationship	39. Many studies suggest that the most important factor in therapeutic success is the _____.
placebo	40. According to Frank, _____ is psychotherapy. The word itself comes from the Latin, meaning, "I shall please."

SELF-QUIZ

MULTIPLE-CHOICE ITEMS

1. Which of the following psychotherapists is *most* likely to also be a researcher?
   a. psychiataric social worker
   b. counselor
   c. clinical psychologist trained in a university
   d. clinical psychologist trained in a professional school

2. Freud believed that psychological distress arises from
   a. subliminal perceptions.
   b. complexes.
   c. conflicts of id and ego.
   d. the superego.

3. In the Freudian technique known as "_____," the patient is asked to say anything that comes into his or her mind, no matter how obscene, unimportant, or silly it may seem.
   a. free association
   b. libido cathexis
   c. ego regression
   d. ego monitoring

4. According to the psychoanalytic view, a patient's resistance during the opening phase of treatment is taken as an indicator of
   a. transference.
   b. countercathexis.
   c. cathexis.
   d. unconscious effect.

5. In psychoanalysis, the concept of transference refers most specifically to the patient's
   a. unconscious conflicts about his or her sexual maturity.
   b. irrational beliefs about the way other people feel about him or her.
   c. perceptions of and relationship to the therapist.
   d. acquired complexes that cause anxiety about basic trust and mistrust.
6. From the standpoint of psychoanalytic theory, the immediate result of catharsis is
   a. resistance and guilt.
   b. emotional trauma.
   c. pleasurable relief.
   d. a countercathexis.
7. From the behavioristic standpoint, psychological disorders are the result of
   a. faulty learning.
   b. neuroses.
   c. catharsis.
   d. irrational beliefs.
8. Which of the following is not among the reconditioning techniques typically used in behavior therapy?
   a. systematic desensitization
   b. free association
   c. flooding
   d. assertiveness training
9. The main difference between behavior therapy and cognitive-behavior therapy is
   a. the former's emphasis on behavior.
   b. the former's emphasis on learning.
   c. the latter's emphasis on the effect of behavior on thinking.
   d. the latter's emphasis on the effect of thinking on behavior.
10. Which of the following is *not* among the four major areas where, according to Beck's cognitive restructuring therapy, a person's thought processes make his/her beliefs self-fulfilling?
    a. absolute thinking
    b. repressing negative thoughts
    c. generalizing from a few negative events
    d. being overselective in perception
11. According to Meichenbaum's stress inoculation approach to therapy, how people deal with stressful problems can be changed by altering the way they
    a. respond to criticism.
    b. react to novelty.
    c. relate to significant others in life.
    d. talk to themselves.
12. Rogers's person-centered therapy is most appropriately characterized as what kind of approach?
    a. neo-Freudian

    b. cognitive
    c. behavioistic
    d. humanistic
13. A common side effect of the strong chemotherapy used for treating cancer is
    a. hysterical conversion reaction.
    b. depression.
    c. epilepsy.
    d. brain damage.
14. Today, electroconvulsive therapy ECT is used in what situation?
    a. to cure epilepsy
    b. only the most severe cases of depression or schizophrenia
    c. routinely for depression but not schizophrenia
    d. once medications have ceased to be effective
15. Which of the following is a commonly prescribed form of pharmacotherapy for the treatment of depression?
    a. monoamine oxidase inhibitors
    b. drugs that reduce the concentration of serotonin in the brain
    c. reserpine
    d. Thorizane
16. _____ are the "most prescribed drugs in America?"
    a. Anti-depressants
    b. Anti-psychotic drugs
    c. Anti-anxiety drugs
    d. Placebos
17. In an early psychotherapy outcome study, Eysenck found that roughly _____ of the neurotic patients he studied perceived that their neurosis vanished, whether or not they received therapy.
    a. 25 percent
    b. half
    c. two-thirds
    d. 90 percent
18. According to Frank, many studies suggest that the most important factor in therapeutic success is
    a. the therapist-client relationship.
    b. belief on the part of the client that he or she will improve.
    c. administration of drugs and/or placebos.
    d. the assignment of new behaviors for the client to practice.

TRUE-FALSE ITEMS

1. T F During the period of the Industrial Revolution, people afflicted with psychological disorders were most typically chained and confined to dungeons with criminals.
2. T F Freud used hypnosis to help his neurotic patients avoid having their anxiety-provoking unconscious thoughts surface to consciousness.

3. T F From the psychoanalytic standpoint, a patient's forgetting or being late for a therapy appointment in the "opening phase" of treatment is a sign of resistance.
4. T F Resolution of transference is the last phase of psychoanalytic therapy.
5. T F Behavior modification is based on the theory of operant conditioning.
6. T F Systematic desensitization is based on the method of free association.
7. T F In the technique known as "flooding," the therapist incessantly presents situations that evoke fear and anxiety in the patient.
8. T F The cognitive-behavioral therapies emphasize the influence of unconscious conflicts underlying the presenting symptom.
9. T F In rational-emotive therapy, the client is confronted *directly* with his or her belief system and forced to examine it against reality.
10. T F A major emphasis in Meichenbaum's stress inoculation therapy is on getting the client to stop talking to him or herself.
11. T F An important aspect of the family therapy approach involves training the client to change from being an observer to being an emotional reactor in his or her interpersonal relationships.
12. T F In Rogers's person-centered therapy, the therapist's positive regard for the patient is made contingent upon the patient's ability to show a dramatic change in behavior.
13. T F Not even prolonged and continued ECT treatments cause any significant brain damage in the patient.
14. T F The drug chlorpromazine is widely prescribed in the treatment of schizophrenia.
15. T F The symptom alleviation produced by administration of antipsychotic drugs typically results in eventually curing the schizophrenic disorder.
16. T F The tricyclics are sedatives.
17. T F Many studies make it clear that the most important factor in determining the success of psychotherapy is the therapist-client relationship.
18. T F Placebos have been found to be effective in the alleviation of postoperative wound pain.
19. T F According to Susan Nolen-Hoeksema, men and women react to depression in remarkably similar ways.
20. T F Results of "meta-analysis" of the studies of psychotherapy show that there is no significant positive effect from "attention placebo."

ANSWER KEY TO SELF-QUIZ

MULTIPLE-CHOICE ITEMS

1. c 2. c 3. a 4. d 5. c 6. c 7. a 8. b 9. d 10. b 11. d 12. d
13. b 14. b 15. a 16. c 17. c 18. a

TRUE-FALSE ITEMS

1. T 2. F 3. T 4. T 5. T 6. F 7. T 8. F 9. T 10. F 11. F 12. F
13. F 14. T 15. F 16. T 17. T 18. T 19. F 20. F

THINKING ABOUT THE PSYCHOLOGY OF YOUR OWN EXPERIENCE

1. From the perspective of modern science, medieval ideas about demonic possession as the cause of mental disorder seem ridiculous, and the "treatment" practices (such as trephining) that were derived from them seem cruelly barbaric. But imagine a psychologist or medical practitioner of the twenty-fourth century looking back on the psychotherapeutics of the late twentieth century. What specific contemporary theories and practices do you think are the most susceptible to being regarded as primitive forms of foolish quackery by "mind scientists" of the future?

2. You read in the chapter that Rational-Emotive Therapy involves attempts to "re-educate" people so that their own irrational beliefs are replaced by more realistic ones. An example of a belief of this kind is the belief that everyone must like you. A related irrational belief is that you should like everyone else, that you should be everyone's friend.

- Can you describe briefly a circumstance in which you or any person in your life ever held such an irrational belief?
- Can you recall situations where such a belief led to correspondingly irrational, maladaptive behavior?

PART V

THE SOCIAL WORLD OF THE ADULT

17
SOCIAL PSYCHOLOGY

GENERAL STUDY QUESTIONS

After reading Chapter 17, you should be able to answer the following questions.

1. Define social psychology.

2. What is behavioral confirmation?

3. What is the difference between a situational attribution and a dispositional attribution? Give an example of the fundamental attribution error.

4. What are four possible reasons for the fundamental attribution error?

5. What is the self-serving bias? Give an example.

6. What are two ways we use attributions to maintain our sense of control?

7. Why do we create illusory correlations? Give an example of an illusory correlation.

8. What is reactance?

9. What is an attitude? What are the three components of attitude?

10. According to Bem's theory of self-perception, how do we form attitudes?

11. Under what conditions is the ordinary view that attitudes can and do cause actions supported?

12. The theory of cognitive dissonance assumes what? Under what conditions is dissonance aroused?

13. Why are attitudes formed through the resolution of dissonance particularly difficult to change?

14. What are stereotypes? How do they work?

15. How does cooperation help eliminate prejudice?

16. In order to be convinced by a persuasive message, what must happen?

17. What are three factors that affect whether a persuasive message works or not?

18. How does social comparison work?

19. What is conformity? How does conformity contribute to groupthink?

20. Under what conditions are people most likely to help someone who needs it?

21. What are seven conditions that contribute to aggression?

22. What is the difference between Freud's theory of aggression and the social learning theory of aggression?

23. What is the difference between conformity and compliance?

24. Why is it making the fundamental attribution error to call the obedient subjects in Milgram's study sadistic?

25. According to Robert Cialdini, what are six social psychological principles used to influence us?

OUTLINE OF KEY TERMS AND CONCEPTS

Observing others: social perception
   Behavioral confirmation
     Snyder's work
Social thinking: attribution
   Attribution theory
     Explaining behavior
       Situational attribution
       Dispositional attribution
   Mistakes and biases in inference
     Kelley's work
     The fundamental attribution error
       Bias toward dispositional attributions
       Ross College Bowl study
     Self-serving bias
       Take credit for success, blame failure on situation
     Maintaining sense of control
       Biases help maintain sense of control
     Illusory correlations
       Linking random events
     Reactance and helplessness
       Resist loss of freedom
       Loss of control over events leads to feelings of helplessness
Attitudes
   ABCs of attitude
     Affect
     Behavior
     Cognition
   Developing attitudes
     Self-perception theory
       Infer own attitudes
   Link between attitudes and behavior
     When attitudes influence behavior
       Perceived control
       Social norms
       How well remembered
     When behavior influences attitudes
       Theory of cognitive dissonance
         Discrepancy between attitude and

                knowledge of behavior
            Can't change behavior so change attitude
                Festinger and Carlsmith's study
                    Boring task
                    Subjects paid $1 or $20 to lie
                    Subjects rated task
                    $1 subjects evaluated task more favorably
    Prejudice
        Stereotype as overextended prototypes
        Discrimination
            Behavior predicted by prejudice
        Countering prejudice: changing attitudes with actions
            Use conformity of attitude to change
            Increased contact
            Cooperation
                Sherif's summer camp study
                    Created cohesive groups
                    Groups competed
                    Caused hostility
                        Eliminating competition didn't lessen ill will
                        Groups became friends through cooperating on vital tasks
                Aronson's jigsaw classroom work
    Persuasion: changing attitudes with words
        Persuasive communications work if:
            Induced to think about message
            If it is relevant to us
            Exposed to it many times
            In written form
        Who says what to whom
            Persuasion works when:
                Source factors: attractive, expert or trustworthy, or similar to us
                Message factors: Vivid - verbal or visual
                    Fear appeals
                    One sided or two?
                    Timing of message
                        Primacy effect
                        Recency effect
                Audience factors
                    Depends on complexity of message
Subtle influences on our thoughts, feelings, and actions
    Social facilitation
    Social comparison
        Bennington study
            Change in attitude from conservative to liberal through changing reference groups
            Changes lasted for 25 years
    Conformity
        Asch's study
            Judging length of lines
            Real subject last
            32 percent conformed to wrong response
        Factors in conformity
            Group unanimity
            Group size
            Importance of group to subject
    Group influence
        Group not simply collection of individuals
        Influence through:
            Norms
            Roles
            Cohesiveness
        Thinking and acting in groups
            Social impact theory
                Each person added has less of individual impact
            Group polarization
                Groups make more extreme decisions than do individuals
                    Social comparison
                    Conformity
                    Developing arguments
            Groupthink
                Disastrous decisions by groups
                    Highly cohesive group
                    Strong, directive leader
                    Reaching premature agreement in crisis
                    Groupthink: characterized by:
                        Feeling of invulnerability
                        Belief in correctness of past decisions
                        High cohesiveness
                        Opponent's stereotypes
                        Groups pressure leading to self-censorship on part of individuals or to conversion
                        Mindguard
                            Member who shields against information
        Avoiding groupthink
            Build contentiousness into group
                Assign role of "devil's advocate"
                Input from nongroup members
            Forming subgroups
                Allow reconsideration of decision

Helping others
   When do people help?
      When alone
   Who helps?
      Not a personality variable
      Likely to help if:
         Life in rural environment
         Parents who lived by high moral standards
         Empathetic
         Oriented to needs of others
         Feel capable
   Who needs help?
      Will help if person is:
         Known
         Similar
         Attractive
         Appears dependent and deserving
   Why do people help?
      Empathetic
Aggression
   Two types
      Hostile—in anger
      Instrumental—means to some other end
   When do people hurt one another?
      Major factors affecting aggression
         Physiological arousal
         Crowding
         Noise
         High temperature
         Alcohol
         Marijuana
         Tranquilizers
   Why are people aggressive?
      Freud
         Thanatos
      Ethology
         Aggression instinctive
         Inhibitions against fatal aggression
            Lack in human beings
      Social learning theory
         Vicarious learning
         Punishment works only when it is:
            Imminent
            Severe
            Highly likely
Overt influences on our thoughts, feelings and actions
   Compliance: deliberate conformity
   Obedience
      Milgram's study
         "Teachers and learners"
         Administer electric shock to learner
         Nearly two-thirds of subjects obeyed experimenter and administered 450 volts
         Influence of social situation
   The situation takes over: A mock prison
      Zimbardo's study
         Male subjects randomly assigned to play role of either prisoner or guard
         Terminated after six days
         Prisoners weak and submissive
         Guards arrogant and cruel
   Countering social influence
      Cialdini's work
         Social trigger features
            Norm of reciprocity
            Need to be consistent
            Social comparison
            Liking
            Deference to authority
            Scarcity

COMPLETION ITEMS

social
intensifies
coaction

1. Human beings are _____ animals. The mere presence of others _____ and directs our behavior. This has been known since the early days of psychology as the _____ effect.

hostile
confirmation

2. Snyder and Swann found that competitive play by subjects who had been led to believe that their partners were hostile elicited _____ behavior from their partners. This was part of a program of research on behavioral _____.

explain

situational

fundamental attribution error

others

the situation
self-serving bias

illusory correlation

Reactance

helplessness

lack of control

behavioral

infer
infer

measured

situational

justifying

consistency
Dissonance

motivates

inconsistent

resistant

the boring task
stereotype

discrimination

3. Attribution theory guides study of the ways in which we _____ the behavior of others. Thinking that Sam failed his midterm because he didn't get enough sleep is making a _____ attribution about the cause of his behavior.

4. The tendency to assign the cause of events to the person rather than to the situation is called the _____.

5. When observing _____, we attribute the cause of events to the person rather than to the situation. But when things go wrong for ourselves, we blame _____. This is _____.

6. The belief that rain is caused by picnics is an example of an _____.

7. _____ is an angry or hostile reaction to loss of freedom. Any time we feel that we have no control over the outcome of events, we experience a sense of _____. Psychologists believe that we learn to be helpless through repeated experiences of _____.

8. An attitude about another person has an affective component, a _____ component, and a cognitive component.

9. According to Daryl Bem's self-perception theory, we _____ our own attitudes in the same way we _____ the attitudes of others.

10. The ordinary view that attitudes can and do cause actions is supported when researchers have carefully and specifically _____ both. But researchers found that, before they can predict behavior from an attitude, they must also take into account such _____ factors as perceived control, and the social norms operating.

11. One of the most effective methods of persuasion is self-persuasion through _____ our behavior. One perspective on this involves cognitive dissonance which assumes the need for cognitive _____.

12. _____ is a discrepancy between an attitude we hold and our knowledge of something we have done or intend to do. We try constantly to resolve discrepancies because, as in any state of disequilibrium, dissonance is uncomfortable and _____ us to reduce it.

13. Dissonance can be reduced by changing one of the cognitions so that it is no longer _____ with the other cognition, or by attempting to reduce the importance of one of the dissonant cognitions. Attitudes changed in this way are often particularly _____ to change.

14. Subjects in the Festinger and Carlsmith $1/$20 study reduced their dissonance about having lied to other subjects by changing their attitude about _____.

15. A _____ is a generalized assumption that attributes identical characteristics to all members of a group. Prejudice is an attitude, _____ is the behavior it predicts.

200

CHAPTER 17 / SOCIAL PSYCHOLOGY

contact 16. One way to reduce prejudice is to increase _____ with the prejudiced group; direct experience dispels the basis for the prejudiced attitude.

17. In Sherif's "robber's cave" experiment, it was found that hostility decreased and cooperation and fellowship increased when the members of two competing groups had to work together toward a common _____.

goal

interdependence 18. Aronson's jigsaw classroom approach to reducing prejudice encourages _____ between the students in the group.

pay attention 19. To be persuaded, we must not only _____ to the message but also understand and remember it. Sometimes, however, we shortcut the process and allow the _____, or attractiveness or the persuader or simply our exposure to the product to change our attitude.

expertise

20. If a message is complex, it will be more convincing if it is _____. Otherwise, a verbal or visual presentation is more effective—the more _____ the better. One such message that is very effective is one that arouses _____.

in writing
vivid
fear

friendly 21. One sided messages work only if the audience is _____ to the position and are unlikely to hear the other side. If the buying or voting is to occur immediately after the presentation, you would want to make your presentation last in order to take advantage of the _____ effect.

recency

less intelligent 22. While _____ people are more persuaded by simple messages, an intelligent person may counterargue a complex message rather than yield to it. Contrary to folk wisdom, _____ are no more persuadable than _____.

women
men

arousing 23. Having others around is _____ and interferes with difficult tasks. But if the task is easy, having others around is _____ and may cause you to outdo yourself.

exciting

social comparison 24. The theory of _____ states that, when in doubt, we compare ourselves to those we admire or believe are like us. The group we choose to compare ourselves with is our _____ group.

reference

25. The students in Newcomb's Bennington College study were found to abandon the attitudes of their conservative families in favor of the liberal attitudes of their new _____ group of the faculty. Even after _____ years, most of the students were still politically liberal.

reference
25

26. In Solomon Asch's classic study in which all of the confederates picked the same obviously incorrect line, 32 percent of the real subjects _____ to the group pressure and gave the incorrect answer.

confirmed

27. People are most likely to conform when confronted with _____ group opinion. Although group _____ is also important, conformity does not seem to increase with more than four people in the group.

unanimous
size

Norms 28. _____ are the rules of behavior established by the group. They exert pressure to _____ and violation will result in pressure from the group.

conform

Social loafing   29. _____ is the idea that we sometimes slack off when our efforts are hidden in a group.

Group polarization   30. _____ happens when groups discuss a problem and those who are for the decision become stronger in their support while those who are against it oppose it even more.

Altruism   31. _____ is a prosocial behavior that is personally costly and engaged in without the expectation of reward. Daniel Batson has found that _____—the capacity to experience the emotions of another—is enough to motivate some people to act for the benefit of another in the absence of any personal reward.

empathy

Hostile   32. _____ aggression is motivated by anger or hatred and is intended only to make the victim suffer. _____ aggression is motivated by an incentive, usually economic.

Instrumental

    33. Some of the factors that affect the aggressive response such as crowding, noise, and high temperatures influence _____ while others, such as alcohol and drugs, reduce _____.

arousal level

inhibitions

Freud   34. _____ held that aggression is one of two fundamental human drives. Calling it _____, he identified it as a destructive energy that accumulates until it is discharged either inwardly or outwardly.

Thanatos

social learning   35. According to _____ theory, the biological basis of aggression is the same as that of all learning. According to this view, aggressive behavior is elicited not merely by learning how to do it, but also by _____, both experienced and anticipated.

rewards and punishments

Conformity   36. _____ is the changing of behavior to go along with the norms of the group. _____ is going along because someone asks you to.

Compliance

    37. When the person asking you to comply to a request is a legitimate authority, going along is called _____.

obedience

    38. In Milgram's experiment, the real subjects were told that as the "teacher" it was their job to administer an electric _____ to the "learner" every time he or she made a mistake. Most of the teachers—62.5 percent—in the experiment complied completely and gave the _____ shock of 450 volts. The results of this experiment show how strongly human beings can be influenced by a social _____.

shock

maximum

situation

    39. Zimbardo sought to investigate the degree to which brutal behavior can be _____ determined in a study simulating a "prison" in the basement of the psychology building at Stanford University. The apparently complete _____ over the prisoners resulted in arrogant, aggressive, and cruel behavior on the part of those who played the guards.

situationally

power

    40. According to Cialdini, our need to do many things _____ makes us vulnerable to people using social psychological principles to influence us. He likens this to the fixed-action patterns of animals and suggests that there are certain "_____" that elicit automatic compliance.

automatically

trigger features

SELF-QUIZ
MULTIPLE-CHOICE ITEMS

1. Assuming that Sally snapped at her roommate because she is tired is an example of
   a. behavioral confirmation.
   b. a situational attribution.
   c. a dispositional attribution.
   d. an illusory correlation.

2. Which of the following is not discussed in the chapter as a possible reason for the fundamental attribution error?
   a. our society-wide belief in personal responsibility
   b. there are more ways to describe individuals than situations
   c. people stand out against the background of a situation
   d. because we need to maintain our sense of control

3. Which of the following is not among the components of attitudes as they are described by social psychologists?
   a. cognitive
   b. attributional
   c. affective
   d. behavioral

4. In Festinger and Carlsmith's study, the subjects who evaluated the dull experimental task most favorably were those who were _____ to lie about how interesting it was.
   a. given extra grade points on their final exam
   b. permitted to compare their reactions to those of other subjects
   c. paid $1
   d. paid $20

5. When a prototype becomes overextended, it becomes an
   a. stereotype.
   b. internal locus of control.
   c. external locus of control.
   d. dissonant cognition.

6. In Sherif's summer camp experiment, hostility between the "eagles" and the "rattlers" was reduced by
   a. eliminating competition between the two groups.
   b. rewarding all of the boys for having performed well in the competitive athletic events.
   c. eliminating the troublemakers from each group.
   d. creating a common goal toward which both groups had to work cooperatively.

7. Which of the following messages will be *least* persuasive?
   a. a complex verbal message
   b. a complex written message
   c. a vivid message
   d. a personally meaningful message

8. According to Festinger's social comparison theory, we are most like to seek out and compare our attitudes and behaviors with those of others when
   a. the standards of such judgments are objective.
   b. there are no objective standards for such judgments.
   c. we are making dispositional attributions.
   d. our cognitions are dissonant.
9. The groups to which we choose to compare our attitudes and behaviors are called _____ groups.
   a. coaction
   b. conformity
   c. peer
   d. reference
10. Newcomb's Bennington College study is a classic illustration of the way people's attitudes change as a function of changes in
    a. dispositional attributions.
    b. situational attributions.
    c. reference groups.
    d. their stereotypes.
11. In the Asch experiment in which subjects were required to judge the relative length of lines, subjects went along with the erroneous judgments of a unanimous majority roughly _____ percent of the time.
    a. 10
    b. 30
    c. 60
    d. 90
12. The phenomenon when groups make more extreme decisions than do individuals is known as
    a. social impact theory.
    b. social loafing.
    c. groupthink.
    d. group polarization.
13. A person is most likely to help someone who needs it when he or she
    a. is alone.
    b. is with friends.
    c. is with strangers.
    d. is an altruistic personality type.
14. Which of the following is an example of instrumental aggression?
    a. being hit by a pop fly
    b. being hit by an angry little brother
    c. being knocked down by someone grabbing your backpack
    d. being tail-gated on the freeway
15. According to social learning theory, punishment works to subdue aggression only if certain conditions are satisfied. Which of the following is *not* among those conditions?
    a. The punishment is observed.
    b. The punishment is imminent.

c. The punishment is severe.

d. The punishment is highly likely.

16. In Milgram's study, _____ of the subjects complied with the experimenter's instructions to the point of administering the maximum shock of 450 volts to the "learner."

    a. none
    b. about 10 percent
    c. one third
    d. over 60 percent

17. The subjects in Zimbardo's mock prison experiment were all

    a. Stanford University students.
    b. police officer trainees.
    c. from a county jail weekend work-release program.
    d. parolees from a state correctional institution.

18. You receive unordered labels with your name and address printed on them. According to Cialdini, which of the social "trigger features" is being used to influence you to donate money to the cause of the sender?

    a. The need to be consistent
    b. The norm of reciprocity
    c. Social comparison
    d. Deference to authority

TRUE-FALSE ITEMS

1. T F Bicyclists have been found to ride faster alone against the clock than when actually racing against other riders.

2. T F Correctly attributing the cause of Sam's behavior to the situation is an example of behavioral confirmation.

3. T F When observing others, we attribute the cause of events to the situation rather than to the person. This is known as the fundamental attribution error.

4. T F When things go wrong and we are asked to account for our own behavior, we blame the situation. But if they go right, we take credit. This is known as the self-serving bias.

5. T F Despite serious effort, Jim fails chemistry for the third time and gives up. This is an example of reactance.

6. T F According to Bem's theory of self-perception, when we are asked to describe our own attitudes, we base our judgment on the same evidence as would an outside observer.

7. T F Researchers have found that they can successfully predict behavior from attitudes when they take into account such situational factors as perceived control and the social norms operating at the time.

8. T F Dissonance can be reduced only by lying to someone about one of the cognitions.

9. T F In Sherif's summer camp experiment, it was found that conflict between groups can be effectively reduced by having them ventilate their anger in athletic contests in which they compete against one another.

10. T F Aronson's "jigsaw classroom" technique is designed to reduce prejudice through cooperative learning experiences.

11. T F A message will not be persuasive if it arouses fear in the audience.
12. T F Overall, the most effective methods of attitude change are those that motivate action.
13. T F Most of the subjects in Newcomb's Bennington College study became more liberal in their political attitudes while they were in the liberal college environment, but were found to be extremely conservative 25 years later.
14. T F People are most likely to conform when faced with unanimous group opinion.
15. T F Social impact theory predicts that adding one more person to a twelve person group has the same impact as adding one more person to a three person group.
16. T F Avoiding groupthink involved building cohesiveness into the group.
17. T F A person is most likely to help another when he or she is alone.
18. T F According to the ethological view, the strength of instinctive inhibitions against acting out fatal aggression within a species corresponds to the strength of a species' offensive weapons.
19. T F In Milgram's study, the maximum level of shock intensity was administered only by those subjects whose anger had been aroused toward the "learner."
20. T F In Zimbardo's prison simulation study, the men who played the role of "guards" were disappointed with the early termination of the experiment.

ANSWER KEY TO SELF-QUIZ

MULTIPLE-CHOICE ITEMS

1. b 2. d 3. b 4. d 5. a 6. d 7. a 8. b 9. d 10. c 11. b 12. d 13. a 14. c 15. a 16. d 17. a 18. b

TRUE-FALSE ITEMS

1. F 2. F 3. F 4. T 5. F 6. T 7. T 8. F 9. F 10. T 11. F 12. T 13. F 14. T 15. F 16. F 17. T 18. T 19. F 20. T

THINKING ABOUT THE PSYCHOLOGY OF YOUR OWN EXPERIENCE

1. One reason for the biases in our social thinking is that they help us to maintain our sense of control over events. We believe that other people also control the events in their lives and so we sometimes find ourselves "blaming the victim." For example, after the 1989 earthquake, many of us in the Bay Area received phone calls from friends in other states checking to see if we were all right and telling us," that is what you get for living in California."

- Can you recall ever "comforting" someone who has been mugged or otherwise victimized by telling them that they "shouldn't have been in that neighborhood at that time of night?"

    What remains unspoken is, "And I know better, so nothing like that will ever happen to me." This helps us to maintain our own sense of safety instead of having to confront the randomness of a violent event.

2. You read in Chapter 17 about Newcomb's Bennington College study. To what extent is there an identifiable political orientation at the school you are currently attending?
   - In what ways, if at all, have your political (or other) attitudes been altered in the direction of those that you feel are prevalent by the general social environment of your school?
   - In what ways, if at all, have your political (or other) attitudes been altered by your specific reference group(s) (for example fraternity, sorority, athletic team, and so on)?
   - Has this created conflict with your family?

18 HUMAN INTIMACY

GENERAL STUDY QUESTIONS

After reading Chapter 18, you should be able to answer the following questions.

1. What is an estrus cycle?

2. According to the text, why is human sexuality unique?

3. What forms the basis of the family?

4. According to the text, in what ways does the human style of sex allow a foundation for a stable society?

5. Why are males "more expendable" than females?

6. What determines who dominates?

7. What is the basic difference in reproductive strategies of males and females?

8. In evolutionary terms, why is sex more important than aggression?

9. In what way is sex different for human beings than for other animals?

10. What are pheromones?

11. What are the four major phases of the sexual response cycle?

12. Why might the age of sexual maturity contribute to homosexuality in males?

13. What are three characteristics that researchers have found to be indicators of interpersonal interest?

15. Why do we sometimes hate someone we once loved?

16. Describe the seven characteristics of passionate love.

17. What are Sternberg's three components of love?

18. At what stage of a relationship is physical attractiveness most important?

19. What is the relationship between attractiveness and criminal behavior?

OUTLINE OF KEY TERMS AND CONCEPTS

Attractiveness, love, and sexuality
   Human sexuality unique
      Ovulation
      Estrus cucle
      Menstrual cycle
   Pair bonding
      Frequency of sex
      Visual sex signals
      Sexual bonding
Sex differences and division of labor
   Men hunt/women gather
   Men fight/women raise children
   Male dominance
      Control protein source
      Control society's valued resources
   Differences in sexuality
      Discord in sexual relationships
      Roles in reproduction
      Sexual expression
      Sexual desire
      Reproductive strategies
      Changes in society
   Cooperation in human society
      Mating systems
      Lessening competition among males
Human sexuality: intimate feelings
   The sexual animal
      Frequency of sex
      Upright posture
         Visual signs of sexuality
   Sexual response cycle
      Excitement
      Plateau
      Orgasm
      Resolution
   Homosexuality
      Changing attitudes
      Not a disorder
      Internal arousal and imprinting
      Age of sexual maturity
Love and attraction
   Importance of scientific research in this area
   Characteristics of people in love
      Inclination
      Closeness
      Gaze
   Excitement of sexual love
      Walster's work
   Importance of arousal in sexual atttraction
      Wobbly bridge study
      Love turning to hate
      Obstacles to love
   Passionate and companionate love
      Intense absorption, arousal
      Involuntary
   Companionate
      Friendly affection
      Deep attachment
   Falling in love
      Men more romantic
      Men fall faster
      Women usually end affairs
   Ingredients of love
      Intimate feelings
      Passion
      Commitment
Attractiveness and loving
   Attractiveness in college students
      Only determinants of interest
      Related to popularity for women
   Nature of attractiveness
      Human sensitivity to scarcity
      Height and success
   Attractiveness and criminals
      Likelihood of getting caught
      Leniency in court
         Attractive defendant gets lighter sentence

COMPLETION ITEMS

love

family

estrus

ovulating, menstrual

conception, bonding

resources

evolutionary
reproduction

cooperation

mental
emotions

estrus

pheromones

contact

menstrual

resolution

10

early

1. As far as we can tell, the emotion of _____ seems to be unique to human beings. The father-mother-child unit is bonded by love into the _____ unit that is typical of our species.

2. Most female mammals other than human beings have an _____ cycle, which means that they ovulate only a few times a year. Also, all female mammals except human beings are physically capable of receiving a sexually aroused male only when they are _____. In the human _____ cycle, however, with ovulation occurring every month, a woman is capable of sexual intercourse at virtually any time.

3. From an evolutionary viewpoint, the pleasure derived from heterosexual activity can be seen as adaptively advantageous insofar as it motivates increased frequency of sexual relations, thereby increasing the probability of _____. Sexual or pair _____ is the basis of the family.

4. Largely because men have historically controlled the supply of the most valued _____ in a society, they typically occupy a dominant status over females.

5. One view on the discord in human sexual relationships comes from _____ theory. It emphasizes that males and females, because of their different roles in _____, have different ways of behaving so that they gain the greatest advantage. Male homosexuality is thought to be a "hypermale" kind of sexuality, uninhibited by females.

6. With the replacement of an estrus by a menstrual cycle and the emergence of pair bonding in the human species, the continual sexual competition between males was lessened, and _____ increased generally throughout the species.

7. Sex is different for human beings than for other animals in that the signals for sex are _____ as well as biological. More significant, however, is the role of _____ and our interpretation of love experiences.

8. During _____, the female of a species produces an odor that arouses the male of the species. Such chemical substances used to communicate are called _____. It has been found that the female scent can diffuse through a room and be effective, whereas the male scent requires close _____.

9. Women who spend a lot of time together tend to have their _____ periods at the same time.

10. The four major phases of the sexual response cycle are excitement, plateau, orgasm, and _____.

11. Almost _____ percent of males are homosexual. The internal arousal and imprinting view predicts that _____ sexual maturers are more likely to be homosexual, and the data seem to support this prediction.

lean

eyes

sexual

bridge

Passionate

companionate

faster

passion, Intimate

physical

taller

shoplifters

average

unattractive

12. Studies of postural status in interpersonal situations have shown that we tend to _____ toward people we like and away from those we dislike. People who like one another tend to look more into each other's _____ than do people who do not.

13. Many studies confirm the importance of arousal in _____ attraction. The men on the wobbly _____ in Dutton and Aron's experiment interpreted their arousal as attraction.

15. _____ love is the strong form of "being in love." The more sober kind of "everyday" love is known as _____ love, which involves less arousal and excitement but more friendly affection and deep attachment.

16. Hobart's research indicates that men fall in love _____ and have a more romantic view of love relationships than women do.

17. Sternberg describes loving as having three components: Intimacy, _____, and commitment. _____ feelings include a desire to promote the welfare of the other, holding the loved one in high esteem, and sharing mutual understanding.

18. In the dance staged for college freshman by Walster and colleagues, _____ attractiveness was the only determinant of interest in the date with whom the students were randomly paired.

19. In all Presidential elections from 1900 to 1968, the _____ of the two candidates won.

20. In Mace's study, it was found that customers in a retail store are more likely to report _____ of undesirable appearance.

21. Salomon and Schopler's research has indicated that, other things being equal, an _____-looking female defendant is likely to get the harshest sentence.

22. Other research has indicated that an _____ man accused of rape is more likely to be seen as guilty and given a harsh sentence than is a handsome man.

SELF QUIZ

MULTIPLE-CHOICE ITEMS

1. As noted in the text, the sexual bond in human beings is
   a. at the root of most aggression and violence between members of our own species.
   b. the basis of the family.
   c. not nearly as strong as in most other species.
   d. antagonistic to the development of cooperation.

2. According to the viewpoint based on evolutionary biology, the discord in sexual relationships between males and females is due to
   a. their differences in size and strength.
   b. the different resources they control.

c. the different rates at which they reach sexual maturity.
d. their different roles in reproduction.

3. _____ form(s) the basis of the family.
   a. The estrus cycle
   b. The sexual bond
   c. Female sexual strategies
   c. Male sexual strategies

4. Sex is different for human beings than for other animals in that _____
   a. the signals for sex are mental as well as biological.
   b. human females are potentially ready for sex at all times.
   c. upright posture transfers emphasis from odor to visual sexual signs.
   d. all of the above.

5. In what way do male and female scents act differently?
   a. female scent can diffuse through a room, male scent requires close contact
   b. female scent is musky, male scent is feral
   c. females respond to male scent, males respond to female scent
   d. all of the above

6. Which of the following is *not* one of the four major phases of the sexual response cycle?
   a. arousal
   b. excitement
   c. plateau
   d. orgasm

7. What percentage of males are homosexual?
   a. 1 percent
   b. 5 percent
   c. 10 percent
   d. 25 percent

8. According to the internal arousal and imprinting hypothesis, homosexuality is predicted to be more likely to develop in people who are
   a. only children.
   b. early sexual maturers.
   c. late sexual maturers.
   d. raised by a same sex parent with the opposite sex parent missing.

9. According to the text, which of the following is not among the "characteristics of people in love" that researchers have observed as indicators of interest?
   a. Sudden feelings of warmth when the other is present
   b. "Inclination" toward another
   c. Standing close
   d. Looking directly into each other's eyes

10. Which of the following is not one of the "ingredients" of love described by Robert Sternberg?
    a. intimate feelings
    b. dependency
    c. passion
    d. commitment
11. If a person is good looking,
    a. he or she is less likely to be caught when committing a crime.
    b. he or she is likely to receive a harsher sentence than an average-looking person.
    c. he or she is more likely to be caught when committing a crime.
    d. he or she will receive a harsher sentence than an average person but a lighter sentence than an unattractive person.

TRUE-FALSE ITEMS

1. T F Human fathers are the only males among primates who take a signifcant role in the care of their own offspring.
2. T F Publications like *Playboy* magazine have created a need for men to look at women sexually.
3. T F From an evolutionary point of view, females are more expendable than males.
4. T F According to Kinsey, "Among all peoples, everywhere in the world, it is understood that the male is more likely than the female to desire sexual relations with a variety of partners."
5. T F Male homosexuality is thought to be a "hypermale" sexuality, uninhibited by females.
6. T F According to the text, survival is related more to sex than to aggression.
7. T F Most animals communicate their sexual receptivity through visual stimuli.
8. T F Women who have intimate contact (usually sexual intercourse) with men at least once a week have longer menstrual cycles, fewer infertility problems, and a less difficult menopause.
9. T F About 10 percent of females are homosexual.
10. T F The report that some people strongly hate someone they once loved is thought to be due to the arousal component of sexual love.
11. T F Women are more romantic than men.
12. T F Men usually end relationships more often than women do.
13. T F According to Sternberg, romantic love is a combination of passion and commitment.
14. T F Good-looking people are more likely to be caught when committing a crime than are unattractive people.
15. T F In one study, observers thought that a well-dressed women caught shop-lifting would be more upset and suffer more from being caught than would a poorly-dressed woman.

ANSWER KEY TO SELF-QUIZ

MULTIPLE-CHOICE ITEMS

1. b 2. b 3. b 4. d 5. a 6. a 7. c 8. b 9. a 10. b 11. a

TRUE-FALSE ITEMS

1. T 2. F 3. F 4. T 5. T 6. T 7. F 8. T 9. F 10. T 11. F 12. F 13. F 14. F 15. T

THINKING ABOUT THE PSYCHOLOGY OF YOUR OWN EXPERIENCE

1. According to Robert Sternberg, perfect love is comprised of all three components of love: passion, intimacy, and commitment. Passion is the state of longing for the other, intimacy is the desire to promote the welfare of the other, and commitment is the ability to give up others for the moment or to stay with the loved one over the ups and downs of life.

- Recall the first time you "fell in love." What components were involved?
- Recall the first time that love led to a relationship that lasted more than three months. What components were involved in that relationship?
- If you have been married for more than two years, again consider the components of love that are primary in the relationship.
- Talk to someone who has been married for more than twenty years. Ask that person about the importance of the various components of love over the course of their marriage.

Does the relative importance of these components seem to change as relationships lengthen? If so why do you think that is true? If not, why not?

19
HEALTH PSYCHOLOGY

GENERAL STUDY QUESTIONS

After reading Chapter 19, you should be able to answer the following questions.

1. What is behavioral medicine? What is the assumption underlying Engel's biopsychosocial and Weiner's psychobiological model of medicine?

2. Why is the fight-or-flight response adaptive? What are the seven physiological changes experienced during this response?

3. What is the general adaptation syndrome? What are its three stages?

4. Define stress. Describe three types of stress.

5. Which of the three types of stress best predicts psychosomatic and physical symptoms? Why?

6. What are three childhood experiences that foster hardiness?

7. How does control mediate the effect of stress?

8. Why might denial be good for your health?

9. Describe the three components of "sense of coherence." How do they contribute to health?

10. What is the difference between the "main-effect or direct hypothesis" and the "stress-buffering hypothesis" of social support?

11. What is the "diathesis-stress" model?

12. What are four treatments for stress-related disorders?

13. What are the three levels of the "health belief model"?

14. Describe the "control and predictability model" of health.

15. What two factors are important in patient compliance?

16. Describe the "parallel process model" of fear and attitude change.

17. What is the "gate-control theory of pain"?

18. Describe the three methods for treating chronic pain.

19. What is "relapse prevention"? What is the difference between a "slip," a "lapse," and a "relapse?"

20. What are the major risk factors for coronary heart disease? What are the minor risk factors?

21. What is the relationship between hostility, self-involvement, and Type A behavior pattern?

22. What has been the focus of treatment and prevention of coronary heart disease?

23. One can lower blood pressure by changing any one of what three factors?

24. What is the single largest reducible cause of cancer?

25. Under what condition will a single exposure to the AIDS virus result in becoming infected with the virus?

OUTLINE OF KEY TERMS AND CONCEPTS

About health psychology
  Psychosomatic medicine
    Biopsychosocial model
    Psychobiological model
Stress: adapting to changes in the world
  Emergency reaction
    Fight-or-flight response
      Physiological changes
    Selye and the stress concept
    General adaptation syndrome
      Alarm reaction
      Resistance
      Exhaustion
    Mediators of the emergency reactions
      Sympathetic nervous system
      ACTH
  Stress as a failure to adapt
    Catastrophes
    Major life changes
      Rating life events
    Chronic life strains
      Hassles
      Uplifts
  Mediation of stress
    Hardiness in the face of stress: coping mechanisms
      Kobasa and Maddi's work
        Components of psychological hardiness
          Commitment to self, work, and family
          Sense of control over life
          Change seen as challenge
      Hardiness induction
        Teach hardiness skills
    Control
      Mediates stress
      Perceived control
      Learned helplessness
    Man-made health
      Optimistic attitudes

- Pessimistic attitudes
- Denial of our feelings
  - Lazarus's work
    - Avoiders
    - Vigilant
  - Sense of coherence and health
    - Antonovsky's work
      - Comprehensibility
      - Manageability
      - Meaningfulness
  - Social support
    - Esteem support
    - Informational support
    - Social companionship
    - Instrumental support
    - Main effect or direct hypothesis
    - Stress-buffering hypothesis
  - Exercise
    - Helps relieve depression
- The effects of stress: the diathesis-stress theory
  - Two parts
    - Constitutional predisposition
    - Inadequate homeostatic restraints
- Treating stress and stress-related disorders
  - Cognitive-behavior therapy
  - Biofeedback
  - Relaxation
  - Conditioned immune responses
- How people behave as medical patients
  - Coping with chronic illness
    - Health belief model
      - Patient's readiness to act
      - Costs and benefits of compliance
      - Existence of a cue to action
    - Control and predictability model
      - Illness brings on helplessness
  - Adherence to medical regimens
    - Factors influencing compliance
      - Patient satisfaction with physician
      - Comprehension
- Preventive health behaviors
  - Changing attitudes
  - Changing behaviors
  - Opposing gradient of reinforcement
  - Increase level of fear about destructive behaviors
    - Fear plus instructions for action
      - Parallel process model
        - Danger control
          - Reduce or eliminate threat
        - Fear control
          - Adjust to threat
- Pain
  - Perception of pain
    - Gate-control theory of pain
      - Sensory input modified by gate before pain perceived
      - Psychological aspect
    - Complex combination of:
      - Stimulation
      - Processing
      - Learning
      - Behavior
  - Psychological treatment methods
    - Hypnosis
    - Acupuncture
    - Cognitive strategies
      - Distracting imagery
      - Stress inoculation
      - Pain clinic
        - Decrease "pain behavior"
      - Functional restoration
- Addictive behavior: smoking
  - Psychoanalytic understanding
    - Oral stage
    - Psychosocial struggle
  - Social learning
    - Peer approval plus imitation
  - Evans' work
    - Behavioral inoculation
  - Effective programs combine:
    - Aversive techniques
    - Stimulus control
    - Reinforcement of nonsmoking
    - Substitute behaviors
    - Chewing nicotine gum
  - Relapse prevention
  - Maintenance
    - Slips
    - Lapse
    - Relapse
- Major causes of death
  - Coronary heart disease
    - Type A and B behaviors and the heart
      - Type A
        - Aggressive
        - Impatient

   Time urgent
  Type B
   Placid
   Speak slowly
 Hostility
  Destructive component of Type A behavior
  Self-involvement
 Treatment and prevention
  Community intervention
  Intervention with large groups
   Stanford Heart Disease Prevention Project
   Multiple Risk Factor Intervention Trial
Hypertension
  Lowering blood pressure
  Treating obesity
  Restricting sodium
  Reduce psychological stress
  Transactional psychophysiology
  Change communication patterns
Cancer
  Second highest cause of death
  Smoking is largest reducible cause
  Nutritional factors affect cancer
AIDS
  Compromised immune system
  Transmission through exchange of bodily fluids
  Encourage safe sex

COMPLETION ITEMS

psychosomatic medicine

Behavioral medicine

emergency reaction, fight-or-flight

fight-or-flight

symbolic

stress

general adaptation syndrome

exhaustion
adapt
Stress

hassles

changes
Hassles

1. Originally a subdiscipline of psychiatry, not psychology, _____ has been based on the premise that particular personality traits are components of the cause of particular illnesses.

2. _____, an interdisciplinary field, attempts to intervene in health maintenance with behavioral changes.

3. Our most basic and immediate reaction to stress is called the _____. It includes both the _____ response and the general adaptation syndrome.

4. The _____ response that evolved to mobilize the body to cope with physical threats is now regularly elicited by _____ ones.

5. The key to Hans Selye's understanding of _____ was that he saw it as a response, not as the environmental stimulus or as a situation where the demand exceeds the individual's abilities to cope. He called this response the _____.

6. The third stage of the general adaptation syndrome is _____. This occurs when the body's ability to _____ uses up all of its resources.

7. _____ is the failure to adapt. Stressful situations are of several types: catastrophes, such as earthquakes, wars, and fires; major life changes, such as unemployment or the death of a spouse; chronic life strains, such as poor working conditions; and _____, such as having a check bounce.

8. People who score high on Holmes and Rahe's measure of major life _____ have been found to show a higher likelihood of becoming ill than do those with lower scores. _____ better predict psychosomatic and physical symptoms than do major life events.

commitment

challenge

acceptance

illusion of control

learned helplessness

healthy

objective

Denial

pathology

vigilance

coherence

meaningfulness

main effect

stress-buffering

diathesis-stress

Biofeedback
Relaxation

compliance

uncontrollable

compliance

comprehension

9. Kobasa and her colleagues found that high stress/low illness executives have a strong _____ to self, work, family, and other important values and tend to perceive change as a welcome _____ rather than as a threat.

10. Kobasa and Maddi's research has also indicated that development of a child's sense of commitment is facilitated by a family environment in which there is strong parental encouragement and _____.

11. Even the _____ may reduce stress. The extreme of having no control is _____.

12. People who rate their health as "poor" tend to die earlier and be more likely to get sick than do their counterparts who see themselves as _____. In fact, such subjective, self-reported health ratings have been found to be more accurately predictive of who will die than _____ measures ascertained by physicians.

13. _____ is the mental operation by which thoughts, feelings, acts, threats, or demands are minimized. It is often considered to lead to _____.

14. Richard Lazarus found two basic coping strategies, avoidance and _____, when he asked patients who were about to undergo elective surgery how much he or she wanted to know about the disease and the operation.

15. Antonovsky has referred to the complex of health-promoting resistance resources as a sense of _____. The three basic attributes he has identified as components of this sense are comprehensibility, manageability, and _____.

16. The _____ hypothesis proposes that social support directly benefits health, regardless of stress.

17. The _____ hypothesis proposes that social support reduces the effects of stress.

18. The belief that people react to stress with different physiological patterns is known as the _____ model.

19. _____ is a method of training people to become aware of and control their internal processes. _____ exercises may be as effective as biofeedback for controlling the bodily part of the stress response.

20. The "health belief model" proposes three levels: the patient's readiness to act, the costs and benefits of _____, and the existence of a cue to action.

21. The "control and predictability model" proposes that chronic diseases pose a stressful and potentially _____ crisis for patients.

22. One factor that appears very important in _____ is the patient's satisfaction with the physician. Another factor is _____ of instructions and information presented by the doctors.

fear

behavioral

parallel processing

Danger control

gate-control

pain

hypnosis

clinic

pain behavior

oral

drug effects

Quitting

maintenance

lapses

relapse prevention

coronary heart disease

Type A

hostility

Type A

large groups

23. The level of _____ stimulated by information about destructive behaviors has an effect on attitude change. Generally, higher levels lead to more attitude change and somewhat more _____ change in use of seat belts, dental care, smoking, and inoculations.

24. The _____ model of fear and attitude change includes two ways people cope with fear communications. _____ involves reducing or eliminating the source of fear while fear control consists of coping to make one feel better despite the threat.

25. The _____ theory of pain suggests that neurophysiological mechanisms in the dorsal horns of the spinal cord function as a gate, increasing or decreasing the flow of nerve impulses from peripheral nerve fibers to the central nervous system.

26. Any approach to the treatment of _____ must take into account that it is a complex combination of stimulation, processing, learning, and behavior.

27. Among the psychological treatment methods for chronic pain are _____, acupuncture, and various cognitive strategies.

28. The most comprehensive approach to cognitive pain treatment is the pain _____. In this approach, environmental consequences, such as attention of family, and the clinic staff, are made contingent on the decreased frequency of _____.

29. The psychoanalytic understanding of cigarette smoking stresses arrested development at the _____ stage.

30. The smoking habit is a complex combination of social factors, individual habits, and _____ and any attempt to help smokers quit should take all these into account.

31. _____ is only the first stage of change. The _____ stage is much more difficult and lasts a longer time. People are expected to experiences slips, or small episodes of the old habit; _____, or more serious episodes; and perhaps relapse, full-blown recurrences.

32. The key difference between _____ and other approaches is that it views these problems not as failures but as learning experiences.

33. Type A behavior pattern is one of the major risk factors for _____.

34. A person demonstrating _____ behavior pattern is one who reacts to challenge with aggressiveness, impatience, and time urgency.

35. Easily provoked _____ is an important indicator of heart disease. It is currently the most popular candidate in the search for the destructive _____ component.

36. Most of the research into treatment and prevention of coronary heart disease has focused on community intervention and intervention with _____.

hypertension

37. People whose blood pressure is consistently high have _____ and hypertension contributes to strokes and heart attacks.

38. Lowering blood pressure can be accomplished by changing any one of the factors that affect it, such as obesity, high sodium levels, and chronic _____.

psychological stress

smoking

39. Cancer is the second highest cause of death in the United States and _____ is the single largest reducible cause of cancer.

human immunodeficiency virus, immune

40. AIDS is caused by the _____ (HIV), which attacks lymphocytes directly. This compromises the _____ function of those who contract it, making them susceptible to infections that they could easily have fought off otherwise.

exchange of bodily fluids
sexual encounter

41. HIV is spread by _____. It normally requires more than one _____ to become infected, but direct exposure through breaks in the skin are exceptions to this.

SELF-QUIZ
MULTIPLE-CHOICE ITEMS

1. Which of the following is an interdisciplinary field that attempts to intervene in health maintenance and change?
   a. psychosomatic medicine
   b. behavioral medicine
   c. medical psychology
   d. biopsychosocial approach

2. Which of the following is *not* one of the physiological changes experienced during the fight-or-flight response?
   a. respiration deepens
   b. pupils dilate
   c. blood's ability to seal wounds is increased
   d. increased perspiration

3. Which of the following is not among the stages of the general adaptation syndrome as described by Selye?
   a. alarm
   b. denial
   c. resistance
   d. exhaustion

4. _____ is the expression that was used to describe the condition of extreme psychological distress observed in military combat personnel in the Vietnam War.
   a. Acute combat reaction
   b. Shell shock
   c. Combat neurosis
   d. Combat fatigue

5. An LCU score of 185 on the Holmes and Rarhe scale would be classified as indicative of a _____ level of recent past stress.
   a. mild
   b. moderate
   c. high
   d. excessive
6. Hassles have been found to be more accurately predictive of _____ than are major life events.
   a. job satisfaction
   b. psychosomatic symptoms
   c. marital compatibility
   d. attitudes toward school
7. Kobasa and colleagues found that high stress/low illness business executives tended to regard change as
   a. the enemy to be defeated.
   b. a challenge.
   c. a threat to growth and achievement.
   d. distressing only because it disrupts the daily routine.
8. Kobasa and Maddi found that development of a sense of control tends to be cultivated in children who encounter
   a. intense trauma and survive it.
   b. very few difficult challenges in life.
   c. mostly challenges that they surmount easily.
   d. a variety of tasks that are neither too simple nor too difficult.
9. Maddi and Kobasa's "hardiness induction groups" were designed to encourage all of the following *except*
   a. commitment.
   b. control.
   c. calm.
   d. challenge.
10. Which of the following is not one of the components of Antonovsky's concept of "sense of coherence?"
    a. comprehensibility
    b. manageability
    c. deniability
    d. meaningfulness
11. The kind of social support you receive from friends when you need practical help is called _____ support.
    a. esteem support
    b. informational support
    c. social companionship
    d. instrumental support
12. Which of the following is not discussed in the chapter as a stress mediator?
    a. exercise
    b. biofeedback
    c. relaxation
    d. all of the above are used to mediate stress

13. The health belief model proposed by Rosenman and Friedman is composed of three levels: the patient's readiness to act, the costs and benefits of compliance, and
    a. relaxation.
    b. denial.
    c. a cue to action.
    d. the perceived severity of illness.
14. The two components of the parallel process model of fear and attitude change are
    a. danger control and fear control.
    b. fear control and denial.
    c. comprehension and compliance.
    d. fear control and compliance.
15. The treatment of chronic pain known as _____ considers a data base of how other people with similar injuries have recovered.
    a. stress inoculation
    b. relaxation
    c. the pain clinic
    d. functional restoration
16. The most difficult stage of change is _____.
    a. quitting
    b. maintenance
    c. taking responsibility for being down
    d. taking responsibility for getting up
17. Which of the following is not a major risk factor in coronary heart disease?
    a. obesity
    b. high blood cholesterol
    c. hypertension
    d. cigarette smoking
18. HIV is spread by _____.
    a. sneezes
    b. mosquitoes
    c. exchange of bodily fluids
    d. any close physical contact

TRUE-FALSE ITEMS

1. T F The fight-or-flight response is regularly elicited by symbolic threats in the modern world.
2. T F Alarm, the first stage of Selye's general adaptation syndrome is the same as the fight-or flight emergency reaction.
3. T F Stress is the failure to adapt.
4. T F High scores on Holmes and Rahe's "life change" measure tend to be predictive of both psychological disorders and physical illnesses such as leukemia and cardiovascular diseases.
5. T F The ratings of stressful life events is consistent across cultures.
6. T F There is considerable research evidence indicating that uplifts are associated with improvements in a person's physical health.

7. T F In order to remain healthy it is important to avoid stress.
8. T F Simply having the illusion of control may reduce stress.
9. T F Denial is always detrimental to your health.
10. T F When a person's sense of coherence is disrupted, he or she is more likely to become ill.
11. T F Exercise mediates stress.
12. T F Medical procedures that enhance the patient's sense of control improve treatment outcome.
13. T F The expression of pain depends primarily on where in the body the pain centered.
14. T F Hypnosis is useless against severe pain.
15. T F Cigarette smoking is responsible for more deaths in the United States that crack addiction.
16. T F The model of relapse prevention puts responsibility on the individual without blaming him or her for being addicted.
17. T F In a study by Lynda Powell, heart attack victims with great self-involvement were more likely to have a second heart attack.
18. T F Hypertension is another way of describing a state of severe stress.
19. T F Smoking is the single largest reducible cause of cancer.
20. T F Everyone exposed to the human immunodeficiency virus (HIV) contracts AIDS.

ANSWER KEY TO SELF-QUIZ

MULTIPLE-CHOICE ITEMS

1. b 2. d 3. b 4. a 5. a 6. b 7. b 8. d 9. c 10. c 11. d 12. d
13. c 14. a 15. d 16. b 17. a 18. c

TRUE-FALSE ITEMS

1. T 2. T 3. T 4. T 5. F 6. F 7. F 8. T 9. F 10. T 11. T 12. T
13. F 14. F 15. T 16. T 17. T 18. F 19. T 20. F

THINKING ABOUT THE PSYCHOLOGY OF YOUR OWN EXPERIENCE

1. As you read in Chapter 19, the psychological study of human adjustment has focused on the experience of life change.

Consider the following:

- What kinds of positive life changes have you experienced over the past six months and how have they affected your feelings of well-being?
- What kinds of negative life changes have you experienced over the past few months or so and how have they affected your feelings of well-being?
- Research has shown that susceptibility to illness may be partly from external stressors and partly from internal makeup. To what extent is this stress-illness hypothesis supported by your own experience in general?

- Do you see this pattern over the past six months?
- Do you see this pattern looking back over the past ten years of your life?

2. Given what you have learned in Chapter 19, imagine that you have just been assigned the task of designing a Life Adjustment Education Curriculum for elementary school children in your community.
- What would be some of the key objectives of your program?
- What broad goals would you set for the children?
- What specific skills and strategies would you want the children to acquire? Why?
- How would you go about implementing them (for example role-playing exercises, parent-teacher groups, and other activities.)

20 ADAPTING TO THE MODERN WORLD

GENERAL STUDY QUESTIONS

After reading Chapter 20, you should be able to answer the following questions.

1. Modern human development is what kind of development?

2. How do people misuse comparisons?

3. How do insensitivity to old problems and sensitivity to scarcity affect our behavior?

4. How does the process of habituation affect our decision making and attention processes?

5. What is proxemics?

6. What are two factors that contribute to the experience of crowding? How does crowding influence our behavior?

7. What do computers have to do with deskilling or upgrading jobs?

8. What does a human factors psychologist study?

9. What are two characteristics that make machines easy to use.

10. How does an expert system work? What are its limitations?

11. What is one argument against the use of computers in the classroom?

12. What is the relationship between education and cardiovascular disease?

OUTLINE OF KEY TERMS AND CONCEPTS

How and why our world is different
    Ability to judge lags behind ability to create
        Population explosion
        Inventions
        Cultural evolution faster than genetic evolution
Mental adaptations to a world long gone
    Modern development is cultural
    Mistakes in judgment
        Mental emphasis on the new and exciting
        Misuse of comparisons
        Self-based analysis
        Insensitivity to old problems
            Vivid new information commands attention
        Sensitivity to scarcity
    How we are manipulated by comparisons and categories
        Pricing strategies
Adapting to density
    Crowding
    Personal space
        Individual distance
            Intimate
            Personal
            Social
            Public
    Privacy
    Experience of crowding
        Population density
        Social pathology
        Calhoun's work
        Responses to density
            Population "crash" in Sika Deer
            In mock jury deliberations
    Built environment
        Churchill's observation
            Rebuilding House of Commons
        Pruit-Igoe Housing Project
            High-rise to replace slum
Adapting to computers and mechanization
    Quality of work
        Deskilling
        Upgrading
    Designing machines for people to use
        Human factors psychology
            Ergonomics
        Visibility

Feedback
Easy to use computers
　Macintosh
　　Direct manipulation
　Models of cognitive processes
Expert system
　Artificial intelligence

MYCIN
Organizational structure and decision making
Computers in education
Get ahead
Education correlated with improved health and disease resistance
Sense of mastery and competence from education

COMPLETION ITEMS

evolution, cultural

1. Many of society's current difficulties are rooted in our _____. Our _____ evolution had proceeded enormously faster than our genetic evolution.

gradually

2. Until comparatively recently in the course of human evolution, the changes to which we were adapted occurred _____ in relatively stable environments. Throughout our evolution, there have been no radical changes in the _____.

brain

agricultural

3. The stability to which human beings were adapted began to disappear at about the time of the _____ revolution.

4. Because of the characteristics of the sensory-brain system,

current

_____ information often has a disproportionately powerful influence in our decision making.

comparisons

5. Human judgments are, to a large extent, based on _____. This often leads to some remarkably stupid errors of judgment such as

Watergate

those which culminated in the _____ break-in that brought down the Nixon presidency.

6. Among our mind's simplifying heuristics is the tendency to analyze every-

personal

thing as an immediate _____ phenomenon: "What does this mean to me?"

7. Little is done about the chronic dangers of highway safety or the 300 murders per week or the 100 billion cigarettes smoked each year—because

familiar

they are _____ problems.

scarcity

8. A sensitivity to _____ of resources, especially a sudden change, is a default program in all animals. A sudden

decrease

_____ in the number of game animals or the fruit and grain supply needs immediate attention and action.

hard-to-get

9. This sensitivity to scarcity explains why _____ people are usually thought to be attractive.

comparisons

10. Categories can affect _____. The shifting nature of our comparisons is shown by the fact that there was little decline in gasoline consumption as gas rose from 38 cents to 95 cents per gallon; but once gasoline was above $1.00 per gallon, there was a marked decrease in usage.

Proxemics

11. _____ is the method developed by E. T. Hall to analyze

Privacy

human spatial behavior. _____ refers to the need to be alone when one so chooses.

Crowding

12. _____ is having more people around than one desires.

experience

The _____ of crowding depends upon a number of factors, including population density and the way that density is interpreted.

crash 13. When an animal population in the wild becomes too large, it may suddenly decline or "_____".

shape 14. Winston Churchill said, "We shape our buildings, and thereafter out buildings _____ us." The inadequacy of many urban housing projects can be traced to a failure to consider the psychological

needs _____ of the people for whom they are presumably designed.

deskilling 15. According to the _____ view, computers will tend to decrease the status and satisfaction qualities of work life. An alternative view is that the primary effects of computers will be to

upgrade _____ the quality of life in work settings where they are used.

16. The branch of psychology concerned with designing machines that are easy for people to use is called human-factors psychology or

ergonomics _____.

17. Two characteristics that make machines easy to use are visibility and

feedback _____.

intelligence 18. Artificial _____ programs used to help make decisions ordinarily made by human experts are often called

expert _____ systems.

19. The Macintosh computer has been very successful, in part because people

direct manipulation find its style of interaction, called _____, easy to use.

20. Groups that communicate via computers to make decisions participate

equally more _____ in the decision-making process but take longer to come to a consensus than face-to-face groups.

SELF-QUIZ
MULTIPLE-CHOICE ITEMS

1. According to the text, the human brain evolved to
   a. aid the survival of genes.
   b. aid the survival of families.
   c. aid the survival of individuals.
   d. none of the above.
2. We constantly judge things
   a. by how they look.
   b. by how they work.
   c. by comparison.
   d. by how well we remember them.
3. Which cookie was valued most highly by subjects in Worchel's cookie jar experiment?
   a. the cookie from the two-cookie jar
   b. the cookie from the ten-cookie jar
   c. the cookie from the ten-cookie jar once the ten-cookie jar had been replaced by a two-cookie jar
   d. the cookie from the two-cookie jar once the two-cookie jar had been

replaced by a ten-cookie jar

4. According to Hall, personal space extends _____.
   a. from actually touching to 18 inches
   b. up to 4 feet
   c. 4 feet to 12 feet
   d. more than 12 feet

5. Mice populations that were allowed to increase without external restraint by predators, disease, or lack of food and water _____.
   a. flourished
   b. showed no change
   c. died out completely
   d. none of the above

6. According to the text, what is the effect of crowding on behavior?
   a. It encourages aggressive behavior.
   b. It encourages altruistic behavior.
   c. It depends on where the crowding occurs.
   d. It amplifies what is occurring.

7. The branch of psychology concerned with designing machines for human use is known as_____.
   a. ergonomics
   b. human-factors psychology
   c. industrial psychology
   d. a and b

8. Artificial intelligence programs that are used to make decisions that ordinarily are made by human experts are often called _____.
   a. human factors
   b. human interface
   c. expert factors
   d. expert systems

9. Which of the following characterizes groups that communicate through computers to make decisions?
   a. They participate more equally in the decision making process.
   b. They take longer to come to a consensus than a face-to-face group.
   c. They engage in more uninhibited verbal behavior.
   d. All of the above.

TRUE-FALSE ITEMS

1. T F There were no radical changes in the brain in the course of human evolution.
2. T F Genetic evolution is enormously faster than cultural.
3. T F The same neural procedures that originally developed to judge brightness now affect such decisions as, which items to buy, and whether to harm or help someone.
4. T F Among our mind's simplifying heuristics is the tendency to analyze everything as an immediate, personal phenomenon.
5. T F The reason that "special, limited time" offers attract us is that they force us to make comparisons that we might not otherwise make.

6. T F Both individuals and cultures differ on what is "too many people."
7. T F When an animal population in the wild becomes too large, it adjusts itself to a proper size through limiting reproduction.
8. T F In general, crowding amplifies what is occurring, whether it is positive or negative.
9. T F Whether computers will deskill or upgrade jobs depends on how managers choose to use them.
10. T F Two characteristics that make machines easy to use are visibility and feedback.

ANSWER KEY TO SELF-QUIZ

MULTIPLE-CHOICE ITEMS

1. c 2. c 3. c 4. b 5. c 6. d 7. d 8. d 9. d

TRUE-FALSE ITEMS

1. T 2. F 3. T 4. T 5. F 6. T 7. F 8. T 9. T 10. T

THINKING ABOUT THE PSYCHOLOGY OF YOUR OWN EXPERIENCE

1. As noted in Chapter 19, the late Prime Minister of England, Winston Churchill, once said that "We shape our buildings, and thereafter our buildings shape us." In this regard, imagine that you have just been appointed Human Environmental Engineering Consultant to a project aimed at redesigning your school. What are some of the structural changes you would recommend, and how do you feel they might help to enhance the quality of life for the people who function within them?

2. According to Edward T. Hall, the space we live in is a medium of communication. Take note of the distance between people as they interact.

- Try to guess how well people know one another by noting the distance they leave between them when they talk.
- Purposely stand a little closer to a person than you normally would and see what happens.
  - Try it with someone you know fairly well.
  - Try it with a stranger—someone standing in front of you in a line.

    What happened? Did it make you feel uncomfortable? Did the person move away?

21
OLD AGE

GENERAL STUDY QUESTIONS

After reading Chapter 21, you should be able to answer the following questions.
1. What is gerontology?

2. When does old age begin? Why this age and not another?

3. What are cohort effects?

4. Describe the programmed senescence theory of aging.

5. The increase in life expectancy over the years is due primarily to what?

6. How long *can* a person live?

7. What is the hallmark of biological aging?

8. What is the difference between normal aging and abnormal aging?

9. What are presbyopia and presbycusis?

10. What part of the body changes *least* due to aging?

11. What is meant by the statement, "Aging is a process of differentiation."

12. What is the best predictor of functioning in old age?

13. What is the "terminal drop?"

14. What is the "swan song effect?"

15. Does retirement present a major crisis for older adults?

16. What is the relationship between social isolation and the death rate?

17. What are some of the reasons that widowhood may be more difficult for males than for females?

18. What are some of the reasons that widowhood may be more difficult for females than for males?

19. What does the availability heuristic have to do the perception of old people's lives?

20. According to Rodin, what are three reasons that the connection between health and sense of control is strong in the elderly?

21. What is the "survivor effect" and why is it a problem for longitudinal studies?

22. What is the difference between crystallized intelligence and fluid intelligence?

23. What is the "anniversary effect?"

24. What are the five stages that a dying person goes through, according to Kübler-Ross? What are some of the problems with this model?

25. What is the best predictor of happiness in old age?

OUTLINE OF KEY TERMS AND CONCEPTS

Special issues and terms
   How old is old?
      Gerontology
         Old age begins at 65
      Generation not age differences
         Cohort effect
Why do we age?
   Programmed senescence theory of aging
      Hayflick's work
   Immune system changes
      Antigens
      Autoantibodies
   Neuroendocrine system
How long can we live?
   Increased life expectancy
      Improvements in sanitation and public health
   Ratio of older to younger changing
   Maximal life span (115–120)
Biological aging
   Slowing
   Birren's work
      Impairments a function of disease not age
   Normal (primary) aging
   Abnormal (secondary) aging
      Dementia
   Normal changes
      Presbyopia
      Presbycusis
      Kyphosis
      Neuronal atrophy
      Climacteric
      Menopause
   Abnormal changes
      Secondary or disease related changes
         Chronic conditions more likely among old
         Health influenced by behavior
   Gender differences in old age
      Men die younger
      Women live longer but under harsh circumstances
   Health and daily functioning
      Level of functioning
      Obstacles to daily functioning
      Age as predictor of change
         Process of differentiation
         Three levels of old age
            Young-old (60–74)

                Old-old (75–84)
                    Very-old (85–older)
                Terminal drop
            Race and Gender
                Women live longer than men
            Social changes
                Retirement
                Support for elderly
                Forms of social support
                    Family
                    Friends
                    Community
                    Organizations
                Comparison with other societies
                    Japanese, in Japan, have less heart disease
                Widowhood
                    Difficulties for men
                    Difficulties for women
                Grief of widowhood
            Psychological change
                Availability heuristic
                Expectations and attitudes about old age
                    Behavioral confirmation
                Dependence
                Mindfulness
                Self-efficacy and cognitive aging

                Importance of control
                Changes in cognitions
                    Intelligence
                        Longitudinal studies
                            Crystallized intelligence
                            Fluid intelligence
                    Memory
                        Declines with age
                    Personality
                        Men and women may age differently
                        Stability of personality
            Death and dying
                Years before death
                    Anniversary effect
                Stages of death
                    Kübler-Ross's work
                        Denial and isolation
                        Isolation
                        Bargain with fate
                        Depression
                        Acceptance
                    Criticisms of Kübler-Ross
                        Risk of too literal interpretation
                        Stages not sequential
                        Correlates?

COMPLETION ITEMS

gerontology

arbitrary

1. In _____, the scientific discipline that studies aging, there is a general agreement that old age begins at 65. This is an _____ number that was chosen by the U.S. government when it established the Social Security Act and had to decide when people could begin receiving their social security benefits.

decline
What goes right

2. Scientists generally approach the study of old age as the study of _____. Instead of asking "_____?," they ask, "What goes wrong?"

experience
cohort

3. Differences in people reflect not only their age but their _____. These differences in what people have lived through are called _____ effect.

programmed senescence

4. The _____ theory of aging proposes that aging and death occur due to built-in clocks in our genetic structure.

neuroendocrine

5. Recent studies on aging focus on the immune and _____ systems as the basic mechanism of aging in human beings.

antigens
autoantibodies

6. As we age, our immune systems become less competent, less able to fight off _____, such as infections and cancers. We then develop _____ which can attack our own organs and joints.

medical care
sanitation

over-80

115–120

slowing
disease

Normal
Abnormal

Presbyopia

presbycusis

kyphosis

lungs
brain

Menopause
climacteric

86

age-related

behavior

7

Five
elderly

age

health status

one stage

terminal drop

7. It is a common misconception that people are living much longer today because of improvements in _____. Improvements in _____ and public health, not medical treatments for disease, account for most of the reduction in infant mortality.

8. The fastest growing segment of the population is the _____ group.

9. Most scientists agree that the maximal human life span is _____ years.

10. The hallmark of biological aging is _____. Impairments in old age are often more a function of _____ than of old age.

11. _____ aging reflects changes that are age related, gradual, and irreversible. _____ aging refers to age-related diseases that, at least in theory, are reversible.

12. _____ is a form of farsightedness that is considered a normal part of aging. Age-related hearing loss is known as _____.

13. Most people are about two inches shorter in their later years compared to their maximum height because of _____, the minor bending of the spine and the settling of the vertebrae.

14. Normal aging causes changes in the gastrointestinal system, the cardiovascular system, and the _____. There is less change in the aging _____ than in the rest of the body,

15. _____ is the cessation of menstruation and ovulation. In men, the _____ is more gradual and never complete.

16. Approximately _____ percent of people over 65 require medical care for some kind of health problem. This is because normal _____ changes leave us less able to ward off disease.

17. Health in old age is influenced by our _____ and the environments we were exposed to in younger days.

18. On average, women live _____ years longer than men but they are more likely than men to live out those years under harsh circumstances.

19. _____ percent of people over 65 live in nursing homes. Most caregivers for the elderly are in the _____ age group.

20. By adulthood, _____ begins to lose its power as a predictor of physical ability, intellectual functioning, and social behavior. By old age, _____ is a better predictor of functioning.

21. Researchers have become aware that to classify the last 30 years of life as _____ is not adequate because people who are 65 are very different from people who are 85.

22. The phenomenon known as the _____ suggests that there is a rapid decline in physical and intellectual performance about five years before death.

creativity   23. There is some evidence that _____ increases during the final years of life and then gradually declines until death.

isolation   24. Old age increases the risk of social _____ which somehow increases susceptibility to disease in general. In a study of Alameda County residents, it was found that those who tended not to join or participate in community organizations died at a rate 2 to 5 times

greater   _____ than those with more extensive social ties.

                       25. A study of victims of a heart attack one year later revealed that pet owners had _____ the death rate of non-pet owners.

one-fifth

                       26. Marmot and colleagues found that in spite of eating Western foods, having high serum cholesterol, smoking cigarettes, and having high blood pressure, those Japanese immigrants who maintained close ties with the Japanese community had rates of heart disease one-fifth as high as those

social relationships   who adopted a Western pattern of _____.

                       27. Most women live longer than men and marry men older than themselves; thus they have a much higher chance of being _____

widowed   than men do.

mortality   28. Widowhood results in marked increases in _____ in men but not in women.

                       29. A *Los Angeles Times* poll found that more than two-thirds of respondents

very satisfied   over the age of 65 reported being _____ with the way things were going in their lives.

distorted   30. Most of us hold a _____ image of old age which may be because we segregate ourselves by age.

                       31. When we do come into contact with old people we may treat them as feeble or dependent and they may respond in ways that

confirm   _____ our distorted expectations of how old people behave.

                       32. Margaret Baltes found that nursing home residents became conditioned to

dependent   be _____ because the staff responded to them only when they needed assistance.

control   33. According to Rodin, _____ is important to older people because they seek to organize their lives more than do the young.

                       34. The apparent decline in intelligence among older groups is due to

historical   _____ rather than aging factors.

Longitudinal   35. _____ studies attempt to control for this problem by selecting a group or panel of subjects to be studied over a number of years or decades.

                       36. One problem with these studies is that people who are more intelligent and better educated tend to live longer and continue as participants and

increases   may make it appear as if intelligence _____. This is
survivor effect   known as the _____.

crystallized   37. Verbal abilities, or _____ intelligence seem to remain relatively constant or to increase slightly with age.

Fluid   _____ intelligence, or measures of performance, decline.

stability

5

denial and isolation

sequential

38. According to Costa and McCrae, the _____ of personality is so striking that the interesting question is not how it changes in old age, but how people live through so many changes and maintain a consistent personality.

39. Kübler-Ross's theory describes _____ stages that a dying person goes through. The first of these is _____ which may function to keep the person from being overwhelmed with grief.

40. While these stages reflect common characteristics of the terminally ill, they are not _____.

SELF- QUIZ

MULTIPLE-CHOICE ITEMS

1. Who decided that age 65 is the beginning of old age?
   a. researchers who found that age 65 is when most people can no longer work
   b. researchers who found that around age 65 there is a dramatic decrease in the number of brain cells
   c. the U.S. government
   d. artisans during the Renaissance who began a tradition of retirement at that age

2. The scientific discipline that studies aging is known as
   a. psychology.
   b. developmental psychology.
   c. senescence theory.
   d. gerontology.

3. For the purposes of longitudinal research, a cohort is a
   a. gang.
   b. a group of friends.
   c. people of the same age.
   d. people of the same culture.

4. Autoantibodies
   a. fight off "foreign invaders" in the body, such as infections.
   b. are complex neuroendocrines.
   c. can attack our own organs and joints.
   d. slow down the aging process.

5. Today, the life expectancy for Caucasian American men is
   a. 65.
   b. 69.
   c. 72.
   d. 77.

6. People are living longer today because
   a. of improved medical care.
   b. of improved public health.
   c. they are better educated.
   d. they know ways to counteract stress.
7. Abnormal (or secondary) aging is defined by
   a. your age.
   b. your health status.
   c. your genes.
   d. your psychotherapist.
8. Which part of the body changes the *least* as we age?
   a. the brain
   b. the eyes
   c. the gastrointestinal system
   d. the cardiovascular system
9. According to the textbook, why does coronary artery disease account for 50 percent of deaths among older people?
   a. because of their thickened blood vessels
   b. loss of elasticity in blood vessels
   c. Older people have higher rates of hypertension.
   d. all of the above
10. What percentage of people over the age of 65 live in nursing homes?
    a. 5 percent
    b. 10 percent
    c. 25 percent
    d. 35 percent
11. If a woman marries a man 10 years older than herself, she stands an 80 percent chance of being widowed by age
    a. 35.
    b. 45.
    c. 50.
    d. 55.
12. The feeling of _____ constitutes a pathological reaction to bereavement.
    a. guilt
    b. emptiness
    c. hostility
    d. all of the above
13. In a poll conducted by the *Los Angeles Times* _____ of respondents over the age of 65 reported being very satisfied with the way things were going in their lives.
    a. one-tenth
    b. one-quarter
    c. one-half
    d. two-thirds

14. According to the text, which of the following is the best predictor of functioning in old age?
    a. age
    b. health status
    c. sex
    c. intelligence
15. On the basis of research such as the study in which plants were given to elderly people in nursing homes, Rodin concluded that psychological interventions can greatly enhance the lives of the elderly, provided the need for _____ is taken into account.
    a. generativity
    b. unconditonal positive regard
    c. cognitive consistency
    d. self-determination
16. Longitudinal studies of changes in intelligence with age are especially susceptible to error due to
    a. the cohort effect
    b. historical factors
    c. nonrepresentative sampling
    d. the survivor effect
17. Which of the following best describes what happens to our intellectual capacity as we age?
    a. Crystallized intelligence remains constant while fluid intelligence declines.
    b. Fluid intelligence remains constant while crystallized intelligence declines.
    c. Both types of intelligence decline.
    d. There is no change in intelligence as we age.
18. Which of the following is not one of Kübler-Ross's 5 stages that a dying person experiences?
    a. denial and isolation
    b. anger
    c. regression
    d. depression

TRUE-FALSE ITEMS

1. T F Differences that reflect what people have lived through as opposed to how many years they have lived are called cohort effects.
2. T F Recent studies of aging in humans have tended to focus on genetic mechanisms such as limitations on cell division.
3. T F Caucasian women are the longest-lived group in our country
4. T F In 1900, the average life expectancy was 47 which means that if you had been born in that year, you could expect to live approximately 47 years.
5. T F The hallmark of biological aging is *slowing*.
6. T F People who are classified as abnormally aging are those who have not adjusted to their advancing years.

7. T F Even with normal levels of stimulation there is considerable decline in brain functioning in the aged.
8. T F Experts predict that the hearing of the future old will be worse than what we observe today because of the widespread appeal of loud music among today's young people.
9. T F Roughly half the elderly in the country are institutionalized.
10. T F Old people are much more alike than are people in early adulthood.
11. T F The so-called terminal drop refers to a marked decrease in intelligence scores a few months or a year before death.
12. T F Currently, researchers believe that for the average person, retirement presents a major crisis for older adults.
13. T F A study of heart attack victims one year later revealed that those who were petless had a death rate 5 times higher than did pet owners.
14. T F Comparative studies show that Japanese immigrants who have maintained close ties with the traditional Japanese community have less heart disease than those who have adopted Western ways.
15. T F Only 35 percent of women over 65 are married.
16. T F Researchers have found that older people are less lonely and less depressed than middle-aged adults.
17. T F If we were to take a cross-section of people aged 20, 40, 60, and 80, we would find that IQ scores decrease with age.
18. T F Crystallized intelligence seems to decline steadily with age.
19. T F Old people take longer to learn new things.
20. T F As we age, our personalities change slowly but steadily.

ANSWER KEY TO SELF-QUIZ

MULTIPLE-CHOICE ITEMS

1. c 2. d 3. c 4. c 5. c 6. b 7. b 8. a 9. d 10. a 11. d 12. d 13. d 14. b 15. d 16. d 17. a 18. c

TRUE-FALSE ITEMS

1. T 2. F 3. T 4. F 5. T 6. F 7. F 8. T 9. F 10. F 11. F 12. F 13. T 14. T 15. T 16. T 17. T 18. F 19. T 20. F

THINKING ABOUT THE PSYCHOLOGY OF YOUR OWN EXPERIENCE

1. Spend an afternoon with someone who is over the age of 70, but is not a relative. It might take a little arranging to find such a person because of the age segregation in our society. Think about it, how many such people to you know?

Once you have found someone, the relative of a friend for example, ask that person to tell you the story of his or her life.

- Ask about his or her family of origin
- Ask how he or she came to be married (if that is the case).
- Ask how he or she came to his or her work.

You probably won't have to say much after that. Just listen and think about the similarities and differences between the life you are hearing about and your own.

2. There have been discussions throughout the text about the way the brain grows with experiences and how people can adapt to new and challenging situations.

- How has this information changed your views of your own development and possibilities?
- How has this changed your relationships with those older than yourself?
- What changes do you think society should make regarding the treatment of and opportunities provided to the elderly?